Greenhill Books

KESSELRING

GREENHILL MILITARY PAPERBACKS ON THE SECOND WORLD WAR

BATTLE OF BRITAIN DAY

BOMBER OFFENSIVE

DISASTER AT D-DAY

GUDERIAN

THE HITLER OPTIONS

I FLEW FOR THE FÜHRER

INVASION

KESSELRING: GERMAN MASTER STRATEGIST

LONG RANGE DESERT GROUP

THE MEMOIRS OF FIELD MARSHAL KESSELRING

SAS: WITH THE MAQUIS

THE SKY MY KINGDOM

WAR ON THE EASTERN FRONT

WHY THE GERMANS LOSE AT WAR

KESSELRING

German Master Strategist of the Second World War

KENNETH MACKSEY

Greenhill Books, London
Stackpole Books, Pennsylvania

Greenhill Books

This edition of
Kesselring: German Master Strategist of the Second World War
first published 2000 by Greenhill Books, Lionel Leventhal Limited,
Park House, 1 Russell Gardens, London NW11 9NN
and
Stackpole Books, 5067 Ritter Road, Mechanicsburg, PA 17055, USA

British Library Cataloguing in Publication Data
Macksey, Kenneth, 1923-
Kesselring : German master strategist of the Second World War. -
(Greenhill military paperback)
1.Kesselring, Albert, 1885-1960 2.Germany. Luftwaffe - History 3.Germany.
Wehrmacht - Officers - Biography 4.Marshals - Germany - Biography
I.Title
943'.086'092

ISBN 1-85367-422-2

Library of Congress Cataloging-in-Publication Data
Macksey, Kenneth.
Kesselring : German master strategist of the Second World War / Kenneth Macksey.
p.   cm. — (Greenhill military paperbacks)
Includes bibliographical references and index.
ISBN 1-85367-422-2
1. Kesselring, Albert, 1885-1960. 2. Generals—Germany—Biography.
3. Germany. Heer—Biography. 4. World War, 1939-1945—Germany.
I. Title. II. Series.
DD247.K5 M33 2000
355'.0092—dc21
[B]   00-038078

Publishing History
This book was first published in 1978 by B.T. Batsford as *Kesselring:
The Making of the Luftwaffe*, and as *Kesselring: German Master Strategist of the
Second World War* in 1996 by Greenhill Books. This new paperback edition
reproduces the original edition, complete and unabridged.

Printed in Great Britain by the Alden Group, Oxford

Contents

List of Illustrations   vii
List of Maps   ix

   Introduction   11
1 Determined, Militaristic, Amiable   15
2 The Organiser   32
3 Airman in the Ascendant   56
4 The Nemesis of Incomprehension   66
5 Night Bombing and the Russian
     Interlude   85
6 A Glorified Quartermaster   104
7 Back to Soldiering   126
8 Sicily and the Road to Cassibile   158
9 Against Rommel   175
10 The Consul   187
11 Reputations at Stake   206
12 A Study in Obstinacy   224
13 By Trial and Error   232
14 A Man on His Own   247
   Bibliography   253
   Index   255

List of Illustrations

Between pages 128 and 129

Carl Adolf Kesselring
Rosina Kesselring
Albert Kesselring, aged four
The gunner lieutenant, 1904
At Metz, 1912
The staff officer, 1917
Reichswehr days
Building the *Luftwaffe*: cartoon
Kesselring, Rommel and Hitler
Kesselring, Göring and Milch
The Field-Marshal, July 1940
A Russian airfield under bombardment
Kesselring with Löhr, Göring and Loerzer
September 1940, directing the Battle of Britain
North Africa: Frölich, Rommel, Kesselring,
    Crüwell, Gause
Desert conference
Berchtesgaden: Kesselring, Hitler, Mussolini
    and Keitel
Tunis: Kesselring and Walther Nehring
German tanks and infantry at Tebourba
Frascatti: Kesselring, Cavallero and Hans von
    Mackensen
Kesselring in Italy
Anzio: Kesselring, Westphal and von
    Richthofen
Command Group in Italy: Kesselring, von
    Vietinghoff, von Senger and Westphal

Acknowledgements

Illustrations from the private collection of the Kesselring family.

List of Maps

The Invasion of Poland, 1939   61
The Campaign in Holland, Belgium
   and Northern France, May/June 1940   70
The Battle of Britain, 1940   80
The Invasion of Russia, 1941   93
Axis Convoy Routes, 1941/42   108
The Advance to El Alamein, 1942   120
The Retreat to Tunis, 1942/43   131
Operation 'Avalanche' and Operation
   'Husky', 1943   170
Conquest of Italy, July 1943–May 1945   191

Introduction

This is the biography of a liberal classicist who became one of the most formidable technicians of war known to the twentieth century. It is about a great strategist and organiser who became enmeshed in a pernicious political environment, one who has become side-tracked in terms of public esteem but who has been rated, by a prominent German Chief of Staff, as one of the top three German soldiers with 'a hold on the troops' – Erwin Rommel and Heinz Guderian being the others. Although this is not intended to be a history of the campaigns Albert Kesselring fought it must, of course, introduce material and opinions which, up to now, have been obscure, for Kesselring was addicted to modesty, the last man on earth to boast loudly about his considerable accomplishments. And yet it is to him that much credit must be given for laying the foundations of the *Wehrmacht* and *Luftwaffe* which, by their originality and prowess, won significant initial victories for Adolf Hitler at the beginning of the Second World War. Without his determined contribution, by obstinacy and charm, to a system, these organisations might well have been of average quality. As a result battles that would have been drawn were won and those which might have been lost were drawn. Furthermore, deprived of generalship, Adolf Hitler's most grandiose military schemes might have been squashed at the outset and the long retreat Kesselring was to conduct after 1942 might never have been necessary.

Why then has Kesselring been overshadowed in popularity by men such as Rommel, Guderian, Montgomery, Patton and the other 'propaganda marvels' whose deeds were considerable but who flourished mainly in the upsurge of victories rather than thrived in adversity – as did Kesselring for nearly six years? To some extent the answer is to be found, of course, in the realisation that the lives of Hitler's generals remain

11

obscure, even though so many have published their memoirs and historians have benefited by the availability of a mass of relevant material. Disclosures have yet to be made, not all the official histories have been published, and only in the past decade has the diminution of old hostilities made possible a more liberal attitude to the exposure of points of view which were unpublishable in the 1950s. Maybe the sheer volume of material is to blame; there has been too much to digest and, so far as the English-speaking peoples are concerned with regard to German sources, too few interpreters available. Therefore only a minority of the available papers have been translated. In consequence only a discreet élite is as yet apprised of the inside story relating to several important episodes as well as aware of the full range of German sensitivities in those traumatic years. It is information which, after all, is denied to the German people too, let alone to outsiders. The majority of popular books in English about the Germans depend upon only a few familiar sources – sources which, in many instances, reflect the *immediate* post-war biases. Kesselring's story suffers in the classic manner from this repetitive process. Not for him, when he was writing his 'Memoirs', was there an almost uninhibited access to private references or published works such as his British or American opponents in battle could avail themselves when writing their memoirs. He wrote secretly when he was in prison, cut off from the essential records and frequently under supervision. Moreover, Kesselring and his contemporaries had to take especial care about every word they uttered in case they inadvertently provided the military tribunals with evidence against comrades or themselves. Long after their exclusion from real power, the German commanders had in their hands fuses to detonate several kinds of political bomb, any one of which might harm individuals, damage the state, or wreck the alliances to which their nation aspired to belong. The fact that they imbibed so profound a loyalty to their past calling and considered any kind of adverse publicity repugnant, went almost without mention.

By upbringing, too, Kesselring was suited to operate effectively in the shadow of exuberant personalities, statesmen and politicians who advertised their achievements while he passed over his own immense contributions to their success and took the blame for their errors. The flamboyance of Herman Göring, the immense ability of Erhard Milch and the adulation accorded to Walther Wever, before and after his premature death, hide the truth of the matter – that the foundation stone of the *Luftwaffe* was laid by Kesselring when he was working for Hans von Seeckt and that the structure upon which it was based was fashioned by him. Likewise it is often customary to blame Kesselring for turning Göring, in 1937, against the creation of a strategic bomber force, although it is overlooked that it was he who actually contrived the instrument of air power that became the *tactical Luftwaffe* which made a vital contribution to the rapid conquest of Poland, Holland, Belgium and France. It is forgotten by some that it was he, controlling the preponderant element of the *Luftwaffe* during the Battle of Britain, who so shook the British and he who, in 1941, ruined the Russian air force.

It was Kesselring's fate to assume the role of a Troubleshooter, the unpopular Axeman whose traditional task it is to destroy myths and kill holy cows. Inevitably, therefore, he became the centre of controversy in the public sector when Hitler sent him to restore order out of chaos in the Mediterranean theatre of war at the end of 1941. There he would have to pit his wits against the hierarchy of an Italian ally who was jealously guarding sovereign rights, and against Erwin Rommel, an extrovert whose exploitation of an assiduously won propaganda reputation left no more room for shared glory than did Göring's. Naturally the task did not enhance his popularity even if he cared very much that it did. Moreover axemen tend to be sent from one hatchet job to another and this, too, was his experience. So it is all the more astonishing that Kesselring, who won far more battles of intrigue than he lost, besides enjoying notable victories against the foreign enemy, emerged smiling at the end.

Unfortunately the compilation of Kesselring's biography is hampered by the almost total absence, obliteration or loss of his personal documents. He neither kept a diary, nor did he correspond very much except in his official capacity, and of this correspondence little has survived. Fortunately the years he was to spend in prison after the Second World War presented him with the opportunity to write prolifically for the American Historical Division. It is from the products of these labours, conducted with consummate skill, balanced judgement, and enjoyment, that it is possible to understand much about a man of cool appreciation and high intellect. For the rest there are the surviving German records, and the reminiscences of his colleagues, friends and enemies to draw upon in some profusion, scattered though those sources may be. There is also the transcript of the Military Tribunal in Venice where he was tried as a war criminal. In gathering this information and obtaining the essential background to the Kesselring family, I have had the good fortune to receive the collaboration and reminiscences of Albert Kesselring's adopted son, Dr Rainer Kesselring, who has helped me cut several corners in tracking down new facts and opinions. The 'Memoirs' I have drawn upon to the least possible extent in so far as matters of fact are concerned, employing them mainly as a source of his reflections, some of which may well be more revealing than he intended, others of which are misleading. Where I have quoted facts from the 'Memoirs' I have endeavoured to find some corroborative primary source from the archives, such as war diaries and accounts from unimpeachable witnesses. In this latter connection I am particularly indebted to the assistance and evidence I have received from *Generalmajor* K.-H. von Barsewisch, *Oberst* Graf von Klinckowstroem, *Oberst* K.-A. Mügge, *General der Panzertruppe* W. Nehring, *Oberst* Dr K.-H. Schroeder, Dr D. H. Robinson, Vice-Admiral F. Ruge, *General der Artillerie* W. Warlimont, *General der Kavallerie* S. Westphal and Wing Commander W. Winterbotham.

Considerable assistance was rendered too by the Imperial War Museum, London; the Library of the British Ministry of Defence, London; The National Archives and Records Service, Washington and The Bavarian Kriegsarchivs, Munich, all of which have in their possession documents that added considerably to my researches.

I am extremely grateful, too, for their immense and vital assistance in the translation of documents from the German, to Reinhold Drepper and Helga Ashworth; for typing the manuscript to Margaret Dunn; and drawing the maps Michael Haine. And as usual there was my wife who criticised, read proofs and gave encouragement whenever it was needed. Finally, Brigadier E. D. Smith read the draft and made most valuable comments and suggestions.

1
Determined, Militaristic, Amiable

In the faded splendour of the old Venetian court house on the Grand Canal in Venice, the powerfully built figure of *Generalfeldmarschall* Albert Kesselring stood ready to open his defence against accusations of committing war crimes. On this, the twelfth day of a trial that was to drag on for fifty-nine days (with Kesselring in the witness stand for twelve of them), the British major-general and five lieutenant-colonels who comprised the court were to hear, for the first time, from the formidable fighting man who was before them on trial for his life, accused of responsibility for the death of some 1,400 Italians. His defence lawyer, Dr Hans Laternser, a veteran of many War Tribunals who had but recently defended the German General Staff in the Nürnberg Trials, rose to begin the examination of the famous German soldier who, deprived of his martial dignity by the obligation to wear civilian dress, could call now on force of character and clear expression alone to make an impression.

'When were you born?'

'On 30th November, 1885,' came the reply in the crisp, rapid-fire German that was, at certain periods in the trial, to cause difficulties for court and interpreters who found it hard to keep pace with a man whose speed of thought was quicker than his interlocutors'.

'Would you give us a short description of your career?'

A slight pause for translation and then the court heard a record of service such as no other commander in the Second World War had surpassed or equalled.

Kesselring: '*Leutnant* in the Artillery, 1904; in the First World War at troop service and General Staff. After the World War 1918/1919 first General Staff Officer at the HQ at Nürnberg and fighting against the revolution . . .' The staccato relation of his achievements hushed the court room. Interspersed with the interpreters' explanations they moved

15

to a culminating announcement, '1940 promoted to the rank of *Generalfeldmarschall*. From my position at Moscow [sic] where I had my last position I was transferred to the South of Italy.'

The President: 'What year was that?'

Kesselring: 'November 1941.'

Dr Laternser: 'What are your decorations?'

Kesselring: '*Ritterkreuz* with swords and brilliants and diamonds and *verdienst kreuz* for personal services, for merit as an officer and also personal courage. *Flugzengführer* pilot decoration as an officer serving as a pilot; class 4 front fighting for front flying and for 200 operations.' (He did not bother to mention the four awards he had won between 1914 and 1918.)

Dr Laternser: 'Have you been shot down?'

Kesselring: 'Several times.'

Dr Laternser: 'How often were you shot down?'

Kesselring: 'Five times.'

And now the story behind these achievements unfolded and with it the bizarre reasons for his appearance on a criminal charge arraigned by enemies who had already encompassed his defeat in the field along with that of his country. But if those past enemies were under any illusions that the prisoner at the bar was to plead merely for his per 9n l safety and honour they were sadly mistaken. Albert Kesselring, having lost his last physical battle, was set upon winning a final moral victory for the sake of his country and also for the *Wehrmacht* he had helped design and which he had served so loyally for so much of his career.

*   *   *

The dignified arrogance with which Kesselring faced his accusers was a natural by-product of breeding. As a member of one of Bavaria's most ancient families, which had been established in the leadership of central southern Europe as far back as the 7th century (at least), he was accustomed to exercising command and power. His distant ancestors had been tribal knights who stood firm against peasant revolts and the eternal threat of invasion from the east by Avars and Hungarians, to name but two predators. They had gradually settled among the free cities of Germany, such as Colmar; engaged, between innumerable bouts of hostilities, in the beer and wine trade, to become wealthy merchant adventurers besides soldiers of fortune. Kilian Kesselring had been in command of Swiss forces during the Thirty Years War and had fought in a skirmish against the Swedes under General Horn at Rheinfelden in Alsace in 1633. This quite wealthy family had established itself firmly in Lower Franconia (which is, today, a stronghold of Bavarian right-wing political parties), adopted the Protestant faith and assumed an important role in local politics.

The branch of the family into which Kesselring was born was one which steered a different course to the rest but, nevertheless, adhered to the alliance of Kesselrings. His father, Carl Adolf (born 20 July 1846), had taken up an academic career in teaching that may not have provided a great income by Kesselring standards. But, supplemented by the dowry of the woman he married in 1872 – his second cousin (not first as some will have it) Rosina Margaretha Maria Kesselring, it sufficed. The making of this match in itself demonstrates typical Kesselring determination to prosper in the face of strong opposition, for although the concept of an arranged marriage was normal, there were family objections on the grounds that the relationship was too close. Professor Kesselring, despite his gentler calling, was a martinet whose word was law within a liberal family framework which, paradoxically, allowed his children some freedom of choice in their selection of careers. It may be that Rosina Kesselring's role was a minor one. Indeed, so far as Albert Kesselring was to be concerned, women – notably those of grace and beauty – were fit mainly to charm but not rule: and steadfastly he declined to be influenced by them. Nevertheless Rosina modulated Albert by her kindness: he always spoke endearingly of her, with gentle affection. Into these stern surroundings she introduced that humanising element which is so essential in the civilising of offspring when a father's omnipresence is harsh. Of the six children she bore, four survived infancy and received sound educations at upper-middle-class schools in Bayreuth. One became a doctor (and remained a bachelor), another studied for the law but as a student committed suicide, and a girl remained a spinster. The system under which they were brought up would appear to have come closer to that of the Prussians than the somewhat easier relationships upon which Bavarians like to pride themselves. Strict emphasis was placed upon the virtues of honour and duty in preparing the children for responsibilities that were intended to fit them for a leading role within society. The destiny of the Kesselrings was never considered in the slightest doubt; debate on any subject of change and of personal choice was permitted, usually in accord with a code that encouraged dispute – up to the point of ultimate decision that is. Under these exacting, but far from oppressive, conditions Albert, the youngest son, born at Marktsteft on 30 November

1885, grew up at Wunsiedel and received a classical education in the Latin School at Bayreuth.

Practically every facet of Kesselring's character and subsequent accomplishments can in some way be traced with a fair degree of certainty to one part or another of his early upbringing, for he was an empiricist who took careful note of events, and analysed and stored away in a capacious memory the conclusions for future reference. Systematically he created a formula which rejected waste, regularised method, and stimulated originality. Though he was popular at school and well endowed with scholarly attributes that won respect from his teachers, he was without a single close friend and developed as a maverick. Educated in Bayreuth as he was, it would have been surprising had he not imbibed the strong cultural wine of the city which Wagner had made his own, and where the great composer had died but two years prior to Kesselring's birth. For ever an admirer of Wagner (though not himself a musician) and heavily influenced by the egalitarian, liberal policy of his school, it was perfectly natural that he should assimilate the habit of hard work from the start and become a cultured classicist. It may therefore have come as a surprise to his parents when he showed leanings towards technology and decided to join the army. He knew his own mind and says in his memoirs 'I wanted to be a soldier, indeed I was set on it . . .'. But then, of course, diversity of interests was always among his attributes: at one moment he could be wrapped in the adulation of scenery, a sunset, architecture or literature, and the next absorbed in the grapple with some military problem.

Kesselring's eccentric choice of the army as an expression of his own independence of mind is of crucial importance in understanding the man's attitude to authority and the environment surrounding him. Unfortunately he does little to explain himself: he forbore to keep a diary, wrote only the briefest of letters and destroyed all incoming correspondence no sooner had he dealt with it – which was strange in a man who would depend so much on filed reports. Therefore it is easier to pin-point some of the causes for this departure into military life and make fairly reasonable surmises than it is to discover his inner thoughts. Bayreuth, with its connections with Prussia, with patriotism and with Wagnerian nationalism, undoubtedly moulded him into a German first and a Bavarian second – though there is nothing to show that he was also influenced in any way by the anti-Semitic trend of Wagnerian philosophy or that he was interested in the fundamentals of the Jewish question. That Prussia had a profound effect upon Bavarians, once their state had been absorbed into Greater Germany by Otto von Bismarck in 1871, is undeniable. But because Germany was plunging into the machine age and acquiring the wealth and trappings of an industrial nation to set alongside the prestige she had acquired through Prussia's recent military victories over Denmark, Austria and France, it was becoming increasingly fashionable for young Bavarian men to enter industry or the army. Systematically the soldiers received a strict training in the Prussian style – leavened as it was by the looser informality practised in the organically separate Bavarian Army. An indication of Kesselring's ingrained flexibility of application is revealed in the way he could deliberately depart from the cosier academic atmosphere of the family circle to tackle the hard reality of life in the 2nd Bavarian Foot Artillery Regiment. Not that the choice of regiment necessarily denoted that he rejected academics or that he was in search of a Spartan code of behaviour. It amounted to this: never could he be accused of careless career planning; each step forward was to be his own choice, supported by careful reasoning – though it must be added that the precise reasons themselves, from a man who habitually kept his own counsel, are not always possible to ascertain.

He became a gunner for a variety of considerations. The cavalry he avoided because of the expense and the infantry because he was not immensely fond of walking. To a very good horseman, with a splendid eye for country, the artillery held an added attraction since it promised better riding besides involvement with machines. At heart, too, he looked down on infantry officers. 'The cavalryman,' he wrote in a paper about the German General Staff, 'acquired a freer and broader outlook than, for example, the infantryman serving in a company. He learned to think on a larger scale without making any special effort to do so and thus acquired something by practice which is indispensible for a General Staff Officer. . . . The rich cavalryman's lack of concern about the future also saved his nervous energy to a far greater degree.' Presumably the superior qualities of artillerymen were so little in dispute that he felt no need to mention them (and it is true that, in the Second World War, a very high percentage of gunners rose to the heights in the services), but of the infantry he felt bound to remark with typical irony that they '. . . did not gain this knowledge and ability without a great deal of sweat'.

Because his father was not an officer and he had not attended one of the Cadet Schools, his entry into the 2nd Foot Artillery Regiment, in 1904, had to be by nomination of the regimental commander as a volunteer, potential officer (*fahnenjunker*) immediately after he left school. The next two years were spent under the regime of the War Academy in Munich

before he joined his regiment as a *Leutnant* in 1906 at the garrison town of
Metz. Metz, for the German army, provided a sort of colonial service in
recently acquired territory within gunshot of a frontier on the other side of
which lay a defeated enemy and a threatening opponent – France. For
Kesselring, the man who one day would hold a considerable portion of the
architectural and cultural heritage of Europe at his mercy, the city, and in
particular its cathedral, was a source of wonder, pleasure and adulation.
The surrounding Lorraine countryside, too, enthralled him with its
beauty and provided him with ample opportunity to extend his already
deep study of modern history by close examination of the battlefields upon
which the German Army had triumphed in 1870. In another respect, also,
it broadened his mind as a European so that, one day, he would find it
possible to solicit the incorporation of a German army into a European
defence force.

   Political pursuits held little attraction for Kesselring in the early years of
his career, however. Though he had developed an outlook which paid
homage to German nationalism, he avoided pronounced party alignments
out of sheer lack of interest. For him it was the army life which
predominated, as successive reports by his senior officers show. They
paint a picture of growing involvement with the service and a quite
outstanding enthusiasm and aptitude for the profession of his choice.
Already, as a cadet in 1904, he had been remarked upon for his talent,
industry and enjoyment of authority. In 1907 it was observed that he had
flair, great energy, loyalty, diligence and, 'Shows great interest in the
training of his subordinates as well as pursuing his further education.'
Skilful in commanding his men, as it was said, he was also of a kindly and
reserved disposition, with great tact, with a pronounced social grace and
'entitled to hope for a great future'. The interest he was taking in technical
matters became clear in the 1909 report, since here it was noted that he had
done well at the School of Artillery and Engineering, the reporting officer
concluding, with unrestrained praise, 'Kesselring is by far the best of my
officers.' That was saying something of so young a member of an élite in
the Bavarian Army. The same pattern is to be found in all the subsequent
reports, along with the information that he was exemplary in making
himself understood, though reserved socially; not over forceful with
senior officers, but always helpful. Now appeared recommendations that
he should be sent to the Military Academy, with a General Staff career in
prospect, or as an instructor at the Artillery School: he was beginning to
develop into that rare bird, the technical staff officer of mature education
who knew how to balance the requirements of tactics and technology. In

the report for 1914, the last before his training would meet the test of war, his determination and endurance were recorded along with the announcement that he had shouldered the duties of battalion adjutant with ease and that he was suitable for the appointment of Regimental Adjutant. This proposal was confirmed by General Kreppel, the Regimental Commander, who had formed an excellent impression of this up and coming young man who had already shown powers of insight in work that was important to the future of artillery.

The 2nd Bavarian Foot Artillery Regiment had an interesting role as a fortress regiment entrusted with the manning and exploitation of heavy artillery, along with experiments to enhance its effectiveness in action. The precise part that Kesselring played in the series of trials aimed at improving the accuracy and flexibility of shellfire which took place during his years of service at Metz from 1906 to 1914 (less the two years he spent at the Artillery School in Munich from 1909 to 1910), cannot be ascertained. He mentions experiments with 'the latest gadgets used by reconnaissance, observation and liaison units' and how 'I was able, for the first time, to be instrumental in an important change' – without disclosing its nature. He also revels in his intense interest in balloons and his delight in this means of transport, both as a way of observing the enemy and for the direction of artillery fire from tethered kite balloons, as well as the sheer pleasure of being airborne, particularly in free flight. Of far-reaching importance, he had received practical indoctrination into the essential principles of two key weapons of modern war – heavy artillery and air power.

By the standards of the years immediately prior to the outbreak of the First World War in August 1914, Metz was a centre for flight. There were no less than four Balloon Companies there whose role in war was primarily laid down as adjuncts to the static fortress batteries whose role excluded them from a part in the kind of mobile campaign that the rest of the army expected. Though Kaiser Wilhelm II and his successive Chiefs of Staff, spurred on by the few enthusiasts of heavy artillery, insisted upon the big guns being made as mobile as possible, their protracted employment in this role was rarely taken seriously by field gunners or by the cavalry and infantry; they assumed it was their ordained and exclusive destiny to settle any disputes that arose. Balloons therefore fell out of favour. But it was already apparent to the Chief of Staff, Helmuth von Moltke, from trials held in 1912, that the newly invented aeroplanes, with their ability to fly over the enemy, were likely to be superior observation platforms. In any case, with the optics then in use, balloon observers could see but 4½ miles into enemy territory. Naturally there was a distinct yearning among fortress officers to do all in their power to avoid this uninspiring duty, so it is a measure of Kesselring's detachment from an overwhelming sense of ambition that he was content to remain in Metz and, perhaps, sacrifice his prospects. Let it be noted that, recommended at the beginning of 1914 for accelerated promotion though he was, he had still not received a nomination to the Military Academy and that more junior officers than he were already there. Possibly it was to his advantage when war broke out in August 1914, for all courses were terminated upon mobilisation and the students were returned to the units. Everybody was placed on an equal footing. By practical demonstrations, the true nature of each officer's proficiency would be revealed and war would take its toll. In Kesselring's case war would resolve any hesitancy about his career.

One irrevocable step into the future he had already taken – or, rather, had been persuaded to take. In 1911 he had married, an arranged match that was the product of a typically forceful and hard-headed move by his father in negotiation with the widowed mother of Pauline Anna Kayssler, both of whom seem to have placed the spiritual needs of bride and groom low in the matter of priorities. Security was uppermost in their calculations: the widow wanted a home and the father knew that an aspiring young officer needed funds. Certainly this was no love match; undeniably the elder Kesselring put the acquisition of the thirty to fifty thousand Kayssler Marks at a premium, and presumably his son concurred. Unhappily the forceful widow Kayssler was part of the deal: she would make her home with the newly married couple – a dubious arrangement her son-in-law would rue. From the outset the marriage was in difficulty and also barren of children to assuage their discontent. But there could be no retreat even when it became plain, over the years, that they were unsuited. Both Albert and Pauline possessed staunch religious scruples; divorce was not to be contemplated though separation would come as the product of the exigencies of service in the army. For him the palliative was to be an increasingly wholehearted devotion to unremitting work without the slightest evidence of dalliance or extra-marital diversions. In this way of escape his dedication to work was a spur to ambition.

It is most unlikely that Kesselring visualised the unexpected course that land war was to assume. As a seer he had no claim at any time, though undoubtedly his work with heavy artillery prior to 1914 had stimulated his hopes, based upon enthusiasm, that these monster pieces might play a more important part in combat than many people thought possible.

During the opening weeks of the war Kesselring stayed with his unit at Metz, that strong hinge upon which revolved the gigantic turning movement being undertaken by the German armies into northern France towards Paris through Belgium. For him nothing very dramatic occurred by way of action except from desultory exchanges of fire: the French declined an assault on a well-established fortress and their offensive on the southern flank, aimed at Saarbrücken, met defeat. His first experience of offensive warfare also provided a taste of defeat since he was at Nancy during Crown Prince Rupprecht of Bavaria's abortive and ill-considered attempt on 4 September, on the eve of the German rebuff at the Marne, to breach the French fortress line. These tactical setbacks and strategic reverses were important omens. Within but a few weeks the entire front from the Swiss frontier to the North Sea had been linked into an almost invulnerable fortified zone of trenches defended by artillery and machine-guns, and the Germans had been held at Ypres. Positional warfare was to be Kesselring's preoccupation for the next four years after he arrived in Flanders with his regiment in November.

Commensurate with that move his career made a crucial advance. On 5 December as *Oberleutnant* (the rank to which he had been promoted in 1913) he had been appointed Regimental Adjutant to the 1st Bavarian Foot Artillery, and thus became involved in the higher staff work with which, except for a spell of four months, he was to be enthralled until 1919. From an unassuming aesthete he was converted into an efficient mechanic serving a machine. He was to spend the larger part of the war on the Western Front, engaged, alternately, in action against the British and the French, witness to some of the most wasteful and yet significant battles. He was, for example, in Flanders throughout the winter of 1914–15 (and promoted *Hauptmann* in March as a mark of the high regard in which he was already held for his frenetic energy and superb organising ability) and thus close (though unengaged) to the first gas attack at Ypres in April. At about this time, too, the artillery staff to which he belonged began its frequent association with the Sixth Army under Rupprecht and thus were initiated the contacts he was to have with this much admired commander who was to play so important a part in moulding him and, to some extent, steering his future. The autumn of 1915 found him back with Sixth Army, after a summer spent in the Vosges, in time to take part in the repulse of the French in their final assault on Vimy Ridge. For the better part of two gruelling years, though in different appointments within the artillery branches of Sixth Army, he was to remain in that region and assist the guns to assume an ever more commanding role in operational procedures, to the extent that it was Gunners who, virtually, decided the tactics to be employed. From this period he drew the conclusion that artillery could not win wars – not even 'flying artillery'.

The crowning moments of his battle experience occurred in the spring and early summer of 1917, when the British and Canadians launched what, up to then, proved their most effective attacks in Artois and in Flanders, using vastly improved artillery techniques. On 9 April, when Kesselring, as adjutant to the 3rd Bavarian Artillery, was out of the line, the German front from the northern slopes of Vimy Ridge to the plains that ran southward from the environs of Arras, was ripped open. Enemy infantry, tanks and cavalry thrust up to three miles into a gap that was some eight miles wide in the German lines. For seventy-two hours it seemed certain that a wholesale German retirement would be unavoidable, that a British tactical victory was creating for them a strategic advantage. On the 10th they had only to push steadily ahead east of Arras and the Germans, whose artillery had been overrun and whose infantry (notably a Bavarian division) were failing, would have been in dire straits. Only a combination of poor organisation, lack of leadership, exhaustion and terrible weather paralysed the further advance of the British that day. Yet, when Kesselring arrived on the 11th, in the midst of a renewed enemy attack of some strength and purpose against Monchy-le-Preux, there again seemed every likelihood of a renewed debâcle. A freshly arrived Bavarian regiment had been destroyed almost at once and again a large gap had appeared in the defences.

It was at this perilous moment that Kesselring, striving heroically to establish order on a front which had been devastated by shellfire, where the gun sites were saturated by enemy gas attacks and in which men suffered extremes of exposure to cold and wet besides acute shortages of food and ammunition, made an indelible impression upon all who saw him in action. Here he saw the effect on men of defeat and here he learned ways of restoring their confidence when in adversity. Visiting the trenches at frequent intervals, going aloft in a kite balloon to see for himself, and working like a fury to reknit the artillery defences and communications which alone would stem the rot among the infantry, he earned for himself a reputation and the highest praise and gratitude of Keppler, his commander, who reported on him as

... extremely capable ... with quick comprehension and great power of decision. He has sound tactical knowledge and insight into the larger tactical situations. An independent, loyal, zealous and quick worker with very good nerves. Independent in judgement, subtle in expression, clear and concise in delivery, besides his good artillery grounding, he also possesses very good all-round knowledge . . . he especially distinguished himself during a week's activity at Arras by his indefatigable industry while compiling clear and precise orders. Despite 20 hours work a day he never gave way. To me he was a staunch supporter and a loyal, conscientious helper and advisor, absolutely suitable for his present appointment and as a Battery commander. I consider him especially suitable for the General Staff.

The same report also told of the way, two months later, he had 'performed wonders' during the battle of Messines in which the British had reached all their objectives in a classical siege warfare operation.

Two points are pre-eminent in this period. First, the unqualified recommendation for appointment to the General Staff which he was granted in 1918 without even the necessity of attending the special staff course then being held at Sedan – a notable acknowledgement of his accomplishments – and, secondly, the lasting impression that British methods of making war seem to have made upon him. Of them he acquired a notion of timidity or laggardliness in exploiting hard advantages won in combat. Both at Arras and Messines they had punched holes in the German lines and wrought confusion; at neither place had they zealously obtained the full benefit from their initial success. Opportunities had been wasted. This lesson was stored away with all the rest, and was to be extracted and re-applied nearly three decades hence in situations which were every bit as harrowing for him (in a much higher office) and demanding again of every scrap of knowledge he could call upon in holding the British in check. He also acquired a much deeper understanding of the workings of air power which, on the Arras front, was omnipresent and prosecuted with particular ferocity. He would have been aware of the unremitting attempts by the British to carry out reconnaissance and offensive operations in the face of a qualitative superiority then enjoyed by the Imperial German Air Force. Frequently he had to integrate his own demands for air observation posts in controlling artillery shoots with the stipulations insisted upon by the airmen, and thus he came to understand their point of view in the most practical way. Overhead he must frequently have seen the most famous of all German fighter circuses in action, that of Manfred von Richthofen which played havoc with the British in April 1917 but never quite prevented them from continuing to come over and attempt to bomb the

German ammunition dumps, sometimes to disrupt the artillery programmes Kesselring was attempting to organise.

Apart from a month spent on the Eastern Front in November 1917 as a General Staff officer of the 2nd Bavarian *Landwehr* Division, the Western Front was his 'home' throughout the war. That spell in the East, however, in which he found himself engaged in arranging the armistice with the Russians on the River Duna, also made a vivid impression upon him. Not only was this his introduction to diplomacy with foreign nationals, it was his first contact with the products of communism, its members in the Bolshevik Russian Army. His disgust is recorded in his memoirs, an undeniably true reflection of the feelings engendered at the time and one which was to remain with him for ever thereafter. Here one reads of his utter repugnance for the manifestations of this new political creed which was about to infest Europe. Of the members of the soldiers' councils he wrote, 'They struck me as callow, uneducated oafs who interfered with practical discussions and peacocked as if they were the officers' bosses.' The foundation of his social conscience was shaken.

Thoughts such as these could only be momentary. The New Year found him back in the West, newly appointed to the ranks of the General Staff and as a Staff Officer on the Quartermaster's Branch, on 4 January 1918, to the II Bavarian Army Corps with Sixth Army, which fell under Rupprecht's Army Group. These were the days of preparation for the greatest artillery concentrations ever undertaken by the Germans during their last massive attempt to win the war, days when his life was conditioned by the duties of supply. At this time too, he found himself invited to the Crown Prince's table, there to receive lessons in the courtier's art, listening to a prince and soldier of deep and wide-ranging education whose insight into statecraft far out-reached that of the Kaiser and was a match for the team of Generals, Paul von Hindenburg and Eric Ludendorff, who were then driving the German war machine to destruction. At the seat of war he was made keenly aware of the necessity of a civilising influence, a lesson that was both invaluable and lasting: nothing was to be wasted in this schooling of his intellect along with its close association with humanitarian ideals.

The record of his service that year can be stated briefly, comprising though it did many of the most exacting battles – from the breakthrough towards Armentièrres against the Portuguese and British in April and the ensuing grapple in the approaches to the Channel Ports, prior to a shift to the south with III Army Corps as Chief Intelligence Staff Officer, to entering the line of the Marne and Vesle rivers and there suffer the final repulse as Ludendorff's throws became weaker and less effective at each attempt. It was on this front that the German attack met its doom and here, for a few days, their exhausted and demoralised troops reclined once more into positional warfare. But from the beginning of August 1918, as Allied counter-attacks mounted in violence, he was to see something new and terrible. For as the enemy pressed it was found that the German soldiers would no longer respond with their old fervour to the call of their commanders and staff. In the defence of the River Oise and Aisne, of the line between Arras and Bapaume and before Cambrai, Kesselring, for the first time in his career, came to understand what it meant to give orders that would not necessarily be obeyed and to realise that there was a limit beyond which men could not be pushed. These things he saw for himself: they were not just the subjects of reports at his desk. Frequently he was sent forward as liaison officer with divisions or regiments to make arrangements at crucial points during the battles. At the front he relearned the value of personal example and leadership. To the last day of the war his assignments seem to have been presciently arranged as practice for the future. He who, one day as a field-marshal, would spend more than two hectic years selecting and designing delaying positions and successive lines of defence against an enemy advance to the Fatherland, was given the task, as a captain, of laying out a fresh line of defence from Antwerp along the River Maas, a job that was denied completion by the Armistice on 11 November as the German people found themselves defeated and in revolution.

If there was any agreement at all between the soldiers of all nations as they came home from that war, it was to the effect that nothing like it must ever take place again. Yet there were variations in their approach to that matter, a total dissimilarity in the reception awaiting the officers and men of the Central Powers and their victorious opponents in the West. A young and dedicated British, French, American or German regular officer, returning to peace-time soldiering, might well bring with him a resolve and new ideas as to the redesign of armies and air forces with radically new methods to obviate the possibility of prolonged positional warfare in the future. But whereas the victors felt that time for making changes was on their side, the vanquished Germans had time against them. First they had to set their house in order before beginning to contemplate the armies of the future.

The communist-inspired revolution which spread through Germany in November (led in its initial stages by sailors' and soldiers' councils of the same kind as Kesselring had come to loath in the previous year on the

Duna) treated their leaders with contempt. Some of the proudest officers, knowing that to wear uniform in public was to invite ostracism and violence, felt so downtrodden by defeat and had such anxiety for their families who were starving at home, that they gave up the struggle and threw off uniform. Kesselring, on his own admission, seriously contemplated resignation but was dissuaded by 'my politically minded GOC' who 'insisted on my staying on to carry through the demobilisation of the III Bavarian Army Corps in the Nürnberg area'. It cannot have been an easy decision. Though childless and unhappy at home he felt responsibility to Pauline, though it is made plain that his career took first priority over his marriage. He had also seen for himself, during the march home, the uncontrolled and libidinous behaviour of the men in Cologne and so could appreciate the magnitude of the work before him. Moreover, in a service whose prospects looked anything but bright, he had seriously to contemplate adopting quite another sort of career. What sort of employment might an ex-officer find in an anarchic communist state? The fortune Pauline had brought was being wiped out by post-war inflation. Was there any future worth considering?

Yet, in complying with the request to stay a soldier, he resolved his dilemma besides thrusting himself deeply into the struggle to preserve something of the old system in the republic which now replaced the wreck of the monarchy. The job at Nürnberg as Ia (senior operational staff officer) to the deputy commander of III Corps was both disruptive, in that he had to help dismember the formation which so recently had been a cohesive body, and productive, in that from the residue of soldiers who still showed fight they were endeavouring to recruit and constitute units for the *Freikorps* in Northern Bavaria. This force, under the German Socialist Party (SPD), was to combat the communist Spartacists and their kin who were endeavouring to take over the government of Bavaria in Munich in the South. In plain terms they were engaging in civil war and so what he was to write after 1945 has an important bearing on his development in 1919. 'Even this work had its educational value, although this period called for very heavy personal sacrifices.' He came to detest this kind of war as, inevitably, he found himself tossed from side to side by vicious factions which, for months on end, were to plot and intrigue for power among outbreaks of terror, coercion and violence. Only the scantiest records survive but the experience was traumatic and the blackest period culminated in what he called 'the most humiliating moment of my life'.

The excesses of the communist perpetrators of the 'Red Terror' which ravaged the principal communities of Bavaria in 1919 are sometimes exaggerated by their opponents, the Nationalists, who were far from innocent themselves of outrages in putting them down. *Freikorps* units such as those raised by Ritter von Epp were among the most ruthless slayers of communists on record and several indignant officers of the old army, who saw everything they stood for being torn down, were among the last to stand in the way of retribution against the Reds. Nobody with responsibility in the midst of that holocaust had clean hands. Loyalties were perpetually under strain and suspect during a struggle against a communist irregular army that rose to several thousand in strength. The worst fighting took place in Munich. Nürnberg was, by comparison, a backwater, though Kesselring makes much of the storming of his GHQ in the Deutschherrn Barracks by the mob. In April and May 1919 the killing rose to its height as the *Freikorps* he had helped raise gradually gained the upper hand. Typically, Kesselring in his 'Memoirs' draws a veil over these terrible events, except to regret their happening. It is a characteristic reaction of nearly all the regular army officers that they tried to erase these events from the records since, one and all, they were compelled, by the uncompromising demands of civil war, to play some objectionable part or another in their perpetration. But none could expunge the memory in its entirety and Kesselring, when faced much later with the prospects of instigating a civil war amidst another nation, instinctively drew back and did all in his power to stifle it.

No man's reputation was safe, though the wise regular officer tried his best to avoid direct contamination from either of the principal political factions for fear of jeopardising his career. Already the separatism from politics, which was to become *de rigueur* in the new army when under reformation, was being implanted by sheer necessity of survival. Kesselring, whose detachment from party politics was inherent, should have found it easier than most to comply, yet such was the prevalent confusion and so pernicious the whirlpool of intrigue and counter-intrigue which sucked them all into the turmoil, even he failed to stay wholly free of contamination. In his 'Memoirs' (which are the only positive record of this event that can be traced) he says, 'My cup of bitterness was full when I saw my devoted work rewarded by a warrant for an alleged *putsch* against the socialist-influenced command of III Bavarian Corps'. When writing that passage Kesselring displayed his obtuse knack of evasiveness in covering up his personal miscalculations. In this case, which can only have been a passing misdemeanour at a time when every army officer was suffering agonies of misgiving, there were no lasting ill-effects. Indeed, a few weeks later, the report on him of 10 August 1919 by his immediate superior, Major Seyler, was entirely favourable except where it clearly refers to this incident. Seyler stated: 'In general no adverse feelings about him, but failed to observe the necessary discretion in a special case. His great obstinacy frequently hampers his activities due to sticking to a preconceived opinion.' But his general took a much stronger line about this turbulent staff officer of 'great abilities and zeal' adding: 'His long employment on higher staffs when young has led him to over-estimate his person and sometimes the difficulties which face the troops in executing orders especially in difficult times. The special case in which Kesselring showed a lack of discretion gave me occasion to change his employment.'

From these terse reports there is more to be learned about the future field-marshal than from almost anything else written about him. Not only did they punish and, probably, guide his footsteps in the future, they provide a clear and economic insight into the essentials of his character. To begin with, Kesselring, it may be fairly assumed, had indulged in a persistent attack upon his commander on grounds of political objection and had persisted in the face of dissuasion by his immediate superior. It would not be the last occasion. He had exposed a weakness in his character, the tendency to pursue a vendetta if he took exception to an individual or if he found himself in conflict with communistic influences. He also had demonstrated a susceptibility to cross the thin dividing line between well-judged determination and bigoted obstinacy – a common enough fault in the greatest of men, let it be added. The accusation of over-estimation of his person by an outraged commander, unjust and severe though it might have seemed, could soon be rectified, just as his too prolonged detachment from regimental service could be put right. He had spent forty-three out of fifty-one months with the staff and a spell of duty with the troops, as recommended in his report, was easily and quickly arranged. It was a common complaint in those days that officers who had spent long periods with the staff had lost contact with the true feeling of the fighting men – though Kesselring, by his repeated visits to the front, was probably less guilty than many of this charge.

The most important point to register is that he benefited from this painful brush with authority by learning an invaluable lesson in connection with the handling of politically sensitive commanders. He was not found lacking when he had to deal with a supreme commander – Adolf Hitler – who was pre-eminently political in his judgements. The experience of Nürnberg in 1919 taught him to modify his debating methods to reach objectives by indirect instead of head-on attack; to have his way, when necessary, by diplomacy and sometimes by intrigue. Be these things as they were, the rest of the report of 10 August assumed crucial inportance, coming as it did as his final assessment as a member of the Bavarian Army on the eve of its absorption into the main body of the German forces.

Those who were to read the report in Berlin cannot have been otherwise than impressed, prejudiced though the Prussians among them might have been against a Bavarian. Somebody obviously took exception to the information that, during the war, he had spent forty-three months on the staff and only eight with troops, for the entry was marked in thick blue pencil and corrective action taken immediately to send him to serve with a battery. For the rest there was nothing but praise to match a list of war-time decorations that amounted to four (including the Prussian Iron Cross 1st and 2nd Class). He was, the report said in answer to a questionnaire, of good and quick intellect, very tall, determined, militaristic and with excellent powers of expression, besides being amiable. He had 'an excellent gift for organisation which enables him to pick quick and sure solutions. Very talented in giving orders.' His grading was of the best – 'Excellent' – and he was recommended for promotion, for special employment on the General Staff and in Higher Command posts besides being suitable, as a picked man, for inclusion in the *Reichswehr*.

When Kesselring read that report the clouds should have rolled away. But though the door to stardom had been thrown open, the harsh peace treaty of Versailles which had been so recently announced would reduce the prospects of quick promotion in the future to the barest minimum. There was bound to be an unforeseeable period of doubt and disappointment which, to a man of his inclination towards the progressive evolution of ideas, might be repugnant. Forged in the heat of war as a creative military personality of vigorous independence of mind, it might be fatal if this enthusiasm was so thoroughly quenched by retrenchment that all warmth was drawn from him. Restrained though he was in connection with politics, there was always the danger that his virulent anti-Communist leanings might carry him too far to the right – as had been the cases with other soldiers of genius – and involve him with factions that were to be excluded from the new army. If Ludendorff could go that way, why not Kesselring? On the other hand, if he could be saved from temptations such as that and employed on tasks of a positively constructive nature there was no telling what he, among the most thoughtful and energetic survivors of the war, might not do to create ideas, organisations and methods that were revolutionary.

2

The Organiser

The ruffled calm which followed in the wake of the turbulent confrontations of 1919 and 1920 with Communism in its most virulent and abrasive form, heralded a period of thoughtful tranquillity for the armed forces of Germany that was broken only occasionally by such abrupt eruptions as the Nazi *putsch* in Munich in November 1923. Within an Army and a Navy which, by successive stages, were to be reduced from the multitudes of war-time to (in the case of the Army) a mere 100,000 men, there was inaugurated a drastic re-examination of fundamental procedures and techniques allied to an exorcism of spirit in an effort to replace disarray with cohesion. Top of the priorities of General Hans von Seeckt, the newly appointed chief of the *Truppenamt* (which performed service in lieu of the old proscribed Great General Staff) was the restoration of confidence among the hard cadre of selected officers and men. It was a daunting task demanding unquenchable enthusiasm of the men if only because the weapons with which they were armed were barely adequate to suppress a riot let alone repel an invasion. At any moment one of Germany's neighbours, France, Czechoslovakia or Poland, could carry out their threat to cross the frontiers – as France was eventually to do in January 1923.

The bureaucracy's selection of the leaders for the 100,000-man army was slow – tortuously slow for those of immense ambition whose whole livelihood was at risk. Though Kesselring's financial state, in the terminology of his report, was 'Orderly', his private fortune had been eliminated by the inflation that accompanied revolution, and a captain's pay was certainly insufficient to allow the standard of living he preferred. His eagerness was no doubt frustrated by the enforced period of service with troops to compensate for his long term on the staff, while the apparent enhancement of Prussian influence, attendant upon the merging of the Bavarian Army with the rest, may have stimulated his anxiety for the future. There were traditional causes for a Bavarian to imagine he would lack preferment as a result of the new 1919 German Constitution, and cogent reasons prompting those who strove for independence from the new state. Kesselring, smarting as he was with anger at his treatment by the mob, by the left-wing elements, and appalled by the by-products of civil war, was patently committed to the Prussian cause and to its traditional bias towards the eastern neighbours such as Russia. But, as with so much else, his future performance would be conditioned by his past experience. Prussians such as Heinz Guderian might, at this time, reflect upon the iniquities of being expected to serve alongside renegades whose loyalties were subjugated to the occupying powers. Kesselring wished to serve on because he was committed to doing honest work in a rewarding career which fascinated him – a career in which, he trusted, the depravities of officers who played the stock exchange and manipulated army accounts to their benefit would be eliminated. Of course, it has to be remembered that one of the criteria governing the selection of officers for the 100,000-man army lay in the priority accorded to those of slender means to the exclusion, if vacancies were over-subscribed, of the wealthier candidates. But although Kesselring qualified for selection upon this as well as every other count, the axiom that an officer without private means would abstain from making bold decisions and taking risks with his superiors, or in making decisions involving heavy financial outlay, could never be applied to him. Even so, at this moment of uncertainty, when a strong Bavarian move to break away from Germany was evident (to which the Hitler *putsch* of 1923 may well have been a sort of counter-move) and the destructive forces of inflation were rampant, it was typical of Kesselring that he was temporarily inclined to reconsider his position and contemplate resignation in order to take up civilian employment. It is a sign of his intentions in 1923 that he and Pauline walked for three hours in order to study the jobs vacant advertisements in Berlin – for Kesselring was not fond of walking at the best of times!

Plumb the depths of despair though he may have done, he staunchly turned to face hard times with characteristic good cheer. Poverty notwithstanding, the Kesselrings stretched their resources to give what entertainment they could to their friends. Though never in debt they lived to the limit of their means and did so, moreover, as members of a community that was foreign to them. For in October 1922, after three years in successive appointments as battery commander – first in Amberg, then Erlangen and finally Nürnberg – he was returned to the

staff, to a plum appointment in the *Truppenamt* which reflected the high
opinion that was already held of him in Berlin. Von Seeckt, whom
Kesselring calls 'the most towering phenomenon of the German Army
after World War I', held Kesselring in high esteem among the bright
young men he gathered around him in the inner circle of the *Truppenamt*.
It was in Kesselring's rooms that they frequently met for informal
discussions which covered a multitude of subjects outside the military
curriculum, and here that the *Hauptmann* of 'good all-round knowledge'
and 'excellent powers of expression' sharpened his intellect upon the hone
of his general's vast experience. Von Seeckt, who played a leading part in
manipulating the politicians in the aftermath of Germany's defeat (though
Kesselring doubted his political skill), was, as Wheeler Bennet remarks,
not a typical Prussian officer, but urbane, cosmopolitan and artistic. It
was these attributes which attracted them together, though in
Kesselring's salon the subjects for discussion also ranged around the
central theme of their occupation, the refurbishing of the military
machine upon modern lines. The élitist, von Seeckt, surrounded himself
with an élite of about sixty men who comprised the cream of staff officers,
drawn from all levels, who had survived the post-war period without
contamination by Communism or membership of the *Freikorps*. There
were men of extraordinary ability such as Joachim von Stülpnagel, Kurt
von Schleicher, Johann Hasse and Walter von Brauchitsch, in the upper
bracket, with Kesselring in a lower tier in company with such progressive
personalities in the Inspectorates as Kress von Kressenstein, artillerist;
Heinz Guderian, tank enthusiast; and the future parachute leader, Kurt
Student. It need not have come as a revelation to Kesselring that he, a
Bavarian, was there at all, even though, like other line officers of the
imperial era, he later expressed the opinion that 'the old Prussian nobility
was given preferential treatment in the General Staff; it was thought that
this opportunity was also granted to the wealthy capitalist class'. The new
system, as he also noticed, was not the same in the old Bavarian General
Staff where social distinctions were different. Kress was a Bavarian too, as
was Ritter von Haack, Seeckt's personal Chief of Staff. The
liberal-minded von Seeckt relished such sophisticated company as this
and here Kesselring put a gloss upon his techniques of diplomacy and
organising, learning to negotiate, manipulate, intrigue and dissemble.
Here, too, he was taught to look deeply into men's minds and hearts, how
to act a part and play for time, to take short cuts, to delude and yet to
present his own case with a disarming sincerity. These were the tricks of a
trade which he learnt to perfection in equipping himself for a task which,

with trained foresight, he may even dimly have visualised. For von Seeckt left none of them in doubt as to his principal aims.

Central to von Seeckt's programme of rejuvenation was the gaining of access to the latest tools in the field of technology as well as of tactical technique. Deprived of these essentials as Germany was by the Versailles Treaty, he searched for collaboration with another politically outcast nation, with Soviet Russia, despite her communist system of government. Whatever diplomatic, political and economic advantages may have stemmed from the conclusion of the Treaty of Rapallo in 1922, there is no doubt about its significance in laying the foundations of the future decisive technical fabric of the German armed forces by the establishment of training and experimental bases in Russia where Germans could study and improve the latest weapons of land and air warfare. From Russia to the *Truppenamt* in Berlin, via the technical offices, came the information von Seeckt desired. And the man who found himself dealing most frequently with air matters was Kesselring, the senior staff officer to the Chief of Staff to the Army Training Department (T4) (*Heeresausbildungsabteilung*). Across his desk came every mite of essential information and through him passed the Chief's instructions to the rest of the Army as well as the initiation of training courses that were extended to the Russians as well. As the result of his personal contacts with the airmen throughout the war, he had come to understand the essential part played by aircraft in the land battle, and so he contributed easily and strongly to the discussions that shaped the clandestine air force which was already in existence. For von Seeckt had ensured that a cadre of experienced airmen (some 180 officer pilots) should be incorporated in the 100,000-man army, even though he seems to have had reservations as to their administrative abilities.

Pilots are not necessarily the most foresighted planners nor the greatest of organising geniuses. They have a flair and a comradeship compounded in a dangerous environment which, in the year 1922, was still a matter of instinct rather than the product of rational training. The wartime head of the old Imperial Air Service did not join the 100,000-man army. Therefore fresh younger leaders were in demand. One such was Ernst Brandenburg, with a brilliant war-time record; another Hugo Sperrle, an ex-air observer and air unit commander. There were, too, Kurt Student, Helmut Wilberg, Wilhelm Wimmer and Hellmuth Felmy, all of whom had experienced operational flying in combat and were to rise to the top in the creation of what was to be the *Luftwaffe*. But of the original 180, but few had the complete attributes of the best higher commander. It was non-flyers such as the young infantryman Walther Wever and his friend the artillerist Kesselring (both experienced products of the Great General Staff) who were uniquely supplied with that, and both went in the ministry at this crucially formative period concocting new ideas together. Here the shrewd von Seeckt and his immediate confrères came to detect the aptitudes of Wever and Kesselring as leaders of cool demeanour best suited to create Germany's air force of the future. There was no place in these councils for the hot-headed aces, celebrities like Ernst Udet and Hermann Göring, who were later to play prominent roles in the leadership of the *Luftwaffe*, who had respectively gone barnstorming or had become involved in fascist politics. The members of the *Truppenamt* were the finest products of the old General Staff and Wever and Kesselring were rated outstanding among them.

With the confidence of experience, Kesselring, with faint irony as applied to the pre-1914 candidates for the General Staff via the War Academy, wrote in 1945: 'If a General Staff officer with this [his own] adjutant's background proved a success in the General Staff one could conclude that he was an unusual individual with special talents. It really meant something to compete successfully with comrades who had gone through three years of highly disciplined training, even assuming that only a part of them had acquired this distinction through diligence.' If it is apparent that he had come to despise those who won promotion by influence and that he worshipped at the shrine of Merit, it seems he agreed wholeheartedly with von Seeckt who believed that 'The best General Staff officer is just good enough to be a teacher for my officer students', and found himself engaged upon the advanced training of the Operations Staff Officers of the Reich Ministry of Defence (*Reichswehrministerium*) and as an instructor of students. And if, as Kesselring stated, those same students came to describe their old instructor's qualities 'as when one seeks to express the sublime quality of a first class bottle of wine by referring to the vineyard where it originated', then it can be declared that, both directly and indirectly, Kesselring came to impose his own high standards and example upon the entire Reich Defence Force. It is an accomplishment too readily overlooked when his subsequent career, his influence and the respect in which he was held comes under consideration. It also accounts for certain prejudices that he and those students may have taken in respect of each other and the quality of their future collaboration. When Kesselring, without apparent reason, criticised a commander or staff officer during the war, it could be that he drew from a superb memory and recollection of earlier reports on that same officer. It is possible that any initial bias he harboured against Erwin Rommel took root in his doubts about any high commander who had by-passed the General Staff net. If it appears that Kesselring was a General Staff snob, so be it. The fact remains that he was an excellent one.

Essentially Kesselring was an empiricist, 'a self-made man', as he called himself; or 'a child of actual practice. The numerous generals and General Staff Officers from all branches of the Wehrmacht with whom I came in contact, officially and unofficially, found me an attentive listener and a receptive student.' He came to the conclusion that 'applied instruction is excellent training for those who are resolved of their own accord to make up the missing links in their education by private study'. Written though they were after the Second World War, those few words transmit the heart of Kesselring's personal approach to men and problems. He recognised good communication and efficiency as refined attributes with a beauty distilled by art.

Von Seeckt, by shifting Kesselring from one task to another – dealing with all branches of training, technical problems, legal affairs and matters of international importance – ensured that one of his most favoured younger protégés acquired an almost unique breadth of experience in as wide a variety of posts as possible within a five-year span. That experience provided Kesselring with an acute insight into the minds of diplomats, as well as sailors and airmen, and took him to the heart of the debate which revolved around the rational desirability for centralised control of the separate armed forces, a grouping of those who sometimes behaved and fought as men apart, not members of a team, on sea, land and in the air. In 1923 and 1924 preliminary studies by the Army Organisation Branch (T2) promoted a paper, written largely by Kesselring, which proposed an Armed Forces High Command (*Wehrmachtgedanken*). The responses, as Kesselring remarked, 'were really pitiful, as interest was as low as one could imagine'. But it was an important beginning since, by then, the groundwork of a third service, an air arm, that must enter into competition for resources with the existing naval and land arms, was prepared. Kurt Student's Air Technical Office was amassing information; Johann Hasse had made a promising contact with the Russians and a flying school for German military aviators and for experimental combat aircraft had been founded at Lipetsk; a branch factory of the Junkers Works was being built at Fili, near Moscow; and numerous sports flying schools were being sponsored throughout Germany. At the same time work was in progress on creating the advanced communication equipment which, it was foreseen, would be essential in the control of the air force of the future.

The systematic laying of a foundation for a young air force was aided in 1926 by the expansion of the Air Organisation and Training Office under the Commander-in-Chief, and supplemented early that year by the formation of a civil air firm, *Lufthansa*, by the amalgamation of the existing civil aviation firms, with Erhard Milch as one of its three directors. The proliferating bureaucracy pertaining to the former had, by 1927, fashioned the essential departments that were to be fundamental to a complete new Service when the time was ripe to announce its existence – as then was far from politic. Though there had been considerable relaxation of political hostility towards Germany in the midst of an economic boom in which money – chiefly dollars – flowed in, the suspicions of the Allies were acute. The advent of *Lufthansa* broadened the base of German aviation in that air crews with first-rate qualifications in long-range operations were trained along with the development of the navigation and blind-flying aids which would be as important to bombers as to air lines. Moreover, Milch, by his dynamic energy and superlative talents as a creative administrator, was brought irresistibly to the notice of those in authority, as well as politicians like Adolf Hitler who looked hungrily for power.

These developments were watched and where possible guided by Kesselring (who had been promoted Major in 1925) along the lines von Seeckt (who had resigned in October 1926 after a political gaff) would have wished. From the centre of the spider's web he also, in 1927, came to realise how the ramifications of the *Reichswehr* were becoming overloaded by bureaucrats who stifled the fighting units' initiative, to the detriment of efficiency, besides raising overhead costs at a time of financial stringency. Waste such as Milch frowned upon in *Lufthansa* for commercial reasons, Kesselring abhorred in the Defence Forces. The mercantile breeding of his family, when fused with his inherent zeal in demanding efficiency, prompted him to analyse the disease in a paper. He pointed out the dangers that existed while suggesting ways of counteracting the evil. His solution may not have been strikingly original – most Ministries of Defence are compelled to make an overhaul every decade or so – but it was undeniably constructive in its final objective, even though destructive in its initial impact. He proposed an investigation into organisation and methods and although, in his 'Memoirs', he complains about being appointed to the task himself (as *Reichswehr* Commissioner for Retrenchment and Simplification) he surely was not so naive or really so displeased as he made out? Be that as it may, he threw himself into a task that was more likely to make him enemies than friends. Working within the framework of a national retrenchment scheme and with the full support of Joachim von Stülpnagel, he aimed to release soldiers from administration tasks, to rationalise office procedure and encourage initiative by greater decentralisation of power to selected individuals. Anybody with experience of this sort of exercise will recall the staunch, inbuilt resistance generated within the organisations and by the individuals under examination. This aspect of the operation seems to have been of secondary importance to Kesselring. So long as his wider aims were attained – as undoubtedly they were – it did not vex him when a few small fish escaped the net. The principal intention, so far as he was concerned, was to build afresh upon the old structure, and nowhere is this more clearly visible than when he came, at a quite early stage of his investigation, to advocate expansions in establishments. Never was this more important than his proposal of 1928 to the Chief of Army Organisation (T2), Major Wilhelm Keitel, that an air inspectorate be formed. For this approval in principle was forthcoming before the year was out, though the actual birth of the *Luftwaffe* had to be delayed, for political reasons, for more than five years. It is of more than passing interest that, round about this time too, Wever and Guderian were also formulating a similar project aimed at the creation of an Armoured Inspectorate (a proposal that had also to await a propitious moment) but which clearly denoted the close association of thoughts filling the minds of these three driving forces within the staff machine. Between them, within the Army, they were designing the forthcoming *Luftwaffe* and *Panzerwaffe* – the two 'private armies' which were to dominate the war to come.

The scope of Kesselring's examination of organisation and methods was widened by a second phase (foreseen at the outset) which took him away from the ministry at Berlin to VII *Wehrkreis* headquarters in Munich, there to turn his ideas into a practical model at the next lowest level of command for others to copy. For a year in Munich, as head of Ia, he carried on the routine duties of that appointment besides implementing the products of the retrenchment, or so-called simplification project. Concerning this period he was to reflect, in 1948, upon his life as a staff officer and the conditions surrounding those who worked with him. He had noticed that staff officers were often prevented from benefiting in full from the courses he had run from T4 because they were overworked. Now he began to realise that, although the pressure of official duties and the officers' economic circumstances generally did not permit them to engage much in social life, 'yet social life gradually increased as their official connection with the other institutions of the state and the industrial organisation also served to establish social ties'. He went on to remark on the way 'invitations gradually reached such proportions as to endanger the economic position of certain individuals', a menace which could only be removed by financial subsidies. To Kesselring such pursuits were welcome in a professional sense, particularly if they coincided with personal amusements: '. . . thus, acquaintances were made with country landowners during hunts and this brought variety and relaxation on later occasions'. Although he couched these opinions in general terms they are closely biographical in that they illustrate his own diversion from his original style of living with his wife and among the corps of officers. By moving farther afield, his resources were stretched and that engendered a coolness that led to an undermining of his home life.

Pauline and Albert had, to his immense disappointment, failed to have children, and the day would dawn when he would seek a child to adopt. As for Pauline, popular though she was with the junior officers, she was unhappy in the service environment and resorted to spending even more time with her mother, that formidable character who had shared his home for so long and whom, as a measure of self-protection, her husband sought to avoid. Frau Kayssler was dedicated too much to the technique of direct approach to suit her son-in-law. On one later occasion, in a group that included the Führer when Kesselring was Chief of Air Staff, she had proudly declared, 'Well, Albert, you've not done too badly, though there must surely be another even better post for you somewhere.' Amused though Kesselring was that Hitler looked distinctly uncomfortable (perhaps a little wary that, maybe, the man from Bavaria had his eye on an Austrian's job) it nevertheless embarrassed him. The restraint that senior reporting officers had noted about him as a junior had by no means been lost in success.

At the conclusion of his task in Munich, Kesselring returned to the Ministry in Berlin in 1929 and thereafter for a short spell was to work in the Army Personnel Office, thus having surveillance over such important matters as personnel selection, appointments, and promotions. In so doing he completed his education by now having served in all the principal staff branches. In 1930 he received two steps in promotion – to lieutenant-colonel and then full colonel – a positive indication, in times of appalling financial stringency when the economic recession was worsening and promotion was at a premium, that he was selected for the highest appointments. Along with the economic blizzard of 1929 came the political storm with its violent buffeting between left and right-wing political parties – Communists versus Nazis – that remorselessly threatened the sickly governing parties. In 1929 Hermann Göring – a newly elected Nazi Party member of the *Reichstag*, and cloaked with the prestige of a former commander of the Richthofen *Geschwader* and an ace in his own right – had proclaimed from the floor of the *Reichstag* that Germany must have an air force sooner or later. With that Kesselring and Wever would have agreed. But the former was away from Berlin at the height of the political and economic storm which brought Hitler to power, and at that moment neither guessed at their future association with Göring, Hitler's close and enthusiastic associate. For early in 1931 it had been decided that Kesselring was due for a break from ministry life and another spell with the troops, this time as commander of the 4th Artillery Regiment in Dresden. He left behind a monument to eight years' endeavour, a reconstructed defence force that was to be a model for all to copy in the organisation of the modern armed forces that were to sweep away the armies of the previous epoch. None of this would have been possible had not von Seeckt given the impetus to change and his successor after 1926, Wilhelm Heye, permitted the necessary rationalisation. Naturally there were those who supervised the venture, such as the distinguished chiefs of the *Truppenamt* Otto Hasse (for whom Kesselring had a great admiration) and Werner von Blomberg, but it takes a dynamic organiser of high calibre to put through strong measures in detail and make them work. It needs a man of amiable charm to persuade or compel the paladins of conservative reaction to accept radically new methods. At the centre of every large-scale reorganisation must stand a practical administrator of middle age and rank with the magnetic abilities of an Albert Kesselring to assure continuity and unity.

In Dresden he lived in relative contentment with Pauline, luxuriating in regimental life with its ingrained minutiae though less demanding pressure of work and social life – engrossed most of all with the joy of commanding men after years of desk work. It was the swan song of anything like contented married life for them. The changes that were being rung in Berlin would presently strike a new note for the Kesselrings. Albert well knew that it could not be long before the General Staff reclaimed him – though it seems almost certainly true that he only contemplated a conventional army appointment, perhaps a command despite his obvious leanings to staff work. His fate, however, already had been decided by the precipitate activities of three men round whom his life was to revolve for the next thirteen years or more.

Among the first acts of Chancellor Adolf Hitler was the appointment, in rapid succession, of Göring to four influential posts – as Reich Minister of Forestry and Reich Minister of Hunting (which remained his favourite task until the end); and as Minister of the Interior for Prussia and Reich Commissioner for Aviation – tasks which carried enormous power and which he wielded with fluctuating ruthlessness, benevolence, enthusiasm, diligence and sheer indolence – as befitted a man of eccentric brilliance who was fundamentally idle. Casting around for somebody who would do the actual work of running the Air Ministry, Göring selected Erhard Milch whose reputation as head of the highly successful *Lufthansa* overshadowed everybody else in the German aviation scene. Milch, well favoured by Hitler, became State Secretary for Aviation in February 1933 (only a few days after Hitler became Chancellor), retaining his directorship of *Lufthansa* and thus embodying these two vital aviation appointments in one man under a Minister who was bent on creating a new German Air Force – the *Luftwaffe*.

By September 1933 plans were sufficiently far advanced to make the first senior appointments to the new air arm, moves which had to remain hidden from the world since they were in direct violation of the Versailles Treaty. Kesselring was earmarked as the head of the intended Administrative Office with responsibility for Budgeting, Personnel, Accommodation and Construction, Food and Clothing. There was scarcely another suitable candidate in sight for the job, bearing in mind that it had been decided to give the new arm the best officers available. In his 'Memoirs' Kesselring says that he was not a bit pleased at the prospect and that he countered with the proposal that administration should remain a function of the Army – thus indicating his instinctive belief that the air arm should be part and parcel of the traditional services rather than a separate entity. Kesselring, of course, was backing a loser. The man who was already appointed as Office Chief (virtually Chief of Staff) in the Aviation Ministry, was his old comrade Walther Wever and Wever was not only *persona grata* with Göring and Milch, but a believer in the indivisibility of air power as postulated by the Italian General Douhet in his celebrated book of 1922, *Command of the Air*. Douhet maintained that strategic bombers could subjugate nations and win wars virtually on their own with only minimal assistance from sea and land forces, and the followers of Douhet, such as Air-Marshal Hugh Trenchard in Britain, had need to acquire complete administrative independence in order to implement his ideas. Kesselring's protests were sharply overruled by the Commander-in-Chief. Wever would lay down the aims and shape of the air arm and Kesselring would adapt and institute the principles and would merge the old order with the 'simplified' methods he had incorporated into a new, integrated system. For, as he describes the attributes of the founding *Luftwaffe* officers of General Staff origin, they were

. . . too clear-sighted and too unfettered by tradition to be satisfied with the unimaginative transfer of Army General Staff standards to the *Luftwaffe* . . . It is to the lasting credit of the first Chief of the *Luftwaffe* General Staff, Walther Wever, that his mind was sufficiently clear and open to recognise the diverging factors and that he knew how to reorganise and incorporate them into an efficient organisation.

Kesselring might easily have been talking about himself, as an intellectual equal with Wever.

It is permissible, in connection with Kesselring's expressed objection to being made to resign from the Army and don civilian clothes as a clandestine airman, to suggest he protested too loudly, perhaps indulged his liking for irony. His performance in practice was not that of the disenchanted. Moreover, the British air attaché in Berlin in 1934, Walter Winterbotham, recalls a luncheon party in Berlin that year when he was introduced to Kesselring and another officer, both of whom were dressed in black coat and striped trousers, but who Winterbotham knew were 'camouflaged' air commodores. 'Over lunch', says Winterbotham, 'Kesselring remained sullen and silent: he was, I thought, just being rude.' But it transpired that both Germans were under consideration for the post of air attaché in London and Kesselring was doing his best to make a bad impression, knowing that Winterbotham's opinion would be asked. Winterbotham concluded that Kesselring's sights were aimed high. Later he was to see the man as he really was – affable and friendly. 'I felt instinctively that he was a quick thinker, tough and could be rough if he didn't get where he wanted to be.' These were the qualities also of a good pilot, which Winterbotham knew him to be from personal observation of his technique. This too was a sure pointer to Kesselring's outstanding attributes. It was remarkable that a man aged forty-eight could quickly learn to fly while carrying out his other myriad duties and qualify with outstanding merit in obeying Wever's demand that all his senior officers must be pilots – Wever having set the example himself. From this moment onward when Kesselring was not on duty he was taking every opportunity to fly, a superior substitute for horse-riding which now completely fell out of his favour.

The acquisition of a pilot's skills and the state of mind which came from it were vitalising to Kesselring. He refers to the 'exemplary *esprit de corps* of the air crew', and 'With the exception of parachute jumping, I know at first hand every aspect of flying, with the combined arrogance and humility it gives you.' Winterbotham believes that Kesselring developed charm, but 'it always had a cutting edge'. According to Kesselring, flying also helped give him a sense of detachment from current political events. He says he was flying in south Germany during the massacre of von Schleicher, Ernst Röhm and the other rivals whom Hitler and Göring wished disposed of in 1934. Under examination as a witness during the Nürnberg Trials after the war he admitted flying over the concentration camps of Oranienburg, Dachau and Weimar in 1933, 'but perhaps I may add that, as a matter of principle, I kept aloof from rumours, which were particularly rife during these periods of crisis, in order to devote myself to my own duties which were particularly heavy'. This answer was standard to those questions seeking knowledge of the camps, though there is a basis of truth in his claim of rejecting rumours and a subsequent assertion that this tended to dissuade people from communicating rumours to him. That way he avoided becoming a rumour monger but undeniably he may also have deprived himself of what might have been useful information – and Kesselring normally was a keen searcher after intelligence in preparing his operations at war. On the other hand it is much more likely that he was better informed than he cared to admit.

★   ★   ★

The air force Hitler demanded and the one Göring may have had in mind were neither of them models of what Wever and Kesselring would ideally have liked. At first Hitler only wanted weapons that would quickly enhance Germany's political bargaining power, an aim which Göring accepted just providing it also helped add to his own prestige and strengthened, in the short term, Germany's defences. Conjointly, at the back of their minds, was the primary economic purpose of creating work for the mass of unemployed by getting a stagnant economy on the move again and thereby raising morale and, above all, faith in the Nazi Party's programme. Wever and Kesselring, along with every other patriotic German, wished to see the military and economic aims achieved and were therefore well content to accept the advent of the new règime. Kesselring does not conceal his feelings in this respect. In 1934, in company with every other officer, he had taken the oath to the Führer – an oath which was his 'one guiding star', and he goes on to state that the *Luftwaffe* 'soon came to be known as the National Socialist part of the *Wehrmacht*'. He came to admire the Nazis' 'brilliant and smooth organisation' during the

great Party and *Wehrmacht* occasions, and he was far from averse to a
so-called socialist system which promised all things to all men – curbing
of capitalists, communists and Prussians, sentiments which may well
provide the key to his apparent acquiescence to so many abuses and evils
which were later to come to light of which he cannot have been in entire
ignorance. In understanding Kesselring, or any other senior German
officer brought up before the First World War and under the règime of
von Seeckt, it is essential to be aware of the meaning that obedience held
for them and the absolute sanctity of the oath of allegiance. Those who
assert that oaths are made to be broken propound absurdities when
relating the mere suggestion to men such as Kesselring, who could also
find offence in inefficient or untidy organisations such as the Weimar
Republic.

Both he and Wever knew that it would take a decade to produce a
service well founded in breadth and depth, even assuming that a
disproportionate slice of the economic and industrial cake was theirs. This
would not be so. Already Hitler was also encouraging other arms of the
service in order to produce the same effect – the *Panzertruppe* of Guderian
becoming a major competitor for resources in 1934. Fortunately for the
airmen, Göring carried preponderant influence and was able to obtain
priority of financial support for them. Moreover results were quickly
visible since models of aircraft that were just suitable for service were
sufficiently developed to go into production: in those days it took little
more than two years to develop an aeroplane.

With 210,200,000 Reichsmarks to spend in the financial year 1934/5
and 340 million annually thereafter, Kesselring had ample resources
(about forty per cent of that available in due course) to begin with and it is
typical of the man that he strove to build something refreshingly new
which did not copy past practices. The *Luftwaffe* was to be as
revolutionary as the Nazi règime claimed to be, and not just a symbol of
mass production. True, the secret force when officially unveiled to public
gaze in 1935 had 1,888 aircraft (many of low combat value) and 20,000
officers and men. Praiseworthily it was housed on airfields where the
buildings assured a complete departure in style from that of the old
military barracks, while the aircraft were being built in model factories.
When Kesselring went to Ernst Heinkel in 1933 with the scheme for a
large aircraft factory it was to tempt him with a guarantee of large orders in
the future and insist, with the greatest resort to detail, on the latest
production methods, high standards for the work people and a dispersal
plan in time of war. The aesthetic as well as the human appeal, besides the

strategic necessity of these breaches with the past, gave Kesselring more pleasure and satisfaction than anything else, and provide clear insight into the artistic side of his nature. The infra-structure of the *Luftwaffe* was part and parcel of the extravagance of Nazidom and Kesselring spent the money well, and at a colossal pace. He swept everybody along by a torrent of instructions and saw everything for himself. If some fell by the wayside he was apparently inexhaustible. The high morale of the *Luftwaffe*, that priceless asset in battle, was to be the product of his high standards.

Standing in the way of expansion was Hjalmar Schacht, the President of the Reich Bank as well as the genius controlling the German economic recovery. Overspending and a resurgence of the inflation of the 1920s haunted him. So Kesselring found himself bound to convince Schacht and the financiers that the money was well spent, an advocacy that was reinforced by propaganda disseminated through the *Stock Exchange Gazette*, whose editor was an ex-airman (and who also helped promote the aims of the *Panzerwaffe*), to bankers who needed hard persuasion to give essential backing that Schacht would not find for the arms programme. Kesselring's feat in recruiting and training the cadres of the rapidly expanding air arm, and of moulding an effective and new organisation which was so highly imaginative, was perhaps his greatest achievement. To do so while retaining the respect and affection of people was all the more remarkable, but there were those who suffered too. Hugo Junkers, who abhorred the Nazis, was broken by Göring and Milch and deprived of everything, only escaping trial for treason by a premature death in 1935, and in due course Göring would dismiss Schacht when he made difficulties in 1939. But since Kesselring was the predominant figure in the reorganisation of the Ordnance Department, whereby the technical and supply branches were placed upon a modern footing, it can be claimed that it was he who was the heart and brain behind the sudden and yet relatively smooth emergence of a new factor in the European balance of power in 1935.

In March of that year Göring announced the existence of the *Luftwaffe*, of which he became Commander-in-Chief as well as Air Minister. Simultaneously he and his minions proceeded to emblazon it as a force with capabilities far beyond those it actually possessed. Meanwhile there appeared the first stirrings of dissent among its leaders. Though Wever and Kesselring were unified in working towards the creation of a *Luftwaffe* General Staff, separate from that of the Army, they were not in full agreement over the roles of air power. As an adherent of the theories of Douhet, Wever was committed in principle to the creation of a strategic air force of which a long-range four-engined bomber had to be the mainstay. Projects to develop such a machine – called the Ural bomber – were put in hand in 1932, the name reflecting Wever's belief, based on Hitlerian philosophy, that Germany's most threatening enemy lay to the east and that a long-range bomber would be essential to strike at Russia's manufacturing base. But from the very beginning it was perfectly obvious to anybody such as Kesselring (and Wever too, of course) that Germany's lack of materials, fuel and manufacturing capacity could not support *all* the things that the different services were demanding and that even the *Luftwaffe* would have to sacrifice some of its sacred cows. Wever clung to the Ural bomber concept because of his belief in strategic bombing, but the hard-headed operational philosophy that began to emerge from war games and staff studies moved in the direction of an air force that would give priority of support to operations by land forces. To this strategy Kesselring donated his own pragmatic support, well aware that a war game had prophesied eighty per cent losses for the bombers of the day and that it would be many years before adequate navigation facilities would be available. The state of the art in that field, and bombing too, was still primitive even though Germany was to the forefront in developing directional radio 'beams'.

Against this background of debate and irresolution Germany entered 1936, a year that was to be crucial both for the nation and Kesselring. In February Ernst Udet, an heroic ace of the First World War, was given the post of Inspector of Fighter and Dive-bomber forces (which admirably matched his enthusiastic advocacy of the much more accurate dive-bomber as opposed to the level bomber). Milch became *General der Flieger* in April that year (one step ahead of Kesselring who became *Generalleutnant*) befitting his pre-eminent position as State Secretary – the one man in the upper hierarchy of the *Luftwaffe* who really understood aviation from broad operational experience. Yet Milch deferred to Wever whose charm was probably more seductive, who was not as abrasive as Kesselring and who was given unqualified support by Göring. As for Kesselring, he went his masterly way, annoyed by minor frictions with Milch, whom he considered 'too ambitious', but happy under the superb leadership of Wever who bound them all together. Milch, in any case, stood in isolated objection to the major project for 1936, the inauguration of the *Luftwaffe* General Staff which Göring, Wever and Kesselring were convinced was essential even if it was to be constituted on different lines to the old Army General Staff. For example, they intended to bring the inspectorates under direct command and thus ensure their dominance in the technical sphere – to the immediate alarm of Milch who saw his own influence dangerously threatened by men whose technical qualifications he discounted. In another way Wever and Kesselring tended to differ from the Army by disposing of the traditional 'red stripe' worn by General Staff officers, but Göring overruled them. General Staff officers had to be like the choicest Rhine wines – *Extra Auslese/Spactlese* – with their mark of distinction. Kesselring came to agree and would quote the poet with 'Der Mann muss sich koennen fuehlen' ('A man must feel that he amounts to something').

The General Staff was opposed by Milch out of habit. Not only did he resent its previous rejection of his candidature and the threat to his prestige, but he was, with some justification, worried about Kesselring's expressed opinion that it did not matter if an air staff officer had served in the old air arm or not. This was an affront made more offensive since Göring and Wever were intent upon making the General Staff supreme.

None of these animosities need have broken surface had not Wever been killed as the result of pilot error on 3 June 1936. Though Chief of Staff in practice, Wever had yet to assume the title which now fell to Kesselring as the only possible successor. Almost at once there was a confrontation with Milch who, himself, wasted no time in attempting to retain power over aircraft development by making Udet Chief of the Technical Office – a post demanding deep insight and cool judgement for which the previous barnstormer was most unsuited, both intellectually and temperamentally – where he would be pliable to Milch. To Kesselring, a man of Udet's 'playboy' characteristics allied to an intellectual shallowness was anathemao it is noteworthy that he completely omits him from his 'Memoirs'. For that matter, however, Kesselring's remarks, apropos the next year's hard dealing, are also quite worthless since he glosses over the reasons for the head-on collision which occurred. A wealth of detail, invective and intrigue is left unsaid in the one sentence when he mentions his disagreements with Milch over 'service and personal matters'. But it suited the narrow-minded Göring, who was jealous of Milch, that Kesselring should actively erode Milch's power and influence, particularly in its effect upon Hitler.

Officially Kesselring took up the appointment as Chief of Staff on 15 August, fifteen days after the *Luftwaffe* General Staff itself was promulgated. At the same time the first of the next generation of aircraft were beginning trials – Heinkel He 111 and Dornier Do 17 bombers to replace the stop-gap Junkers Ju 86 and Ju 52s; Messerschmitt Bf 109s and Bf 110s to supplant the biplane Heinkel He 51s as fighters; Junkers Ju 87s as the latest fighter-bombers for direct support of the land forces. The training and advanced development programme was being promoted with enthusiasm along with the inevitable associated teething troubles of a force that was breaching the canons of orthodoxy. Production of the new types was about to start and expand as the factories Kesselring had projected came into being and the labour force, reducing the number of unemployed, moved in. During this formative period clashes between Milch and Kesselring were to be expected but unfortunately they were not confined to matters of everyday detail. Their initial major confrontation, over a subject of important principle, was brought to a head by Milch's demand that the commander of a training wing should be court-martialled after a spate of crashes during experimental flying had led to a suggestion of incompetence. Kesselring demurred on the grounds that this was a *Luftwaffe* disciplinary matter outside the competence of the Ministry and that on such a question he, not the Secretary of State, was the responsible authority. Nevertheless procedures in the training unit were tightened. Professor Richard Suchenwirth in his study of the command and leadership of the *Luftwaffe* defines Kesselring's position at this moment to perfection: 'Despite his wellknown smile, his amiable and winning manner and his ability to "get on" with others, he was every inch a leader and had no intention of becoming a mere "recording" of the directives of his superiors.' Let it be further said that Kesselring, with a touch of arrogance, was not in the least prone to rate Milch as superior, respect his ability though he might.

Concurrent with those skirmishes fought in the halls of government, Kesselring had also to cope with the *Luftwaffe*'s first important active service commitment. It had played no part in the militarisation of the Rhineland in March but events in Spain now made their call. Fighting had begun between the leftish Republican Government and Franco's rebellious Fascists in July 1936, and it was urgently necessary to the latter that 10,000 troops in Morocco, who were loyal to him, should be transported to Spain. The sea routes were impassable because the Spanish navy remained loyal to the Government, so Franco appealed for help to Hitler, through Milch, who was in Spain at the crucial moment. Hitler instructed Göring to respond with the result that the *Luftwaffe*, along with aircraft supplied by Benito Mussolini from *Regia Aeronautica* of Italy, provided air transport to a scale suggested by Milch and fighter cover for six He 51 fighters sent out in advance by Kesselring. The advanced guard of transports and fighters arrived in Morocco on the 27th. Within less than a fortnight 13,523 men and 570,000 lbs of stores had been safely lifted – to

Kesselring's delight and enlightenment. This was a role neither he nor his confrères had envisaged. The strategic employment of transport aircraft found no mention in their key instructional Service Manual 16 which had just been published. But it would be heard of again in darker days.

Along with gratified surprise, however, he admitted to being 'seriously disturbed' – not through German involvement in an act of aggression but because this unscheduled activity threatened the phased construction of the *Luftwaffe*. There was never a moment when Kesselring was not anxiously on guard against some premature over-exertion of a force which was barely out of the cradle, a reflection to which he was to turn prior to every fresh project to which the *Luftwaffe* was committed in the years to come. At this moment, apart from shortages of modern machines, there was the danger of disrupting training by sending the most experienced instructors to war. On the other hand a baptism of fire plus active service investigation of new aircraft might be invaluable so long as the war was contained in strictly limited combat. New machines and techniques could be studied at leisure, including the Ju 87 dive-bombers and the 88-mm anti-aircraft gun – the latter a *Luftwaffe* weapon much favoured by Kesselring, not only in its role in the air defences but also because of its potential as an offensive weapon in land warfare for attacks upon hard, pin-point targets such as pill-boxes and tanks. Airman though he now considered himself, a soldier he continued at heart and with increasing deliberation as the Nazi war psychosis took hold.

If Kesselring and Wever began 1936 in the sincere belief that they were developing a defensive weapon (though Kesselring always freely admitted that air power could only be employed offensively and that fighters alone were quite inadequate), by the end of the year there could be little doubt that Germany was embarked on aggression. Göring had undertaken yet another major responsibility in October, control of the four-year plan for economic expansion. Thus he assumed a role that enabled him to allocate funds to suit himself as necessary. Needless to say the *Luftwaffe*, Göring's personal army, was to benefit from this materially and by expansion of its interests in the military field. For example, war games held that autumn had revealed the need to establish an organisation that would create and run a 'field' airfield system to support the Army in mobile operations. A decision to implement something on these lines was taken later in the year with the full indication of aggressive rather than defensive intent. Clearly, too, the embryo *Luftwaffe* General Staff under Kesselring's direction was thinking in terms of usurping part of the Army's traditional role, particularly in the use of airborne troops.

At Hitler's instigation Göring became more bellicose than ever. Seeing the need to substantiate Germany's claim to be possessor of a formidable air power, the air detachment in Spain was strengthened by generous reinforcements of aircraft and 'volunteer' air crew as part of the Condor Legion, formed in November 1936. A few days later, on 2 December, Göring called for Milch and Kesselring and told them: 'the Press all over the world is excited about the landing of 5,000 German volunteers in Spain . . . The general situation is very serious . . . We are already in a state of war. It is only that no shot is fired so far . . . Beginning 1 January 1937 all factories for aircraft production shall run as if mobilisation has been ordered.' To Kesselring, a practical analyst, this was tantamount to a demand for the adjustment of priorities and emphasis in the build-up of the *Luftwaffe* to enable it to encompass open hostilities on a large scale much sooner than the years 1941 or 1943 as originally envisaged. Projects which would be late maturing or which would overstrain the intensive short-term programme, as now required, would have to be scrapped or retarded. Only those weapon systems about to undergo the test of active service flying in Spain could be continued as major projects. The stage was being set for a crucial change in policy.

At first the debate was over the most controversial aircraft of all – the four-engined strategic Ural bomber which the apostles of air power passionately desired but upon which Milch was back-pedalling. Udet had already made headway in convincing him of the dive-bomber's virtues of accurate delivery, and the forthcoming twin-engined Ju 88 gave promise of supplanting the costly four-engine type. But largely the row was again over the matter of principle as to whether the State Secretary or the Chief of the General Staff was to control the *Luftwaffe*. Wever's legacy, a fully self-contained *Luftwaffe* possessing its own departments detached from the Air Ministry, had yet to be accepted and promulgated. Kesselring, who was committed to fulfil Wever's wishes (as much because they were his own as Wever's) set out, to quote Suchenwirth, 'to strip the State Secretary of every vestige of power', but he was far too sage an administrator to act without making a well-thought-out plan of campaign. The lessons from Nürnberg in 1919 obtruded.

Kesselring, though not a member of Göring's closest circle, had only to stimulate the Commander-in-Chief's known suspicions that Milch was assuming too much the role of Chief of the *Luftwaffe*, to manufacture rapidly a state of crisis when, in the short-term interests of them all, he might have acted as mediator. For example, when Göring accused Milch of behaving almost as though he were the Commander-in-Chief in performing the task of seeing off units to Spain, Milch reminded Göring that it was he who had written a note asking him to act as deputy. But it was Kesselring (according to Milch as reported by David Irving in his biography of Milch) who ordered Milch's Head of Central Office to destroy the letter in order to damage Milch.* And it was Kesselring who, not so long afterwards, took the opportunity to accuse Milch to Göring of having committed high treason for disclosing too much to the British about *Luftwaffe* intentions – even though the disclosures were part of the official scheme of 'bluff'. To the accompaniment of this intractible fermentation between Milch and Kesselring, Germany's future air policy and strategy were resolved in anger. The overthrow of those on the Staff who insisted that possession of a long-range strategic bomber force was an essential prerequisite created lasting schisms within the General Staff, though it was incidental to the departmental struggle. For Kesselring concurred with Milch over the rejection of the Ural bomber. To him the inadequacy of the aircraft industry to build so sophisticated an aircraft; shortages of raw material and fuel; the unresolved problems of long-range navigation and target finding, besides the lack of foreseeable political necessity, were insurmountable problems in the time available. He drew a soldier's conclusion and plumped for a short-range tactical air force which would give the Army close and medium-range support in land operations such as the enemy had done in 1918, a position he was to defend in 1954 in a definitive written answer. In the witness box at Nürnberg, however, he was to admit 'unfortunately we had a low opinion of the four-engined aircraft, an erroneous belief which proved to be a mistake in the course of later years'. Men of proliferate opinions are entitled to a few contradictions, after all!

Under the command and staff system then in use, it was for Kesselring to tender ultimate advice to Göring, and Kesselring was not the kind to be a mouthpiece for anyone. Moreover it was very much in Kesselring's interests, besides his duty, to demonstrate his loyalty to Göring in order to obtain from him the concessions he believed essential for the *Luftwaffe*'s well-being as well as his own advancement, allied to the restraint of Milch. Throughout the ensuing month from the Ural bomber decision Kesselring, master of the bureaucratic machine, pursued his aims along a carefully charted course. At his prompting, Göring agreed in mid-May to

*There is only Milch's word for this rather improbable story. Something underhand may well have taken place but the destruction of a letter in this way is contrary even to the tenets of Nazi bureaucracy and would have left Kesselring wide open to disciplinary action.

the *Luftwaffe* reorganisation that Kesselring desired, with implementation scheduled for 2 June 1937 at which date the executive letter over Göring's signature was issued. Three days prior to that Kesselring resigned as Chief of Air Staff and thus, by implication, gave an impression that he had been defeated by Milch.

It was far from that, even though Milch remained titularly supreme as State Secretary. In effect Milch was, temporarily at least, pushed to one side and into decline by Göring who happened to be in the mood to assert his authority. So why, if Kesselring had broken through, did he suddenly turn away from goal when the ball was at his feet? Why give up the important post of Chief of Staff?

The explanation in his 'Memoirs', while tendering as the cause 'disagreements . . . between myself and my superior, State Secretary Milch', is a glaring disingenuity. It was for Göring, the man in charge, to later give a clue to the real reason when he admitted that the bitter rivalry and command difficulties within the *Luftwaffe* after Wever's death were deeply injurious to the air force and the lack of harmony detrimental to Germany's cause. In a post-war paper, Kesselring, the staff officer *par excellence*, who held the unequivocal opinion that 'there can be no divided command', offers another clue. For he was equally adamant about *one* exception to that rule. 'If the commander of Armed Forces is not a trained soldier he cannot bear the responsibility for purely military actions.' Since neither Göring nor Milch fulfilled that stipulation a division at the top was inevitable. That being so it was advisable to remove one source of discord – himself – to allow at least a modicum of unity to return. Rainer Kesselring feels, quite simply, that it was at the rock bottom of his father's very nature to take such a step since factional strife was not for him – 'he would not waste more of his time quarrelling with Milch'. He could withdraw, moreover, in the safe knowledge that all the major decisions likely to affect the next two years' development of the *Luftwaffe* had been irrevocably taken. The pattern was sealed – for the present. Therefore, assuming that he foresaw for himself a prominent role in the future of the *Luftwaffe* (as indubitably he must have done in his current state of confidence) it was in perfect propriety for him to present Göring with an offer either to resign or a request for a command appointment while submitting the blue-print of an organisation such as his successor could readily implement. This, in a way, was nothing more nor less than a repetition of phase two of the 'simplification' project, eight years ago, when he had moved one link *down* in the chain of command in order to actuate at the lower level the theory of his higher planning. In this way he could prevent some other obdurate commander from preventing or wrecking the labour of years.

It is hardly likely that Kesselring applied even a whiff of blackmail to Göring by suggesting that his own resignation would follow if he were not granted a command, or that Göring ever harboured the slightest intention of dropping one of his most hard-working and knowledgeable officers. The change-over was too cut and dried to be other than pre-planned and the policy document of 2 June, which Göring signed, all too clearly bears the imprint of careful study and final drafting by Kesselring. Its meticulous definition of the relationships which were in future to govern the collaboration between Göring, Milch and the Chief of Staff, besides reflecting past problems, were of a clarity and legalistic thoroughness far beyond Göring's compass. After stating the clear essentials, it went on to reinforce the intention, by repetition and inversions, to lock the door against any possible misrepresentation or error. Irrefutably it was made clear that 'In his long absence, the Reich Minister and C-in-C [Göring] retains the right to delegate to the State Secretary his responsibility.' The separate responsibilities of the Chief of the *Luftwaffe* General Staff were also set out in respect of organisation, training and weapons inspection, and laid it down that 'The [State] office holder does not have immediate command over troops' though he was to 'co-ordinate the Budget with the Finance Minister', and have 'under him the guarantee of uniform ideological training of the troops' – a neat political side-step. 'The Chief of the *Luftwaffe* General Staff', it was written, 'is first military advisor to the C-in-C in all questions of preparation and conduct of war in the area of personnel, finance and material according to the instructions of the Reich Minister and C-in-C.' Furthermore, 'In filling command posts the Chief of the General Staff is to be consulted. The State Secretary and Chief of Staff are to consult each other on fundamental questions in so far as they affect each other. If controversial opinions exist they are entitled to representation at the decisive meeting with the Reich Minister and C-in-C.' And finally, a nice little touch by a master bureaucrat who intended there should be no future misunderstanding or denigration of the authenticity of this crucial document, 'Implemented by the Secretary of State and Chief of the General Staff in mutual agreement.'

Nor did Göring side-track Kesselring to some out-of-the-way appointment; instead he conferred upon him a plum command, the leadership of *Luftkreis* III to oversee the provinces of Silesia, Saxony, and Central Germany, thus making him responsible for defence of the area from whence the most serious danger seemed to be, threatening Berlin and covering the Polish and Czechoslovakian frontiers. Moreover there can be little doubt that, when he left Berlin, it was with an assurance from Göring that Milch's wings would be clipped. Gradually Milch was relieved of responsibility, including technical directorship which was given to Udet; as a result the drive behind the *Luftwaffe* expansion was relaxed and in due course decay set in, for Udet was no organiser.

It was the *Luftwaffe*'s misfortune and to the world's benefit that the complementary brilliance of Milch and Kesselring was not exploited by Göring. All three were to blame but nobody more so than Göring who permitted or stimulated their feud. But Göring, after all, was not of the stuff that commanders-in-chief are made whereas Milch, to some extent was, and Kesselring undeniably had that rare blend of character and competence. So two dynamic commanders of immense potential were to be thwarted and misused by an indolent political opportunist who had hitched himself to the wagon of a successful demagogue.

For the time being Rudolf Stumpff, a keen mentor and firm old friend of Kesselring's whose task it had been to order him in to the *Luftwaffe* in 1933, took over as Chief of Staff. But this was only a transient appointment. Hans Jeschonnek, an ex-infantryman, the man designated for this task since the days he had worked for Milch and who had become Chief of Operations to Kesselring in April, 1937, would become Chief in February, 1939. As one of the élite who had joined with Wever, he was as keen a protagonist of the *Luftwaffe* General Staff as had been Wever and his friend and close collaborator Kesselring. Thus he was by no means a follower of Milch despite – or perhaps because of – their previous association in the Ministry. Beyond any doubt Kesselring sponsored Jeschonnek's rise and Jeschonnek, until the job became too big for him, gave preference (and sometimes deference) to Kesselring on every feasible occasion. So long as Göring did not become averse to either of them or the pressure of events did not overwhelm their policies, they could work as a team virtually dictating, in close consultation, the destiny of the *Luftwaffe*. Young and relatively inexperienced though Jeschonnek was, he always had in Kesselring a strong and staunch preceptor to turn to.

3

Airman in the Ascendant

Insight into the diligence with which Kesselring applied himself to career planning is provided by Walter Winterbotham when he says 'He was a good pilot and flew me back to Berlin in 1937 after the Nürnberg [Rally] in his own plane. By then he was a *General der Flieger* and supremely sure of himself. He told me he would get command of a *Luftflotte* . . .' – and that was in September, six months prior to the event. The long-sightedness of Kesselring's arrangements along with his readiness for the task stand clearly revealed. *Luftkreis* III, when he had taken it over, was merely an administrative organisation, one of several '. . . miniature ministries' (themselves typical products of Kesselring's administrator's talent) which lacked the capacity to wage war since they were innocent of a command facility. In any case, with but 2,000 aircraft of dubious combat value in 1937 that would rise to little more than 2,928 out of a planned establishment of 3,714 on 1 August 1938, the *Luftwaffe* had no justification immediately to adopt a comprehensive operational organisation. Under Kesselring's guidance, Air Divisions had been conceived by June 1937, but after that it was for his successor to select a convenient opportunity to incorporate them into Air Fleets (*Luftflotten*) and thus assume a combat-worthy posture. On 1 April 1938 *Luftkreis* III (along with other such groups) was converted into 1st *Luftwaffe* Group Command to include two Air Divisions to each of which was assigned a variable number of operational squadrons. Also included within the group were Area Commands with administrative tasks, but these were now secondary to the operational echelons. In due course, on 1st April 1939, Kesselring's 1st Group Command was redesignated First Air Fleet, its commander having piloted it through all the formative stages and, in the process, acquired a preponderance of Germany's air strength under his own hand—a pastime at which he became expert.

Kesselring's every moment was now consumed by the task of preparing the *Luftwaffe* for war. 'My heart leaps when I think back to those months of constructive work', he reminisced. He was immersed in planning those operations which were impending against one or other of Germany's eastern neighbours and which thereby became instruments of the massive propaganda campaign intended to strike fear into Europe by the colossal bluff which attributed to the *Luftwaffe* a strength far in excess of reality. Though Kesselring eschewed the limelight for himself he ostensibly brandished the weapon he was forging, sometimes arriving on official visits by air with an escort of the latest fighter planes, always endeavouring to enhance its sense of importance. Already bluff was being superseded by a carefully formulated and deadly strength. The *Luftwaffe*'s Service Manual No. 16 of 1936, written before Wever's death and the Spanish imbroglio, contained little that was inherent in Douhetism and called for the attainment of strategic air superiority through orthodox methods, by combat and bombing of the enemy sources of air power prior to giving direct support of land and sea forces. The policy had been shaped only in part by Kesselring but now, as experience in Spain seemed to suggest that fast bombers could survive in the face of fighter attack and that the dive-bomber was an accurate, close support weapon, he worked to put its tenets into practice. Attack was to be the guiding theme, as the plans laid at the latter end of 1937 and the beginning of 1938 for the containment (if not suppression) of Czechoslovakia demonstrated. By giving the defence of Berlin (for which Kesselring was responsible) relatively low priority, and locating his airfields close to the frontiers, Kesselring displayed his confidence in being able to overwhelm the Czechs. But he was strangely naive if, as the political situation escalated into a crisis generated by Hitler's bellicosity, he could not understand the international consternation caused by Germany's belligerence.

While the majority of Germans sincerely believed that it was essential to gather under German sovereignty all German nationals, such as the Sudeten Germans in Czechoslovakia, and welcomed the Munich solution of autumn 1938 which gave them the Sudetenland, there were a great many who were disturbed when the *Wehrmacht* (its air element under Kesselring's *Luftflotte* 1) occupied the residue of that country in the spring of 1939. It was not simply that the Munich agreement, which had been intended to preserve the Czech state, had been flouted. With the soldiers, sailors and airmen in the know it was a matter of concern that, militarily, they were biting off more than they could chew. In his 'Memoirs' Kesselring avoids the issue and seems to have been less concerned for the moral and political aspects of the Czech case than the danger of extending the *Luftwaffe* too far before it was ready for a general war. It may be true, as he claims, that he was taken by surprise by the timing of the move into Czechoslovakia, but he must surely have read what was on the cards. Of all the professional Service Chiefs at that time he, like everybody in the upper *Luftwaffe* hierarchy, was far better informed of Hitler's intentions than those in the Army. Kesselring revealed his political outlook (which, in modern parlance, was equivalent to that of the Deterrent) when, in the 'Memoirs', he wrote, 'I considered, as did Göring, that the more firmly the will of the German government was supported by superior military strength the more likelihood there would be of a political solution' – but he omits to explain the solution he or anybody else had in mind. There is little doubt that the main guard of army officers would have agreed. If they *spoke* of a *putsch* to remove Hitler, and after the war some were verbose in their protestations of resistance, at the time they *did* nothing about it because it pleased them to see Germany being restored to her old pre-eminence.

Hitler, for his part, was inherently suspicious and frankly repugnant of the old school army officers, particularly some Prussians among them, though, except on rare occasions, he did not express this to their faces. Gradually he surrounded himself with followers whose confidence was infectious and whose arrogance was muted. Instinctively, as suited a revolutionary, he sought enthusiastic revolutionaries among the military hierarchy. The airmen, with their well-known affinity to Nazism, took his fancy, as did the apostles of the latest land warfare weapons, above all Guderian as the driving force behind the *Panzerwaffe*. Prior to September 1939 Hitler conferred far more with Guderian than he did with Guderian's superior, the Army Chief of Staff; and Kesselring, who was restrained with his superiors, he interviewed far more frequently than Guderian. In this way Hitler demonstrated, as is made clear by the accumulated evidence, that although he originally regarded both the air and the tank arms as the prime elements of propaganda in his campaign of bluff, it was the air force in which he really believed as the force with the most potent war-winning characteristics. There is wide agreement now that Hitler, persuaded by Göring, considered that air power, as flying artillery, would be pre-eminent in subjugating the Poles. Hitler, as an infantryman, had been cowed by artillery in the First World War; of tanks he had no experience. Not until after the Polish campaign did he understand, from the evidence of his own eyes, that armoured land forces were every bit as, if not more, important. But in the days when the *Luftwaffe* could do no

wrong in Hitler's eyes, the Führer came to trust Kesselring while
Kesselring learned how best to please the Führer. Disagreements there
would be to spoil the temper of their association, but there was hardly to
be a crucial occasion upon which Kesselring did not finish up riding the
crest of a wave. Hitler, despite the many reservations he was to acquire in
relation to Kesselring, was susceptible to the airman's infectious
optimism. After the war Kesselring would assert that nobody could
prevail over Göring, let alone over Hitler, in decisive questions (a
comment which he probably applied to Hans Jeschonnek when he became
Chief of Air Staff in 1939) but it was the bubbling enthusiasm of creative
empiricists like Kesselring and revolutionary prophets like Student and
Guderian who stimulated Hitler's imagination and gave him an
exaggerated confidence in the capability of the *Wehrmacht*.

Kesselring claims that he believed Hitler understood the danger of
overstretching the *Luftwaffe*'s (and therefore, by implication, the frailty of
Germany's) strength, but it is to be doubted. Once Czechoslovakia had been
consumed, action for the next expansive venture, against Poland, was at
once initiated by a revolutionary dictator who, like all revolutionaries, could
ill afford to remain static. The next move, however, had wider inference in
the political field – and, also, for Kesselring. When Poland was brought
under political pressure, France and Britain took serious alarm and the
Poles made it known they would fight. Automatically Kesselring, as leader
of *Luftflotte* I, became plunged into the planning of what would become his
first live campaign of conquest. He was thrust to the forefront in Hitler's
considerations as the most prominent leader of the arm that was decisive in
Hitler's estimation. The fact that there was serious deficiency in the supply,
quality and size of bombs, for example, and that Germany's war reserves
barely allowed for a campaign lasting much more than six weeks, was
brushed aside by the Führer. And though Kesselring was undoubtedly
confident in respect of the *Luftwaffe*'s ability to acquit itself well against
Poland, within the limits imposed by material, shortage of experience, and
an operational strength in the east that was less than 2,000 aircraft, he
admits to the same nagging worry felt by every senior German officer (as
well as many in the lower orders), a fear of the threat imposed by Soviet
Russia to the east. They all concurred with relief when, on 23 August, it was
announced that a non-aggression pact had been signed with the Russians,
and relaxed still further on the 25th when it became known that the Western
powers were making diplomatic moves and the invasion of Poland was
postponed, perhaps cancelled.

Kesselring conceals his deeper feelings at this time and declines to comment on what, by then if not before, was a clear indication of the underlying intentions of his Führer. On 22 August he had been among the senior officers called to the Berghof to listen to a protracted declamation of Hitlerian aims that included an announcement of the policy of extermination of 'inferior' people in the footsteps of the conquest that the *Luftwaffe* was to lead. These things Kesselring ignored, perhaps because he considered them too incredible. But his Chief of Staff, Wilhelm Speidel, comprehended what they portended and registered in his diary 'unmistakeable dismay' besides his revelation of 'Our weakness in training, equipment and operational readiness' which were 'again and again dutifully reported to higher authority'. In fact, Kesselring's 'Memoirs' are at their least informative and most misleading in their description of the prologue to and the events of the Polish campaign. They give a distorted picture of the trend and effects of the air war besides providing an ambivalent political commentary along with concealment of his personal motives, the latter admitting to little discernment of the moral issues involved.

The Polish campaign, nevertheless and as might be expected, demonstrates Kesselring's development as a leader and commander. Frequently he was in the air, flying among his formations deep into hostile air space in his attempt to assess the enemy resistance as well as evaluate his own men's performance, besides providing that essential encouragement of leadership which every soldier needs. For it must not be thought that each German plunged gaily into battle in 1939 as so many had done in 1914. There was deeply rooted scepticism to be overcome among fighting men whose memories dwelt upon harrowing tales of the wasteful death roll of the previous conflict. The combat troops had to be persuaded to fight and risk all, quite as much as ordered to do their duty. Kesselring, who knew this from experience, was repeatedly in the fore-front of action.

Luftflotte I was responsible for the northern sector of the invasion which included the link-up with East Prussia from the west, the elimination of the Poles in the Corridor and the subsequent drive towards the south alongside Army Group North to join up with Army Group South advancing from that direction. Within its sphere of responsibility fell Warsaw and its environs. To the rear Berlin had to be protected. His strategy complied with Manual 16 – an all-out assault on the Polish Air Force and its bases as a prelude to direct support of the surface forces. But the elements and Göring at once diluted the doctrinal method, while the Polish Air Force took measures that effectively frustrated an enemy

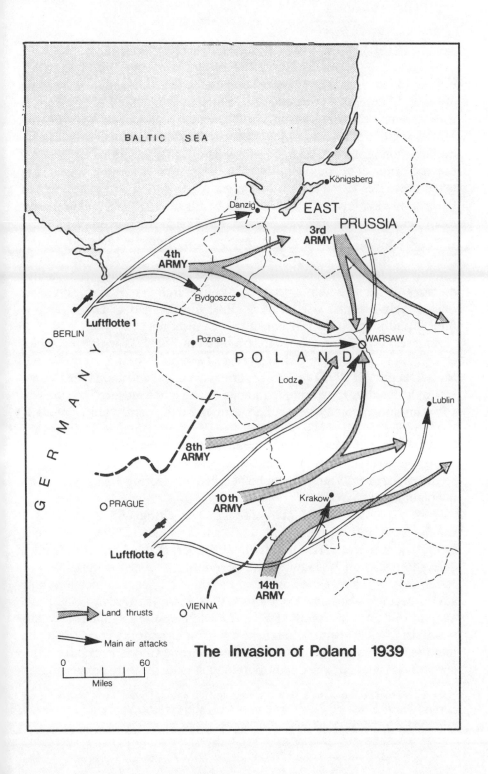

BALTIC SEA

Königsberg

Danzig

EAST PRUSSIA

3rd ARMY

4th ARMY

Bydgoszcz

Luftflotte 1

BERLIN

Poznan

POLAND

WARSAW

Lodz

Lublin

GERMANY

PRAGUE

8th ARMY

10th ARMY

Krakow

Luftflotte 4

14th ARMY

VIENNA

Land thrusts

Main air attacks

0   60

Miles

The Invasion of Poland 1939

assault of this nature. From the outset the defects of air power were exposed.

Low cloud and poor visibility prevented the *Luftwaffe*'s maximum effort on 1 September. Those aircraft which took off had difficulty finding their targets. The mass attack on Warsaw, which Göring had ordered Kesselring to undertake, was postponed: thus this vital communication, mobilisation centre and manufacturing base of the Polish aircraft industry escaped immediate punishment. The 'Memoirs' are again misleading when they refer to having hit the Polish Air Force hard. At the end of a frustrating day, few airfields had been bombed really effectively and not many aerial combats had taken place. The Polish Air Force had, largely, escaped damage because it had dispersed to secret landing strips and found as much difficulty finding the Germans as the Germans had in finding them. Again Kesselring is mistaken (possibly from faulty memory) when he wrote that the Polish fighters 'numerically and qualitatively claimed our respect'. Probably he had a narrow escape himself, although he is reticent in this connection.*

A mere 159 fighters, mostly the obsolescent PSL P 11 with a top speed of 242 mph, were matched against 210 German fighters, chiefly the Messerschmitt Bf 109 D with its superior armament and a top speed above 300 mph. Holding the initiative and possessing much more refined logistic and communication systems, the Germans could hardly fail to prevail. Yet, on the evening of 1 September, though it was plain to Kesselring that his Air Fleet had flown virtually unchallenged, it was also apparent that the enemy remained intact – and this gave rise to concern about what might be in store. Would Berlin be bombed and Göring's assurance of its inviolability exploded?

Quite the most effective intervention by Kesselring's Air Fleet that day was its bombing of Polish naval installations near Danzig and field fortifications in the Corridor in indirect support of the Army, though the delayed attacks on Warsaw towards evening did at last materialise and result in heavy damage to some targets, including communications and aircraft factories. For the next few days the *Luftwaffe* tried with might and main to find and destroy the Polish Air Force on the ground but for the most part hit non-operational types. What few aircraft the Poles could put into the air did quite well, shooting down several German aircraft on the 3rd and carrying out a few light bombing attacks on army targets. But it

*Of the five occasions on which he was forced down it has only been possible, despite an exhaustive search, to identify two, and about these there is little detail since Kesselring, with studied modesty, declined to mention them.

was ground action which settled the air war, the German Army's advance rapidly overrunning the Polish early warning system and forward bases, thus fatally hampering their direction of fighter aircraft, while the supply of spare parts was cut off so that serviceability was seriously impaired. By the 7th the Polish Air Force was indeed broken, but mainly by internal collapse. Not until the 14th was a really telling blow aimed at it on the ground and the bulk of the bomber force at last caught on an airfield at Hutnicki.

After 2 September Kesselring concentrated on support for the Army and accurately presents his attitude to this role in the 'Memoirs': 'I was not subordinate to von Bock [the C-in-C of Army Group North] but voluntarily felt myself to be under his orders in all questions of ground tactics.' Thus the soldier in Kesselring overrode the airman's doctrinal inclinations and there was established the essential motivations which from that moment were to govern his conduct of war. No wonder he was a favourite of von Bock! Committed though he was to the application of air power as a weapon in its own right, he was anything but a bigoted apostle who insisted that air power was indivisible. From deep experience and historical study he new that the ultimate solution with the weapons then available could only be resolved by ground forces and he used everything in his power to ease the task of the Army. It was the newest and most accurate weapons of the *Luftwaffe* armoury (less paratroops which remained as Göring's reserve) which made the heaviest impact, equipment which Kesselring had sponsored all along – the Ju 87 dive-bomber and the 88-mm dual-purpose anti-aircraft gun, the latter deliberately introduced offensively into the forefront of the land battle besides supporting conventional air defence. Here again the combination of soldier with airman promoted within Kesselring his desire to incorporate ground weapons as part of the aggressive air armoury. While on the one hand he would try to make the soldiers appreciate that aircraft, economically and efficiently directed, could swing the battle their way, on the other he directed the *Luftwaffe* towards an innate appreciation of the soldiers' problems. Hence he was very displeased to find, in post-battle analysis, that there were serious shortcomings in collaboration. It was not unexpected that, in a complex highly mobile battle, aircraft should bomb friendly troops and that the *Luftwaffe*'s own anti-aircraft guns should shoot down friendly aircraft, but annoying that deficiencies in close co-operation between the air and land forces were prevalent in the forward edge of the battlefield where the tactical struggle was fiercest. All too obviously the airmen had rather arrogantly concluded that the victory was to be of their exclusive making and that the soldiers would merely follow a lofty lead. Practice had painfully demonstrated that this was not the case and it was for Guderian to show Hitler, on the spot, that the most effective damage in the battle zone had been done by his tanks and guns, not Kesselring's bombers.

The closing stages of the campaign, which lapsed into siege warfare, gave Kesselring the opportunity to restore the *Luftwaffe*'s confidence in itself and to demonstrate, to his own satisfaction as well as to his superiors', his handling of large air formations. Hitler, fearing repercussions from the Russian intervention in eastern Poland (at which he had connived) on 16 September, and an Anglo-French offensive in the west, insisted that Polish resistance in Warsaw should be eliminated without delay by all means possible. At once the Army and the Air Force vied with each other in their endeavours to bring about a solution through bombardment of what they insisted was a fortress – a reasonable enough assumption in the light of the concentration of stores, armaments and fortifications contained within the city.

While Manual 16 was scrupulous in insisting upon observation of international ethics in the conduct of war, it did countenance attacks aimed at undermining enemy morale. There is no doubt that Göring had that in mind when he ordered the initial assaults on Warsaw at the beginning of the war; no practical airmen could reasonably claim that aerial bombardment could be aimed with the same accuracy as artillery fire. At Nürnberg Kesselring stated that the massed attacks executed from 25 to 27 September '   were employed against military targets. I myself was over Warsaw and after practically every air attack I consulted the army commanders about the execution.' There was an attempt to use guns against close-range targets and aircraft against those at longer range in inaccessible locations, but the sight of slow JU 52 transports plodding over the virtually defenceless city with men shovelling incendiary bombs out of the doors is not compatible with the concept of pin-point attack implied by Kesselring and the apologists. Unhappily for Warsaw's defenders the Army's artillery and the *Luftwaffe*'s dual-purpose guns and bombers competed for the honours in magnitude of destruction. As an artillerist himself, Kesselring (post-war) gave credit to the Army's weapons, though throughout this bombardment there was acrimony between the contestants, each complaining that dust thrown up by the other obscured targets from view, both claiming, in the aftermath, that it was *their* weapons which had effected the really important damage. The matter was argued out before Hitler who invested Kesselring with the Knight's Cross of the Iron Cross while snubbing the Army Commander, Johannes Blaskowitz, on the pretext of a minor social misdemeanour. Kesselring was right, however, when he submitted the considered opinion that, 'in this campaign the *Luftwaffe* learnt many lessons . . . and prepared itself for a second, more strenuous and decisive clash of arms'. In 1939 his destiny was obscure since he was left in the backwater of the east, consolidating the Polish conquest. The battle to come in the west was intended to belong to the Old Eagles, to Felmy and Sperrle, with even Milch marching in to steal some of the battle honours.

4

The Nemesis
of Incomprehension

Upon the conclusion of the campaign in Poland it was Kesselring's task to organise the air defences of the conquered territory and establish there, in a zone of relative safety, a base for training the next generation of air crews as well as for the repair of aircraft. For a short spell, too, he returned to his family in Berlin, 'where the happy, intimate atmosphere helped me to forget the mental and bodily strain I had been through'. He was being kind when he wrote that. Family life for him was less attractive now than ever. His mother-in-law was more intractable and there was but little common ground with Pauline; this was almost the last time he was to mention them in the 'Memoirs'. When next Kesselring went on active service it would be for an indefinite term, one that carried him to the forefront of continual action in all the most demanding of Hitler's military campaigns. Totally immersed in the business of war he ceased, thereafter, to take leave. When he returned to Berlin it was on duty to attend the frequent conferences called by Göring and Jeschonnek or, as time went by and his prestige increased, to debate with Hitler in person or the staff of OKW.

He draws a veil over those events in Poland which fell outside his military purview. The herding together of Jews into ghettos and the systematic eviction of the Polish people from one part of the country to another in order to make room for German colonists in the old Prussian territories, is ignored. Yet it is inconceivable that he was unaware of these things, particularly since his opposite number in the army, Johannes Blaskowitz, undoubtedly knew and was loudly indignant at what he saw. For although Blaskowitz regarded the subjugation of Poland as 'a sacred duty' in restoring the old Prussian lands, he was active in condemning the methods employed against the Poles by the SS groups under Governor Frank.

If Kesselring stayed silent one at least among his officers, Blaskowitz's *Luftwaffe* commander, felt unable to do so. Colonel Karl Henning von Barsewisch tells of receiving

. . . in my official capacity from Blaskowitz, documents concerning the unimaginable horrors which have been committed in the east as early as 1939, with the order to fly to Berlin to submit them to the Führer 'who knew nothing about it'. I was intercepted by Milch. He locked up the extensive materials, declaring, in the Führer's name, that Hitler wanted these atrocities. After a long discussion I left the room as an enemy of the system, having entered it as a National Socialist. In this argument the hope remained of preserving the *Wehrmacht* intact so as to maintain an agency to keep order after National Socialism.

But he went on serving his country to the best of his ability; to that there was no apparent, feasible alternative.

The Führer's pronounced intention to invade the West as soon as Poland had been taken might well have led to an offensive in November had not a combination of internal *Wehrmacht* politics and bad weather conspired to prevent it. Both the air force and tank force experts, upon whom all hope of attaining a quick and absolute result depended, were adamant in their insistence upon good weather to accompany their efforts. Kesselring, of course, had nothing to do with these deliberations, occupied as he was in the East where he might have remained had not chance taken a hand. However, the mistaken landing in Belgium of an aeroplane from *Luftflotte* II on 10 January had repercussions outreaching a mere breach of neutrality. Its passenger was carrying the invasion plans and nobody could be sure if they had been destroyed in time. From Hitler, enraged at this serious breach of security, there came a sharp rebuke for the humiliated Göring, who had little option except to sack the commander of *Luftflotte* II, the Old Eagle, Hellmuth Felmy. Into his place stepped Kesselring but not, it seems, as an automatic choice. When announcing the appointment Göring gave nothing away: Kesselring got the job 'because I have nobody else', yet he could have given it to Milch since Milch had asked for it and Göring was agreeable. But once more the General Staff displayed its dislike for Milch, its Chief, Jeschonnek, insisting upon putting in his friend Kesselring.*

The compromising of the invasion plans acted as a blessing in disguise for the Germans in several different ways. The existing scheme had to be

*Soon Milch was to receive the operational command of *Luftflotte* V in the invasion of Norway and was to acquit himself well.

scrapped thus making way for a new, more imaginative strategy with incalculable consequences for the future. Kesselring would take up his new task (in collaboration with von Bock of Army Group B with whom he had worked so well in Poland) in the hope of imposing his own ideas on an existing plan he distrusted. He found that not only was *Luftflotte* II to cover the invasion of Holland by the Army and also act as the spearhead of attack on land as well; this part of the attack was to be a *Luftwaffe* benefit of which the aim was the rapid occupation of the Netherlands through the first large-scale airborne invasion ever undertaken. Felmy, with Student (Kesselring's old comrade of *Reichswehr* days) had hatched the initial scheme, but Hitler, too (ever enthralled by dramatic and large-scale projects), had made a contribution and, as Kesselring soon discovered, was not prepared to allow revision. Kesselring could have argued openly against the Supreme Commander's will, as was his right. Instead he employed what was to become, from then on, an ingrained technique, a process of gradually chipping away the rough edges until the main edifice of the plan had taken a manageable shape. Acting as a sort of Chairman of Governors, he resolved the many differences in technique that had to be settled in order to co-ordinate the air assault with supporting land operations under von Bock, whose troops would have to link up as quickly as possible with Student's men after they had landed deep in enemy territory. In these discussions it was as much the soldier as the airman in Kesselring who participated.

The revolutionary campaign in the Netherlands is an important landmark in the development of Kesselring's career, and probably a turning point. For the first of many occasions he was compelled to take a serious operational risk against his better judgement – launching an unproven airborne army and being ordered to do so *before* the requisite local air superiority had been won. It made him strain every sinew to cultivate surprise by trying to have the transport aircraft reach their drop points before the small Dutch and Belgian air forces could intervene – an almost impossible mission and one that depended as much on luck as anything else. It is therefore interesting to observe Kesselring's main departure from the plan of his predecessor, Felmy, who was cheerfully prepared to rely on air power alone to achieve his objectives. Kesselring was to wrestle fiercely with von Bock for close collaboration of the land forces, as the record of their discussions and those with the other army leaders shows – but in the struggle it was as a soldier that he argued. While guarding *Luftwaffe* interests he took the Army's part and rejected the *Luftwaffe*'s dreams of total independence. Göring and Jeschonnek were arrogantly promoting the invasion of Holland mainly as a way of seizing air bases to facilitate attacks on Britain. In their minds they relegated the Army to a subsidiary role in the forthcoming operations. Kesselring was thoroughly realistic. He protested that the relief force was too small, and therefore was bound to be too late in linking up with the airborne troops. This contention was brushed aside to begin with, but was eventually upheld after he remorselessly pressed his point. On the other hand he was as one with Göring in insisting that the *Luftwaffe* should take all the credit possible and with this in mind he demanded the full commitment of all its resources, including the ground anti-aircraft units.

Kesselring also had strong reservations about the methods employed by the Air Landing Group commander, Kurt Student, particularly to Student flying, in person, with the assault – though Student was only acting in the prescribed German tradition of the day by insisting upon leading from the front. Mainly, however, Kesselring was worried about despatching so many vulnerable aircraft to such a precise schedule in the face of potentially heavy opposition and petulantly he groused about Student's habit of going straight to Hitler whenever his intentions looked like being thwarted – a short-circuiting habit which, to those who recall the Wingate and Churchill relationship, seems to have been endemic among inspired airborne forces commanders the world over. It was orthodoxy in command procedures that was at stake and this disturbed the precise nature of Kesselring's dedication to a formal command system. Already Kesselring was grappling with the intractable problem of keeping Hitler's more bizarre ideas in check. Now he began to understand that, although control of the dictator was impossible and there would be many occasions when to accede was the only course open (even by feeding the Führer with facts he liked), it *was* possible to exert a measure of restraint by providing this extraordinary man with digestible facts prior to stating a case. It became necessary to have the ear of the entourage of younger military liaison officers who were ever in close attendance on Hitler as well as on Göring. In the German corridors of power affairs were settled with quite as much dexterity of secret manoeuvre as in those of other countries – and Kesselring had long been a master of that technique as well.

The invasion of Holland on 10 May was destined to fulfil both the hopes and fears of Kesselring. Though surprise was far from being achieved (since British Intelligence as well as Count Ciano, the Italian Foreign Secretary, were able to warn the Dutch of the exact day danger was threatened), the German parachute and glider troops speedily secured

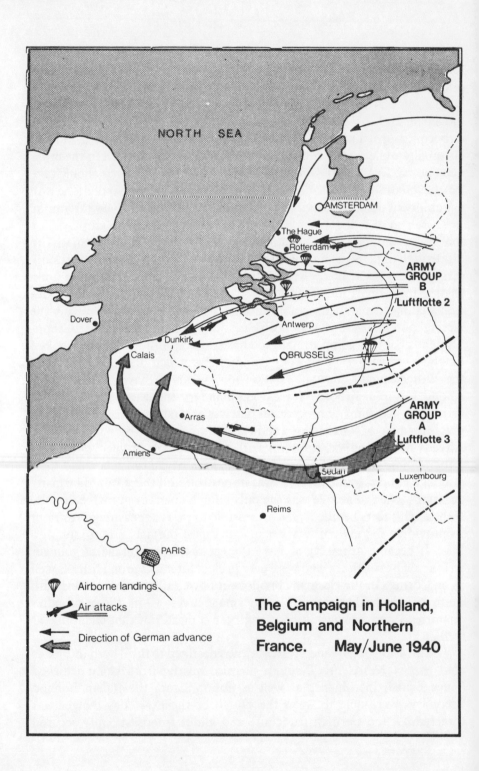

NORTH SEA

AMSTERDAM

The Hague
Rotterdam

Dover

Antwerp

Dunkirk

Calais

BRUSSELS

Arras

Amiens

Sedan

Luxembourg

Reims

PARIS

ARMY
GROUP
B

Luftflotte 2

ARMY
GROUP
A

Luftflotte 3

Airborne landings

Air attacks

Direction of German advance

**The Campaign in Holland,
Belgium and Northern
France.   May/June 1940**

their objectives – the bridges over the River Maas and the Albert Canal, the long bridge at Moerdijk, the airfields at Rotterdam and the Hague. About fifty Dutch aircraft were destroyed on the ground but most of their fighters were airborne early and, as the day progressed (in collaboration with the British RAF) exacted a heavy toll. The slaughter of Ju 52 transports was appalling, each to go down carrying with it a good crew that was an essential part of the training organisation, the cadre upon which the incomplete *Luftwaffe* depended for its maximum expansion in the future. On the 10th on all fronts (including that in Norway), the *Luftwaffe* sustained the heaviest losses it was ever to suffer in a single day – 304 destroyed and 51 damaged – of which no less than 157 were Ju 52s. Some were hacked down in the air (39 in one interception at dawn), more were bombed on the ground. It was a massacre. Moreover the paratroop lodgement at the Hague was eliminated by a Dutch counter-attack long before it could be relieved, and so the only airfield remaining to Student for resupply and reinforcement was at Rotterdam. Kesselring, reinforcing success in the classical manner, instantly and ruthlessly abandoned the Hague project and sent everything he could to help Student at Rotterdam. At the same time he provided the maximum possible bomber and fighter support, though this was attenuated on the 12th when, according to plan, the dive-bombers were diverted to support the main Army offensive as it debouched from the Ardennes and crossed the River Meuse at Sedan.

Time was precious at Rotterdam. Though the land relief forces were nearing the airborne bridgehead on the 13th, and the Dutch were on the verge of collapse, the Germans feared a British seaborne landing and therefore wished quickly to occupy the city and complete the Dutch capitulation. The Germans on the spot threatened the Dutch plenipotentiaries with 'all means necessary' to break resistance if a surrender was not forthcoming on the 14th. The Dutch prevaricated. Meanwhile Kesselring was having a row with Göring over the C-in-C's cavalier approach to bombing Rotterdam, and taking meticulous precautions in briefing the bomber crews who, prior to a final assault by the paratroops, were to carry out a heavy bombardment of the Dutch troops defending the northern perimeter of the city. Radio procedures for stopping the attack if the Dutch had previously given up were arranged as well as the firing of red signal flares by the ground troops if the Dutch surrendered in time and all other communication failed. At the last moment agreement on a cease-fire seemed imminent. But by then the aircraft, high-level bombers with none of the accuracy of dive-bombers, were on their way and, with dreadful portent due to technical reasons, had lost radio contact with control. Moreover haze and smoke in the target area obscured the red signal flares. So the attack went ahead and the centre of Rotterdam was crushed and set alight by fires that grew quite beyond the capacity of the antiquated fire service to prevent. Although there is fairly general acceptance today that Kesselring and many *Luftwaffe* officers really did try their best to prevent the disaster, their C-in-C, Göring, was less scrupulous than his underlings. It was he, against Kesselring's protests, who insisted upon the attack. Of more significance (though it is still accorded far too little weight in assessing the main reasons for the subsequent failure of the *Luftwaffe*, and, indeed, of Germany) was over-reliance upon radio as a means of communication. This not only contributed strongly to the disaster at Rotterdam (which played into the hands of the enemy's propagandists) but was to handicap the Germans thereafter in almost every operation they were to undertake.

Devastating though these air attacks on cities were and provocative of enemy counter-measures against Germany as they were to prove, there is nothing to suggest that Kesselring, the man who was to lead the attack on Coventry, looked upon missions of this kind other than dispassionately. The hatred this bombardment and that previously of Warsaw had helped generate was of far greater magnitude than he can have reckoned with that May. At that time he earnestly believed that a war which was prosecuted to victory by lightning methods would win a more economic and humane solution than one prolonged, as carried on in 1918. To him the air weapon, used with psychological discrimination, was the right, indeed the essential, instrument to help achieve a quick conclusion. For he apprehended that Germany was fighting a poor man's war against opponents who were rich and only temporarily at a disadvantage. They had to be crushed at once; to delay and give them time to recover would be fatal for Germany. These things he told his son Rainer.

The Germans had gone to war in 1939 with what was probably the most comprehensive military communication organisation in the world. They acquired the last word in air and field radio equipment and the *Luftwaffe* and *Panzerwaffe*, which had taken a lead in promoting radio as the best way of commanding and controlling highly mobile units, were lavish in its use. Moreover they had developed highly efficient code and cypher equipment which they fondly believed (and with every good reason) would be proof against breaking by the enemy. Filled to over-confidence with the apparent virtues of radio systems, they used them with abandon, sending over the air even those messages which, if time allowed, might have as easily gone by hand or land-line. The Germans also possessed a highly efficient signal intercept service and could listen to those radio messages sent by the enemy; hence they were well aware how easy it was to glean information by a compilation of even the most innocent traffic. The Germans could not know, however, that the British had constructed a primitive computer which enabled them rapidly to break the top-level codes manufactured by their Enigma encoding machine. Beginning in April, *Luftwaffe* messages were being accurately read in London within only a few minutes of their transmission. The story has been partially revealed by Walter Winterbotham (among others) in *The Ultra Secret* and he records his pleasure at reading everything that his 'old acquaintance' Kesselring sent over the ether. From this moment Kesselring, unbeknown to himself, suffered from a terrible handicap. His secrets and intentions were being exposed to the enemy – as were those of all his colleagues. It was fatal. The Dutch campaign was the last complete victory Kesselring was to win outright, the high-water mark of his success. It was also the last in which his communications were secure.

The plight of the Anglo-French armies penned into Dunkirk by the German Army offered the first opportunity to test whether or not air forces, unassisted, could defeat land forces, though it was neither Kesselring's nor Jeschonnek's idea that the attempt should be made. Both realised that, with their strength attenuated through losses and unserviceability by as much as fifty per cent, their bases too far from the target and with RAF Spitfire fighters based on England well poised to intervene, there was not the slightest chance of mounting a maximum effort, even granted the feasibility of crushing the enemy by fire power alone. At the very moment when the Army spearheads were within hours of entering Dunkirk to complete the envelopment of the British and French armies, it was Göring, eager to win laurels for his *Luftwaffe* – and himself – who ruined everything. He it was who pressed on Hitler the notion of winning a tactical victory by air power alone and he who rejected the reasoned objections of Jeschonnek and Kesselring. Yet there is more than a hint in Kesselring's later writings that, in retrospect, he believed the *Luftwaffe* might have succeeded if it had been up to strength and properly deployed for the task. Here brooded the vibrant optimism that was the essence of Kesselring the man; here too blossomed the very proper faith of a commander in the potential of the force which he had done so much to create. But there too lurked the deadly sin of miscalculation in unison with the inadequate judgement of an operational risk.

Bad weather intervened against the air offensive and prevented the bombers and fighters from achieving the prolonged concentration of attack which success demanded as essential. In any case there was always the cover of darkness to aid the escape of the soldiers and it was by night that the greatest numbers were evacuated by sea. Over 330,000 men were saved, leaving mountains of equipment and stores plus a few thousand prisoners for Kesselring and the others to appraise. What was to follow in France within the next few weeks was almost a formality. The French air force was already broken and the RAF was desisting from too heavy an involvement beyond the British shores since it was conserving its resources for what was to be known as the Battle of Britain, a formal battle between aeroplanes with surface forces largely excluded.

Of the outcome of such a battle Kesselring, early in June, was confident, though haste in its execution was, he knew, essential. It should, he thought, have taken place as an airborne invasion immediately after Dunkirk before the British could recover or prepare. He might have added that any possibility of their recovery might have been unlikely if the German Army had been allowed to prevent the evacuation from Dunkirk. The best of the British Army would have been eliminated. Only a handful of guns and tanks remained in England. Even so he strongly advocated to Göring that the airborne forces should be thrown against England simultaneously with the final attack in France. Reckless though it looked, so imaginative a proposal, which demonstrated his grasp of the conception of mobile warfare, had possibilities. Göring thought so too, as Leonard Mosley points out in a quote from the Reich Marshal who visualised air attacks being concentrated at once on the Royal Navy and the RAF to bring on a battle over the English Channel. 'At the end of the battle', said Göring to Milch, Kesselring, and Jeschonnek in a conference on 5 June, 'both sides would find themselves without anything left and then, with our reserves, with a mere handful of the 5th and 6th Airborne Divisions, [sic] we would bring about the final decision.' This accurately reflects the views Kesselring had put forward with the inherent belief of an artillerist that the war would not be won by artillery, or even 'flying artillery', but by men fighting on the ground.

This proposal which may well have been stimulated by Grand Admiral Erich Raeder's suggestion of 21 May to Hitler that consideration should be given to a long-prepared naval scheme of invasion, was one that went too far for a High Command which had so recently found itself nervously exhausted when sending panzer forces but a few hundred miles by land into France. The prospect of boating or flying across an inhospitable sea terrified Hitler and an entourage who had yet to assimilate the significance and magnitude of their initial and somewhat unexpected victory. So

Kesselring's scheme was rejected, while Raeder hardly bothered to follow his up until compelled to do so. But who can say but what it might not have succeeded? Was it not possible that a surprise lodgement, immediately made, could have been sustained just sufficiently long (even by living off the country and captured enemy arms depots if supply by air and sea temporarily failed) to bring about the same sort of collapse in morale as had brought France to her knees? Two months later Britain, whose people were bewildered in June, had recovered her sense of purpose again and the chances of putting her on the run were remote, even though France had left the struggle and Britain was on her own.

Immediately prior to the Battle of Britain the Germans in numbers, training, experience and, with certain important exceptions, quality of equipment, were superior to the British. Of fighter aircraft the Messerschmitt Bf 109 was the equal of the Spitfire and both could quite easily out-fight respectively the Hurricane and the Messerschmitt Bf 110, the latter, in its turn, being inferior to the Hurricane. The fast, poorly armed German twin-engined bombers were far too vulnerable to go far into enemy territory by day while unescorted by fighters, but the only long-range German fighter was the inferior Bf 110: so the bombers dared not operate by day at long range on their own, while the Ju 87 dive-bombers simply were not battleworthy under any condition in the well-defended English skies. Therefore the most accurate German bombing machine would soon be struck out of the battle while the remaining inaccurate bombers would be reduced in effectiveness. From four campaigns the Germans had gathered a store of battle cunning that far surpassed that of the British who had only one major air battle to their credit. But skill in air fighting came from other factors besides those of the prowess of the air crews. It depended upon the facilities given to controllers to enable them to direct aircraft to an advantageous point of combat to enable the pilots to strike powerfully at the most crucial and sensitive targets in order to achieve telling effect from relatively meagre resources. Both air forces were relatively low in resources. Efficiency demanded good communications and, perhaps above all, excellent intelligence and security against enemy intelligence – and in these things the Germans were notably deficient in one or two important departments.

War against Britain had not at first figured among Germany's intentions and therefore her preparations for such an event had been rudimentary compared with those directed against other countries. The sheer rapidity of the French collapse and Germany's sudden acquisition of almost the entire eastern seaboard of Europe, thus bringing all British targets within close reach of the medium-range bombers, took her leaders by surprise. Hence the effort to acquire intelligence of Britain's defences was relatively meagre prior to 1940 and, concerning Britain's air defences (the prime target of any offensive by the *Wehrmacht* when plans for an invasion were laid), more misleading than definitive.

To begin with the Germans had only an outline picture of the British airfield state. That is to say, they knew where most of them were located but had only the vaguest knowledge of their specific role – a deficiency in detail which also applied to aircraft factories and the RAF repair and maintenance organisation. Therefore it was impossible to be selective in the choice of targets: in the hope of hitting the vital ones, attacks had to be spread over a wide spectrum in a highly uneconomical, and therefore, ineffectual manner. Neither did the Germans know much about the RAF fighter control system; above all they were in ignorance that select airfields also housed the crucial Sector Control Headquarters (in unprotected buildings) which directed interceptions. All they heard, as time went by, was fighters receiving precise directions, but these transmissions they misinterpreted as being of a very local nature, unrelated to a well-balanced and flexible nationwide scheme. Most detrimental of all, they utterly failed to evaluate the excellence of the British radar detection stations which provided the essential information upon which the controllers based their orders. They knew the British possessed, and were using, radar but, from lack of confirmation in detail, rather arrogantly assumed that it could be no better than their own which was, at that time, of only short range and limited use. Hampering too was the inadequacy of their weather forecasting service which was, of course, denied sufficient information from mid-Atlantic where the 'fronts' and 'systems' formed. Finally they were never to know that the British had broken their Enigma cypher and were in full possession of their order of battle and build-up over the weeks of July running into August, along with an insight into their policy and morale and, as time went by, clear indications of the strength and direction of their major attacks. The only times the RAF *could* be surprised were those occasions when certain plans hatched by the Germans were not disseminated on the radio, or when something went awry or was changed at the last moment, causing the attackers to diverge unexpectedly from their assigned missions.

Nevertheless, the *Luftwaffe*'s knowledge of RAF strength at the outset was fairly close to the mark. On 15 July their intelligence branch reckoned there were 675 fighters opposed to them, against an actual operational strength of 603, backed by several hundred machines in reserve and a rising production. Such shortages as existed for the fight against 980 German Bf109s and 110s, were in pilots; only 1,253 were available to fill an establishment of 1,450, a state of affairs the Germans could not be expected to know. Unhappily for the Germans their method of compiling enemy losses was seriously at fault. Because they could not actually see the wrecks in the sea or on enemy territory, over which the battle was to be exclusively fought, they were compelled to rely on their own pilots' claims, which were frequently misleading. An enemy aircraft that smoked and plunged earthward was not necessarily destroyed and very likely the pilot would escape by parachute. Quite regularly claims were two to three times in excess of the true losses, with the result that the intelligence staff accumulated statistics that were wildly divergent from actuality and soon presented an entirely false picture of an RAF in ruins.

The swift redeployment of German air power from its home bases, and its good performance that summer against Britain from less well endowed airfields in the west, was one dividend of Kesselring's pre-war organisation of the force and his first dynamic contribution to launching *Luftflotte* II into its heavy attacks across the English Channel on 17 July 1940. Improvisation was also, of course, heavily invoked. While Kesselring enjoyed comfortably good order in his Brussels headquarters, Johannes Fink, commanding the bombers and fighters of *Kampfgeschwader* II as the spearhead of the offensive againt RAF fighters and shipping, was conducting operations from an omnibus on the cliff-tops. This, to the tidy-minded Kesselring when he saw it, was shocking. He, who had wanted to improvise an invasion of England a little sooner than this, felt bound to comment, 'This is impossible.' Impossible though the command post might look, and vulnerable as it was to enemy air attack, its commanding position was excellent and the work of its occupants exemplary. In the five weeks that elapsed between 10 July and 12 August (the day before Eagle Day when the full fury of the *Luftwaffe* was to be launched against the British air bases on what was, to the Germans, the real beginning of the Battle of Britain) 30,000 tons of shipping were sunk and 148 RAF aircraft, most of them fighters, destroyed. The Germans had lost 286 aircraft of which 105 were fighters, a return that was so unprofitable for the RAF in its fight against odds that it could not be allowed to continue. So shipping was withdrawn by the British from the Channel and the RAF no longer attempted to fight in air space of the enemy's choice but held back until he pushed forward over less favourable territory – above British soil where those RAF pilots shot down might be saved and each German damaged might become a total loss to the *Luftwaffe*. Early in August the *Luftwaffe* began to bomb the southern ports and at once the balance began to alter.

The results of the first month's air fighting were by no means unsatisfactory to the Germans. Their losses were bearable. There was a feeling of victory, particularly since the enemy no longer seemed willing to look for a fight. On 19 July Kesselring's well-being was further stimulated, along with that of eleven other triumphant conquerors of France, by promotion to Field-Marshal. While present in Berlin for the victory celebrations, he could hardly suppress his belief that Britain could not long continue in opposition and would seek peace. But the British decided otherwise and so there was no other alternative left but to destroy them – a privilege claimed by Göring in the belief that his *Luftwaffe* could achieve the essential air superiority that had to be won if an invasion was to take place.

It was Göring's intention to commit some 2,800 aircraft divided into three *Luftflotten* – *Luftflotte* V in Norway with 190 aircraft (mainly bombers) and the rest divided between Hugo Sperrle's *Luftflotte* III and Kesselring's *Luftflotte* II. At that point, as usual, Göring handed over the elucidation of policy and the implementation of control to others – or to put it in the severe words of Völkers, 'his knowledge and capability [of air matters] had remained fixed at the level of a battalion commander'. Squabbles broke out between the contending *Luftflotten* commanders and came to a head on 25 July with the somewhat indolent Sperrle wanting to concentrate the main effort against the enemy's ports and supplies and Kesselring expressing a strong desire to save the *Luftwaffe* from losses as well as to preserve its tenuous reputation of invincibility. He seems to have changed his mind since June. Now he preferred attacks on Britain to be delivered against the Empire's periphery, via the Mediterranean (thus siding with Sperrle for a maritime strategy). But, 'forced into a corner by the High Command', he advocated concentrating maximum strength over a few specified targets, a policy which, to some extent, was adopted by both he and Sperrle, subject to all manner of tactical disagreements over relative strengths, heights of approach and escort duties for the fighters. To Kesselring, faced by the strongest defences of south-east England, went the lion's share of resources, including single-engined fighters in the rough proportion of four and a half to three to those given to Sperrle. But the fighters (though not the bombers) lacked a facility which was of crucial importance – wireless sets which enabled ground controllers to speak to them and through which contact could be made with the bombers. Hence the fighters had to be despatched on carefully pre-planned, free-ranging missions over which there could be no control after they had taken off unless they were instructed to stick close to the bomber formations.

The selection of Eagle Day depended upon the forecasters promising three days' fine weather, conditions which, on 12 August, looked likely for the 13th, 14th, and 15th. Göring's broad directives, converted into detailed orders by Jeschonnek and the General Staff, called for joint assault by *Luftflotten 2* and *3* with *5* joining in in the north once the British fighters had all been committed to the south. Already certain fundamental trends of battle which would shape the campaign had been experienced. The first heavy attacks had been made against airfields and six radar stations in the south of England on 12 August with mixed results. Damage was inflicted but the airfields continued to function and the radar stations were, with one exception, soon restored – and even this one, to German sources, seemed active because the British improvised bogus signals from it. In any case, 'Ultra' provided long-term warning of each day's operations. Discouraged, the Germans bowed to what seemed to them as confirmation of lessons learnt when bombing radio stations in Poland; quite wrongly they concluded these were almost impossible to knock out.

The 13th dawned cloudy and was overlain with confusion. After many of the aircraft had already taken off, the attack was called off but, due to a radio failure, Fink's group did not receive the cancellation while the fighters (who had) could not relay the message. So the attack, of which the British were fully apprised by 'Ultra', went off at half-cock and the unescorted bombers, taking cover in the clouds, were lucky to avert a massacre. As it was, not one of the targets to which they had been sent belonged to Fighter Command, and Kesselring received such a tirade over the telephone from Fink after the angry group leader had landed that he had to go down to the airfield in person from his underground HQ at Cap Blanc Nez (known as 'Kesselring's Holy Mountain') to conciliate him. When in the afternoon the co-ordinated attack was launched, the *Luftwaffe* met a quite unshaken defence, cast its bombs on unimportant targets, and finished with a balance sheet of losses for the day that was thirteen to forty-five in the RAF's favour. Next day the weather again precluded a maximum effort and left Fighter Command still virtually untouched and the *Luftwaffe* angrily frustrated.

At last on the 15th a whole day's fine weather allowed all-out combat. Precisely forewarned by 'Ultra' (and therefore not dependent on the rather vague radar reports as to calculation of numbers) the RAF concentrated on protecting their airfields (which they knew to be the targets) using the economic minimum of fighters demanded. Previously

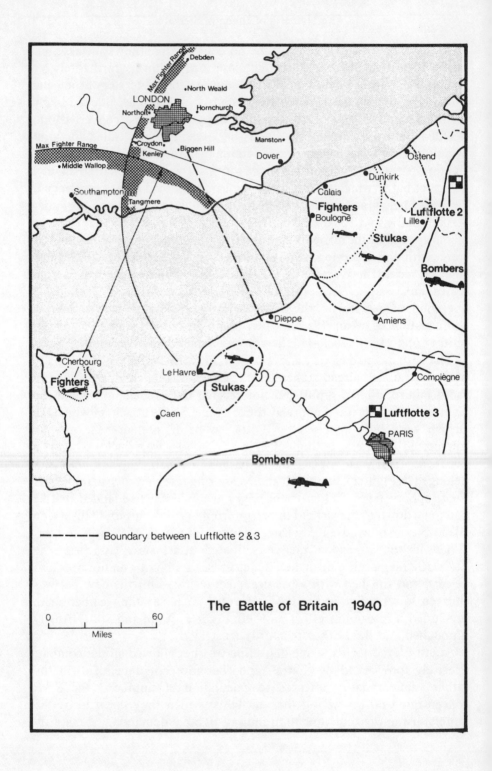

The Battle of Britain 1940

Debden
North Weald
LONDON
Hornchurch
Northolt
Croydon
Manston
Biggen Hill
Kenley
Dover
Max Fighter Range
Middle Wallop
Southampton
Tangmere

Ostend
Dunkirk
Calais
Fighters
Boulogne
Luftflotte 2
Lille
Stukas
Bombers
Dieppe
Amiens

Cherbourg
Compiègne
Fighters
Le Havre
Stukas
Caen
Luftflotte 3
PARIS

Bombers

– – – – – Boundary between Luftflotte 2 & 3

0   60
Miles

Kesselring had concentrated his attacks and done better than Sperrle, the latter having dispersed his formations, and thereby earned a rebuke from Göring for allowing his subordinates too much freedom. Kesselring, satisfied so far with his achievements, achieved full concentration of effect on a day when seventy-three German aircraft (mostly from *Luftflotte* V) failed to return against losses of thirty-four British fighters, a day in which, at last, a number of fighter airfields were damaged – though not always the ones the Germans intended to hit due to vagaries of navigation when under attack by fighters and guns. Of far greater significance was the outcome of the intelligence assessments of the day. The Germans put British losses at 111 with 14 possibles. The RAF had claimed 182, it is true, but their error was not as serious to the outcome of the battle since they worked pessimistically on the assumption of being grossly outnumbered – and profited from the illusion. The Germans, on the other hand, now guessed, quite erroneously, that they had only to mop up a few survivors. For Kesselring, his optimism lifted higher into the ascendant, seems hardly to have challenged intelligence estimates that the RAF was down to about 300 fighters on the 16th (when it was more than twice that number) and pursued a sterile strategy on the assumption that all was going his way. Nevertheless he was beginning to arrive at the conclusion that attacks on airfields were ineffective (as indeed they were if directed against the unimportant ones) and that the best way to destroy Fighter Command was in aerial combat. That being so it was permissible, in his view, to reduce the bomber content of his formations while raising the fighter element. By deploying the fighter swarms in concentrations which not only fought the enemy at a numerical advantage at the critical point but acted also as diversions to throw the RAF defence off balance, he repeatedly prevented the RAF from concentrating its squadrons.

Kesselring had won the initiative and none of the senior air commanders was more eager to exploit it than he. In the days to come, whenever the weather permitted (and there were several spells of reduced activity due to its fluctuations) Kesselring's fighters often caught the RAF at a disadvantage. In so doing they began to inflict unacceptable casualties on the RAF whose case was made worse by two controversial notions of their own. One was the tactic of deploying single squadrons (succeeded later by pairs of squadrons) in order to effect early interception far forward. This played straight into German hands. The other was Hugh Dowding's policy of 'stabilisation' which withdrew, instead of reinforcing, the battered, experienced squadrons from the more hard-pressed sectors to replace them with units that were up to strength but 'green'. In effect Dowding prevented the most efficient killers among his pilots (who were often chief among the survivors) to exploit their hard-won prowess. Thus he persisted in pitting relative amateurs against the Germans who deliberately kept their most expert pilots constantly in action. For the Germans this offered a rich dividend to be gathered since it was only this handful of the best men who scored the most victories and their task was made that much easier when they were saved from meeting opponents of equal experience.

For a moment the battle swung the German way, though almost as much by luck as through Kesselring's undoubtedly shrewd strategy. On the 18th a radar station was knocked out for the rest of the month and for the first time the Sector Control airfields, along with their communication paraphernalia, were hard hit. Unfortunately for the Germans the weather intervened until the 24th when the battle was resumed, but not against the Sector Stations. Again the balance of losses favoured the RAF, helped on the 26th when Sperrle's *Luftflotte* III was given a drubbing near Portsmouth. As a result his part in the day offensive was more or less stopped for the time being and nearly all his fighters transferred to Kesselring, who was only too pleased to acquire the lion's share of these machines in his endeavours to bring the RAF fighters to battle over south-east England. The destiny of the German attack was thus placed in his hands – win or lose it depended upon his judgement, bent as it was at moments of crisis by Göring's whims and Hitler's political demands. Indeed, the latter was about to intervene fatally.

In response to an accidental and ineffectual attack on London by a few of Kesselring's bombers on the night of the 24th, the RAF bombed Berlin with similar ineffectuality on the 26th. At once Hitler demanded retribution and from then on was far less inclined to forbid attacks on targets in the London area. Furthermore the progressive shifting northwards of the German bombing attacks to fulfil the original *Luftwaffe* plan of airfield destruction carried the main air fighting by day in that direction. With the outer airfields of south-east England already in a parlous state by the end of August, the attacks now fell on the inner ones, which just happened to be the Sector Stations. But still they received nothing like the weight their importance justified. There was, in fact, something reminiscent of a First World War creeping artillery barrage about the German method – the progressive advance of a curtain of fire leaving, it was hoped, a dead or neutralised enemy in rear. Perhaps Kesselring's previous experience as an artilleryman had something to do with it. If so, he was flying in the face of history, for creeping barrages only function effectively if the area under bombardment is immediately occupied by troops; to leave it unattended for too long simply gives the enemy time to restore his defences. When the attack shifted to the inner airfields those on the perimeter began to recover. Nevertheless the *Luftwaffe's* basic strategy was prevailing even though it stood well short of victory. RAF fighter losses (destroyed and damaged) for August were 587; those for Messerschmitt 109s, 311 in *all* theatres from *all* causes.

But the autumn storms and the deadline for a sea invasion were close at hand, and Göring's impatience for quick results insistent. Seeking rapid results to satisfy an impatient Führer, he visited the Hague on 3 September with Jeschonnek to discuss with his Air Fleet commanders the apparent tardiness of progress. *Luftwaffe* Intelligence had just produced one of its wilder estimates, saying 1,115 RAF fighters had been destroyed since 8 August, a figure which threw into sharp relief the differences between the realism of Sperrle (who had commanded the Condor Legion in Spain) and the optimism of Kesselring. Sperrle, whose bombers had repeatedly been intercepted well out to sea and badly chopped about, derided the reports; 'the English still had 1,000 fighters available' he declared – and was nearly correct in his estimate. Kesselring, whose fighters were scoring well and to whom the evidence of a falling incidence of interceptions of his bombers was significant, accepted the intelligence estimate and concluded that the 'English have next to nothing left' and 'recently only the bad weather has prevented my bombers reaching their targets'. Therefore, he thought, the range of penetration could safely be extended, the attack on London, which Hitler demanded and Göring felt should no longer be resisted, could be made, even though the primary object of eliminating the RAF remained. It was Kesselring, ebullient in his confidence, who carried the day and supported Göring in giving the Führer his wish – though that is not to say that the sheer destruction of London was Kesselring's aim. He sincerely believed that the RAF could only be destroyed in the air and that the best way to bring them to a final battle was to attack a target they were bound to defend. He failed to realise that attacks upon the airfields were achieving this very purpose already.

The product of his miscalculation is a turning point in history. The RAF did rise to defend London – as, less effectually, it had previously risen to protect the other targets. But now it had more time in which to concentrate for massed interceptions while the *Luftwaffe* fighters, stretched at maximum range with minimum combat endurance, proportionately could do far less to protect the bombers *and*, above all, accomplish what Kesselring sought – the destruction of RAF fighters.

When London was bombed the pressure was relaxed upon the fighter stations; at once their efficiency improved. Now the tactical-cum-technical misjudgements of the past, to which Kesselring had contributed by faulty as well as by correct decisions, began to tell. The 'fast' bombers were unable to outfly the opposition, as they had in Spain and in Poland, and began to suffer punitive losses once they ventured beyond the range of the single-engined fighters which had not been provided with extra fuel tanks. As a result the bomber crews demanded (and obtained via Göring) close rigid fighter escort to the detriment of the independent fighter sweeps which, until then, had proved Kesselring's most effective method for destroying British fighters. In consequence the fighters, deprived of their full mobility and flexibility, themselves fell victims. Of telling effect upon German calculation and morale, however, was the abrupt increase in the number of interceptions by the British. These rose dramatically to a climax on the so-called great day of 15 September when fifty-five (not the claimed 185) *Luftwaffe* aircraft failed to return and the sky seemed alive with Hurricanes and Spitfires. *Luftwaffe* intelligence was shown to be hopelessly in error. Already Hitler had been persuaded by his naval chiefs that a seaborne invasion was impossible and the Navy was complaining that the *Luftwaffe* was unable to prevent the night bombing of its ships. Hitler wavered, clung for a few more days to the dream that air raids on London might bring about a total collapse of British determination, but finally, at *Luftwaffe* insistence that the cost was becoming too high, called off the invasion altogether. Kesselring had suffered his first defeat — one in which absolute success would have been a miracle had he converted such a slim advantage in quantity and quality of men and material against a well-organised opponent into an overwhelming superiority that spelt victory.

5

Night Bombing and
the Russian Interlude

In answering the question as to whether the German bomber force was used strategically or tactically against Britain, the British Air Ministry account, *The Rise and Fall of the German Air Force*, states, with shrewd insight, that, 'The Germans were not clear themselves' and 'they became confused in the extreme. They were forced into improvisation on their original plan and the Chief of Staff found it impossible to draw up any clear alternative amidst the conflicting opinions and advice thrust upon Göring from all sides.' Kesselring, of course, supplied much of that advice but the final arbiter of what was to be done was Hitler whose emotions, as well as his future plans, impelled him to demand a series of improvisations, several of which were conditioned by the inescapable fact that there were only sufficient fighters to escort one-third of the bomber force by day and therefore the bombers must mainly be used at night. The cancellation of the invasion was not the signal for a halt to the air offensive even though the *Luftwaffe* badly needed a respite in order to rebuild its dwindling resources and, particularly, replace its air crews. For a colossal task was in the offing of which only a select few were as yet aware. At the end of July Hitler had instructed the High Command (OKW) to commence planning an invasion of Russia. In the meantime Britain was to be contained.

With the approval of Göring and Jeschonnek (who were encouraged by some thoroughly misleading intelligence reports of riots in London and a collapse of British morale), the air fleet commanders, but mainly Kesselring, persisted in their attempts to bring the RAF to battle by day while trying to hit the aircraft industry at its source, as well as stepping up the attack on London and the major ports. Dilution was the result. With a force whose striking power was strictly curtailed, the *Luftwaffe*'s leaders never settled upon those targets against which it was most lucrative to aim.

No sooner had damage been inflicted on one category of objective than the emphasis was switched to another, permitting the previous target to recover. Everybody was feeling his way and these, of course, were days of experiment – but air power is governed by the military maxims of concentration and economy of effort.

When daylight raids by the twin-engined bombers became too costly, Kesselring tried a new expedient (which he had at first rejected) as a means of delivering bombs and also bringing the RAF fighters to battle. The crews of fighters carrying bombs were trained to dive towards their target from 12,000 feet – a thoroughly inaccurate method of delivery but one which created a threat that could not be ignored by the enemy. Meanwhile the fighter-bombers, once rid of their bombs, could revert to their primary role. These were but pin-pricks from aircraft whose short range denied them deep penetration. Likewise another hit-and-run expedient, of sending single bombers to dive on their targets out of low cloud cover, was condemned to failure since there was no way they could navigate accurately in such conditions. Adolf Galland, one of the most successful and outspoken of the fighter pilots, called the fighters' bombing role 'a violation' of their aircraft and has said there was great bitterness among them at the High Command's attitude to their performance which, as levelled by Göring in a moment of frustration, was insulting. Criticism of Göring, however, was also criticism of Kesselring and in the years to come there was to be a coolness, on his part, to Galland.

The daylight experiments (they really were just that) were doomed to failure as the defences swiftly learned to counter them, as losses mounted and as the autumn weather closed in and made flying more perilous. They were at last called off on 20 October. Kesselring, as a leading exponent of this, the first major attempt to subjugate a nation by air power alone, could only learn by trial and error, making the best of equipment which was totally unsuitable for the purpose – as it still would have been even if the long-range, four-engined bomber had been produced. It was not that the twin-engined bombers could not reach their targets or drop a fairly useful bomb load. It was simply that accuracy was unobtainable and that the inverse psychological effect on a population's morale, and the way it could be actually stiffened instead of weakened by bombing, had yet to be evaluated and understood. In this genuine attempt at strategic bombing, Kesselring was in the forefront of developing a long-term technique and, in the short term, learning valuable lessons and adding vastly to the *Luftwaffe*'s prowess for the tougher campaigns to come. To his credit he never allowed an experiment to go on for too long or to become costly.

That he was sceptical of expediency is plain. He had resisted the introduction of the fighter-bombers – 'light Kesselrings' as derisively they came to be known – well knowing their limitations. Early in October he was fully apprised, too, that the British were interfering with the radio beams which offered the best hope of his bombers finding their targets by night. But he was realistic in promoting the 'path-finder' techniques whereby intersecting radio beams were laid to help picked crews drop incendiary bombs in the vicinity of the target, to start fires which acted as markers for the main follow-up force. Call it an attack upon military objectives though he might, this was area bombing, the methods that, in a much more sophisticated form, were later to be developed by the RAF night-bomber force. Of course Kesselring was perfectly aware that civilians would suffer from the inevitable misses from a fundamentally haphazard bombardment, as was amply demonstrated by the first major essay in this technique against the factories of Coventry on 14 November. Kesselring flew in person to watch the attack first-hand and could appreciate to a limited extent the immense destruction that was inflicted on the city and its industry, though with industry alone the damage was by no means fatal and production was soon restored. The successive cities that were to be attacked as the weeks passed, were only occasionally struck with the same cataclysmic effect. The defences, happily warned by 'Ultra' (which could give 48 hours notice) and by the German habit of 'laying' the beams some hours before the attack, were provided with time to prepare and were, in any case, slowly improving. A subsequently planned attack on Wolverhampton was to be cancelled when a last-minute photographic reconnaissance revealed British guns taking up position.

It is remarkable that the Germans seem not to have investigated thoroughly the reason for this leakage of information particularly since Kesselring was taking a far more critical view of Intelligence estimates now that he had good reason for doubting the value of the assessments which had been made that summer. Post-attack aerial photography told but a part of the story, though it did seem to satisfy the Germans that the factories of Coventry had received a heavy blow. So they refrained from returning again in strength and, instead, spread their attacks over different targets. Again their ignorance of conditions in the target areas (shared with the RAF at that time) was apparent. There was little chance of immense damage being caused to cities by high explosive since most of their bombs in use were only 110-pounders. Havoc was caused by the fires that incendiary devices started, the classic example of their destructive power being the attack by Kesselring's bombers on the City of London on the night of 29 December, an attack he called off two hours after its commencement because of impending bad weather over the airfields in France. Losses from crashes in bad weather were far higher than those caused by the British defences.

Already Kesselring was in profound doubt about the value of continuing the attack upon Britain. Clearly the British were obstinately determined in their resistance. Moreover the fatal dispersion of German forces – land as well as sea – was under way. Units were being subtracted – wisely – from the West to recuperate at home, but also they were being sent to the Mediterranean to stiffen the Italians who had been badly mauled by the British and the Greeks, and were in danger of collapse. The naval war in the Atlantic was attracting many of the best long-range units and in March there would be a sudden diversion of strong forces to invade Yugoslavia and Greece and eradicate the danger that had suddenly threatened Germany's southern flank. By mid-March German fighter defences of Western Europe had been reduced to the absolute minimum, to deal with the light but recurrent RAF raids, and the bomber force was down to about 400 aircraft. The latter continued the offensive with increasing efficiency at night in a way that made it appear as if the effort was far larger than was in fact the case. Although some crews flew two or three sorties each night it was no longer in the hope of reaching a decision. Now they were merely a diversion, part of the grand scheme intended to convince the enemy that the main German effort remained fixed in the West whereas already it was directed towards the East, against Russia where the invasion was due to start in June.

Kesselring, it seems, was told about the impending invasion in December, perhaps in November, but kept the knowledge from his staff. He was given the leading airman's role in Russia, as befitted the *Luftwaffe*'s most experienced senior commander. Like Göring, he was high in Hitler's favour (though the Reich Marshal had fallen somewhat in the Führer's estimation due to the failure over Britain). Unlike several prominent members of the military hierarchy, Kesselring seems neither to have doubted the practicability of defeating Russia nor the urgent need to do so. He believed in exploiting the *Wehrmacht*'s temporary invincibility and he detested Communism with the vehemence he had acquired in 1919. He echoed his Führer's reaction when the latter was warned by a mission which visited Russian aircraft factories in April of 1941 of the quantity and quality of the Russian machines. 'You see how far these people are already. We must begin immediately.' Not even Göring or Jeschonnek concurred with that. They faced the future in pessimism, tempered by a hope that their inherent belief in the proven ability of the air units would be sufficient to support what, in essence, was to be battle of conquest by *land* forces.

The extent to which the *Luftwaffe* was to be subordinate to the Army in Russia emerges with stark clarity from the OKW Directive No. 21 which laid down the conduct of Operation 'Barbarossa', the invasion plan. It was to be a concentration of the mixture as before – elimination of the enemy air force, assistance to ground operations, cutting of communications and the provision of airborne troops and special units (those with the dual-purpose 88-mm guns). But while there was also a dilution in the subtraction of a strategic ingredient for attacks on enemy industry, such as had been part and parcel of the Polish and Western campaigns, it was recognised that the *Luftwaffe* had neither the strength nor the capability to apply this thoroughly within the depths of Russia.

Kesselring wrote: 'I instructed my air force and flak generals to consider the wishes of the Army as my orders' – a statement which faithfully reflects the desires of the Army Command (OKH) that *Luftwaffe* directives should be subject to its orders and directives. This shift of emphasis in his allegiance from the air force towards that of his original service was that of a genuine pragmatist. In Poland he had conducted the battle as an airman of conviction with only the slightest acquiescence to army demands, and the results had been satisfactory in the circumstances. In Holland the air battle had been uppermost in his mind, too, although adjusted to the requirements of territorial conquest. At Dunkirk and in the skies over Britain he had witnessed a rejection of the theory of air power *á l'outrance*. Henceforward he knew that, with the relatively inefficient tools at his disposal, there must be total collaboration between air and land power if quick and absolute results were to be obtained. On the eve of entering Russia he was the epitome of the ideal modern commander, who shrewdly and unselfishly balances the demands of co-operation between the services and forswears service prejudices. It is a rare virtue. The efficient system of consultation between Army and Air Force officers at all levels, developed by Jeschonnek and put into practice in its most outright form by Kesselring, was irrefutable evidence of the way they had shifted their ground without appearing disloyal to the autonomy of the *Luftwaffe*. That, in Kesselring's case, would come later, though never from choice.

As the diversionary air offensive proceeded against Britain, Kesselring became deeply involved in the progressive planning of Barbarossa while spending as much time as possible in the West in order, by his presence, to mislead the enemy – a split role which caused much inconvenience as well as the need for elaborate subterfuge. Sperrle's *Luftflotte* III would remain in the West and combine the task of *Luftflotte* II which, with its headquarters near Warsaw (having delayed its departure from the West until the last moment in June) was to work with von Bock, the Commander-in-Chief of Army Group Centre, which was to make the principal advance into Russia. Cordiality was assured from the outset due to the previous excellent goodwill established between the two commanders. Kesselring had the complete confidence of von Bock from *Reichswehr* days and could, with perfect safety, enter into the mind of an Army Group commander who was renowned for his bravery and a rather icy manner, and make suggestions that, from another man, might easily have been interpreted as interference in matters outside his concern. We are left by Kesselring with the distinct impression that von Bock, who despised Hitler, took Kesselring into his confidence in many other subjects besides military ones. For once the soldier exuded genuine warmth. All the other senior commanders destined to lead the assault on Russia were present when Hitler harangued them on 17 March, the occasion taken by the Führer to inform them that the invasion 'cannot be conducted in a knightly fashion' and that the struggle would have to be waged with unprecedented, unmerciful and unrelenting harshness. Hitler then announced his intention that all Russian Commissars were to be liquidated, though he absolved the *Wehrmacht* from guilt in the matter! Von Bock was one of those who, afterwards, strenuously voiced his complaints to von Brauchitsch, the Army C-in-C, but neither von Brauchitsch, nor his Chief of Staff, Franz Halder, was strong enough to resist the Führer. Already the Army Command was under Hitler's thumb and slipping into thraldom. Von Bock frequently discussed his fears of the invasion's outcome with those closest to him – the members of his staff (some of whom were seeking ways to curb Hitler) and commanders such as Guderian of 2nd Panzer Group. There can be little doubt that, on the eve of the invasion, when Kesselring found von Bock 'rather dispirited, immersed in cogitation befitting a responsible commander before the beginning of a fateful enterprise' he was referring also to matters besides those of military relevance. But Kesselring was not included among the conspirators. There is no evidence to show he was contacted at that time, probably because they correctly evaluated him as hostile to their aims.

As to the military augury, there was good reason for optimism though not to the same degree as expressed by *Luftwaffe* Intelligence or Kesselring himself. It was thought that the Russian Air Force was quite unequal to withstanding the *Luftwaffe* (an assessment which seems to have been based upon the poor Russian performance in the war against Finland in the winter of 1939/40) and had discounted reports of the extravagant new aircraft industry they knew to be in being, the reorganisation that was taking place and the not entirely unworthy resistance which had been put up against the extremely capable Japanese air force throughout a series of 'incidents' in 1939 in Manchuria. After the war Kesselring was to write, 'On the credit side, in two major and two minor campaigns, we had been able to accumulate experiences against which the Russians had no equivalent advantage.' This was partly true but also transmits a dangerous underestimation of the true Russian capability. It moreover overloooked that *Luftwaffe* methods were now fully appreciated and that its way of gaining initial air superiority by surprise was disclosed; hence the means to counteract them were also known. As shown in Poland and Holland, there was small likelihood of an air force being knocked out on the ground if it was forewarned and had taken the necessary counter-measures of dispersion – as each of the above nations had done with varying degrees of mitigation. The Russians were as well aware as anybody else that this was a key to survival and they knew too, from reports from several sources, that an attack was imminent. Unhappily for them it would appear that Josef Stalin refused to credit the reports in sufficient time to take even the most rudimentary counter-measures. When he changed his mind at the last moment on 21 June and a signal was sent to all the threatened airfields at 0130 hours on Sunday the 22nd, instructing them to disperse and camouflage all aircraft before dawn, it was too late. It was Sunday, after all, and many Russians had been engaged in the routine Saturday night social events. Even if the signal had arrived (and there is scant evidence to show it did) there was hardly anybody ready or fit to comply with the alacrity demanded. Already the first waves of German aircraft from *Luftflotte* II were preparing for take-off.

One of the more contentious items for debate between von Bock and Kesselring had been the resolution of agreed starting times for the invasion between the Army and the Air Force. With right of prior authority on their side, the Army insisted upon attacking at dawn and demanded a guarantee that the Russian Air Force had already been assailed and pinned to its airfields. Kesselring forcibly pointed out that it was impossible to deliver a knock-out blow in darkness: neither men nor equipment were equal to that. He asked that the Army should delay its advance until the Air Force had taken the opportunity of delivering its shattering, pre-emptive blow at first light. Von Bock would not agree and so Kesselring felt bound to adopt a dangerous compromise. With an attack by picked crews on the vital airfields, to be delivered at 0330 hours, it was hoped to create sufficient confusion to keep the Russians on the ground until first light when the main blow would be delivered. Joint surprise and shock would be sacrificed but this, perhaps, was a trivial (albeit extremely worrying) matter for Kesselring. Kesselring also records the monumental row with Göring as he struggled to obtain additional resources for what was intended, after all, as the main blow. Even so he seems only to have acquired a few extra air crew and ground troops, though these, by raising his reserves and administrative strength, would obviously help overcome some of the overriding problems of logistics.

The preponderant strength in aircraft of *Luftflotte* II by comparison with its neighbours in the three-pronged invasion of Russia (excepting operations in the far north) can be seen in the following table:

Luftflotte	Objective	*Flieger Korps*	No. of Combat a c	Width of front (miles)	Depth of adv (miles)
I	Leningrad	I	600	125	528
II	Moscow	II and VIII	910	186	680
IV	Dnieper River	IV and V	430	685	700

Although Kesselring fielded a higher proportion of formations and aircraft to space than those of the flanking *Luftflotten*, he was still conscious of a worrying inadequacy that prevented the full implementation of the prescribed strategy of simultaneous assault. Attention could be given at first to winning air superiority; only after that was achieved could worthwhile assistance be lent to the Army – a limitation von Bock had no option but to accept as one of priority. Moreover, from the initial layout of the Russian Air Force, it was seen that against *Luftflotte* II the heaviest opposition was deployed. Some 3,000 Russian aircraft guarded the frontier regions, with several thousand more in rear, backed up by the defences of Moscow itself. These, in their entirety, lay parked in close parade ground order on their airfields at last light on 21 June while their crews reposed in the remaining hours of peace.

The unwanted bombing overture in darkness at 0330 hours on the 22nd, though it awakened the Russians, failed to save them from their own folly. Never before or again would German air crews have such an array of easy targets presented to them as, with the first streaks of daylight ahead, they dived in swarms upon their helpless prey. With the

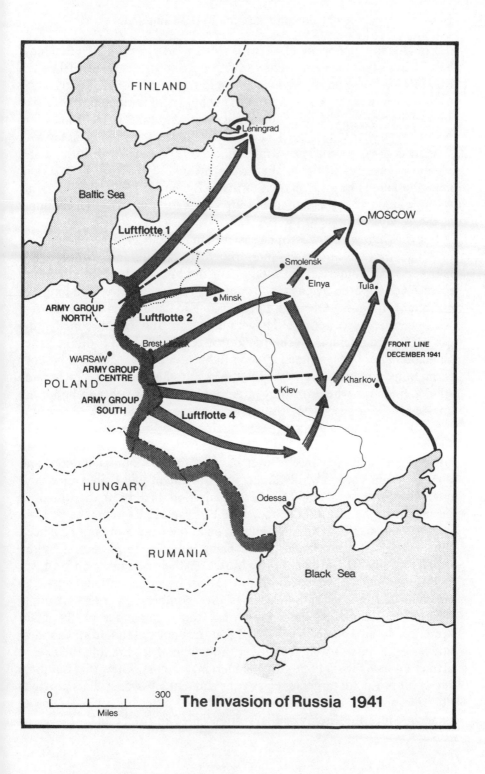

FINLAND

Baltic Sea

Leningrad

Luftflotte 1

MOSCOW

ARMY GROUP
NORTH

Smolensk

Elnya

Tula

Luftflotte 2

Minsk

Brest Litovsk

FRONT LINE
DECEMBER 1941

WARSAW

ARMY GROUP
CENTRE

POLAND

ARMY GROUP
SOUTH

Kharkov

Luftflotte 4

Kiev

HUNGARY

Odessa

RUMANIA

Black Sea

0   300
|____|____|____|
        Miles

The Invasion of Russia 1941

thoroughgoing precision of a drill brought to its peak of efficiency, Kesselring's bombers and fighters, within 24 hours, had demolished the Russian Air Force on almost every airfield within a 185-mile radius of the front. Even Göring was staggered by the initial estimates that 2,500 aircraft had been destroyed for negligible losses, and it was some time before he was convinced of the truth of this figure. It was soon all too easy to gain confirmation. The Army, quickly advancing deep into enemy territory, overran airfields that were littered with rows of wrecked machines piled like junk on their tarmacs. By the 23rd resistance in the air was minimal and it was safe to allocate strong forces to the direct support of the Army.

For the *Luftwaffe* it was much easier than it had been over Britain. Not only had they an absolute superiority in technique and, within a few hours, a local numerical advantage, but the Messerschmitt pilots found themselves opposed by enemy aircraft of a type which they had long ago outfought in Spain. Obsolete Polikarpov I 15s and I 16s fell in droves, whenever they were permitted to get into the air, and were also ineffectual against the bombers, even the Ju 87 dive-bombers which had failed over England. The losses inflicted on their fighters denied the Russian bomber formations adequate escort, with the result that their strikes became suicide missions whenever they attempted in clear weather to bomb the advancing Germans. Kesselring reflects, rather ingenuously, that it was 'infanticide' for the Russians to send their bombers to certain destruction, for he seems to have overlooked the sheer desperation of the Russian situation. To achieve concentration of effort to avert imminent defeat and direct it against worthwhile targets was, for them, impossible once their command structure and control organisation had been disrupted or destroyed in the way that it had. The Russian High Command were in complete ignorance of what was going on at the front and their advanced units, deprived of directions, were being gobbled up piecemeal by the rapidly advancing German Army. Moreover their resistance on land was failing, not so much because of the destruction inflicted by the concentrated attacks of Kesselring's dive-bombers, as by a technique wished on him by General Guderian, the commander of the main armoured force. Guderian had asked that the bombers should spread their attacks over time as well as space with the aim of frightening the enemy artillerists away from their guns. Guderian, a realist, knew that bombers rarely hit pin-point targets such as guns and tanks. Against all its previous doctrine, the *Luftwaffe* dubiously agreed and was richly rewarded for its temerity since the enemy artillery often failed to fire at all.

Of much farther reaching importance was the long-lasting effect of the loss to the Russians of their best air crews. Not only were they stripped of their immediate front-line strength but deprived also of the cadre upon which a future effective air force could be built. As the war progressed, new and better types of Russian aeroplane were to appear, but the men who flew them never came to equal the Germans. They failed to acquire the older techniques let alone the new ones and were destroyed by a more skilful opponent almost as fast as they were introduced into battle. For this the superb *Luftwaffe*, by its shattering annihilation of June 1941, took the entire credit.

Now began the rapid advance on Minsk, Smolensk, Kiev and Moscow to garner a rich harvest from the initial victory in the first week of the campaign. With complete air superiority the German reconnaissance aircraft could gather information at will, while the bombers were free to attack with the minimum escort, leaving the fighters at liberty also to join in the attack on ground targets. Kesselring has left us with a picture of his command technique in those days of glory. We see him restlessly on the move or in conference with his superiors, equals or subordinates. At the HQs of Armies and Panzer Groups, *Luftwaffe* liaison officers kept in close touch with the commanders. Von Barsewisch, for example, went almost everywhere with Guderian of the 2nd Panzer Group, piloting him whenever possible in his own aeroplane and travelling with him in a command vehicle when flight was impracticable. The reports from these liaison officers came back direct to the HQ of the *Luftflotte* and to the *Luftwaffe* liaison officer with von Bock at HQ of Army Group, and they would be authenticated by Kesselring in person, flying his Focke Wulf 189 to scan the battle front and reporting on what he saw, quite often after landing at a forward airfield adjacent to the army headquarters involved for discussions with the local commander. As often as possible, too, he would land at airfields to interview the crews just returned from their missions – to give praise for their achievements, encouragement for the future, sympathy at their bereavement for the loss of comrades and offer help in an endeavour to profit from their experience and make their task easier in the future. Never did he attempt to underrate their difficulties and dangers. Always there was the broad smile and the effusive charm designed to instil confidence – and usually there was a willing response from the men, many of whose names he knew from memory, even when things might have gone wrong. There was the occasion, for example, when a new fragmentation bomb, the SD 10, developed a fault which detonated them in mid-air while still in the bomb racks. Several high-level bombers were lost when these bombs exploded inside the fuselage; Kesselring instantly banned their use except on external bomb racks.

In the evening he would return to his main headquarters for the daily conference at which the results of the day's activities were analysed, the tasks for the morrow, based on demands from the Army, debated and allocations of resources made to tasks. Already the liaison officers would have been engaged upon dealing with situations as they arose, putting the *Luftwaffe* point of view to the Army in order to prevent misuse of aircraft against unsuitable targets. When necessary Kesselring frankly passed on his criticisms to the Army Group Command, and did so with compelling determination, though far more tactfully than an extrovert leader such as Guderian. Each morning he would meet Jeschonnek to press upon the Chief of Staff his requirements from the upper echelons of command, above all the support he hoped to obtain from the Führer via Göring. But for the most part Kesselring was in the air (a relatively safe way of covering the battlefield now that the Russian fighters were struck down) and, at times, the only method of seeing everything in the time available. For, as the advance pushed rapidly ahead, it was no longer possible to retain his headquarters at Warsaw. First it occupied a railway train on the frontier at Brest Litovsk. There the line changed to Russian gauge and so the headquarters had to move forward by lorry on roads that deteriorated with usage. More dependence came to be placed on supply by air. Simultaneously the rapid and deep advance of the Panzer Groups posed new problems of ground to air co operation. Since the strike units had to be based close to the spearhead it was no longer possible for an air corps, let alone HQ of the *Luftflotten*, to control the tactical battle in close conjunction with the various, far-flung army headquarters. So a special air headquarters was improvised by II *Flieger Korps* and, under Colonel Martin Fiebig, placed alongside Guderian's 2nd Panzer Group. This was a difficult task for Fiebig because he was inexperienced in the work and hampered by lack of suitable communication equipment in a job that demanded quick reactions to a highly fluid mobile battle of encirclement in which the Russians were either battering themselves to death to avert envelopment or struggling to escape the embrace of the panzer groups.

Guderian complained that Fiebig was not reacting quickly enough to prevent the enemy escaping the army net in the area of Bobruysk which, in all conscience, was thinly enough spread. But Guderian was asking too much. Once more it was shown that bombing does not hold ground and can only slightly hamper enemy movement. Kesselring was quick to defend Fiebig, and point out that 'experience must be acquired first' and later, for his part, constructively pointed out the errors he witnessed being made by the Army. It was a two-way traffic. When Guderian, in the teeth of opposition to his plan by his superior officer, determined to cross the River Dnieper on 10 July and strike hard for Smolensk, Kesselring gave him unreserved help by allocating in support almost the entire *Luftflotte*, placing VIII *Flieger Korps* under II *Flieger Korps*, with forward local control vested in Fiebig. The plan was thrashed out in detail at Guderian's headquarters though never put into full operation since Guderian managed an opportunist crossing of the river prior to the agreed time. As it happened, the Russians scored a few minor successes with air strikes in the aftermath of the crossing and these, too, were the subject of mild (for Guderian) recrimination. But Guderian and Kesselring were kindred spirits and never seriously at cross purposes, though it is just possible that a suspicion got abroad among certain army officers, at this moment, that Kesselring did not always give the assistance that might be expected. Guderian's Ia was Fritz Bayerlein who was soon to join Rommel in Africa, and the commander of 18th Panzer Division, Walther Nehring, was close by and also would go to Africa. Neither suffered too badly just then, but a year later their contacts with Kesselring were to be of a critical nature and the subject of a disenchantment similar to that hinted at by Guderian.

The jaws of a trap to enclose 300,000 Russians were intended to shut at Smolensk. Guderian got there first on 16 July, despite furious Russian counter-attacks and a counter-offensive brewing against his exposed flank from the direction of Elnya to the south-east where a protective German salient took shape. The 3rd Panzer Group under General Hoth had ostensibly closed the gap from the north though, without realising it at first, had left open a chink between Yartsevo and Smolensk. Flying in his FW 189, Kesselring reconnoitred the gap and saw the Russians filtering their way to safety. As an interim measure he could turn his bombers upon the Russians, well knowing that by night the movement would continue and that even by day only ground forces could plug the hole. To von Bock and Hoth he addressed urgent requests that ground units should be sent in, but the Army was as overstretched as the Air Force. Hoth had sent a panzer corps to another front and Guderian was hotly engaged at Elnya and too weak to press northward and close the gap. Warming to his protest, Kesselring pleaded strongly with Göring to ask Hitler to intervene, and himself promised the absolute maximum of air support for whatever was decided. But as he later said 'Unfortunately nothing happened. My proposals . . . by way of the Commander-in-Chief of the *Luftwaffe* were also fruitless.' By his own estimate, 100,000 Russians got away. This was an occasion on which airborne troops, dropped into the gap, would have been invaluable. Given the troops this was what Kesselring would have done, but the airborne divisions, which had provided his first major victory on land in Holland, had been hard hit during the invasion of Crete in May and were not available.

With the Russian air bases at Smolensk in *Luftwaffe* possession, it was at last possible to strike at Moscow in conformity with Manual 16 when it talked of undermining enemy morale. In line with Hitler's demands for the Russian war, strategic bombing was to be prosecuted to the limit of determination by every possible means, though Kesselring no longer had much faith in this method of attack. The experiences over Britain were well registered in his capacious memory. Nor had he sufficient resources to spare or the desire to risk valuable crews over some of the most heavily defended air space in Russia, crews which had not the slightest chance of escape if brought down behind the enemy front. Moreover, as the Germans were quick to learn, it was in the approaches to Moscow that the hottest anti-aircraft fire was to be met, far more intensive than anything they had found over Britain. Indeed, to give Kesselring enough aircraft for the job, machines had to be withdrawn from the West and even then the maximum effort which could be mounted on exclusively night attacks was rarely more than 100 sorties per night and usually between 30 and 40. Damage, of course, was inflicted on the Russians, but on nothing like the scale wrought against Britain. Meanwhile the effect on Muscovite morale was precisely the same as that on the British: initial dismay was soon replaced by anger and a recharged determination to resist – the lesson that almost invariably is to be learned from wild attacks against the civil populace and one which the Germans had failed to understand on innumerable occasions since 1870 when they took to bombarding besieged French cities. I think Kesselring realised this. His record is pretty clean when it comes to deliberate attacks on non-combatants. Gradually this useless harassment of Moscow died away until a point would be reached when, throughout the whole of October, Kesselring was able to mount only a single strategic raid – by one long-range, reconnaissance bomber against Voronezh. In consequence the Russians were able to rebuild their aircraft factories in complete immunity from strategic attacks with the result that the replacement of their air force's material proceeded unimpeded.

At the end of August the German Army stood irresolute, with its spearheads 400 miles into Russia and its administrative tail stretching tenuously to the rear. Men and machines were wearing out but still the enemy resisted and did so, moreover, with increasing asperity. Victory having eluded Hitler at the first cast of the dice, he had now, with his advisers, to botch a fresh strategy. This they wrangled about as the August days drew closer to the autumn months with the onset of the rainy season writing its prologue to deepest winter. In the pause the German armed forces marked time, rebuilt their strength and fended off ill-co-ordinated Russian attacks. The debate within the German hierarchy was prolonged and acrimonious as Hitler imposed a diversive strategy upon generals whose main aim was to strike, united, against Moscow. Kesselring agreed with the generals although he seems to have withheld from the central argument. It was hardly for him to take part since the responsibility was not his. Hitler eventually opted to hold fast in the centre while striking out at the flanks with an advance against Leningrad in the north (helped by VIII *Flieger Korps* transferred from Kesselring for the purpose) and then, at the end of August, a drive southward of Smolensk to trap a horde of Russians in the vicinity of Kiev. These diversions were greatly to Kesselring's annoyance. He was deprived of substantial forces which might otherwise have been used finally to eliminate the Smolensk pocket, and he found it increasingly difficult to help Guderian's 2nd Panzer Group defend the Elyna salient at the very moment when it was desirable to support an attack by General von Weichs' Second Army in an advance on Guderian's right.

In this instance we see Kesselring taking steps once more to shape the ground battle to suit his soldier's instincts – regardless of what the soldiers themselves deemed right. He persuaded Göring to give priority to von Weichs and deprived Guderian of direct air support – a strategy which led the Army Chief of Staff, Franz Halder, as well as von Bock and Guderian, to complain bitterly. At that moment they were trying to hang on at Elnya for use as a springboard for an eventual attack towards Moscow, contrary to Hitler's desire to strike southward. By the end of August, however, the Russian attacks at Elnya distinctly looked like a major offensive and the decision was taken by the Army on 2 September to abandon the salient. Prior to that, according to Guderian's Chief of Staff, von Liebenstein, Hitler had come round to supporting an independent line adopted by Guderian. So Kesselring, by his own account, went to Guderian's HQ on the 2nd to say that Hitler approved Guderian's attempt to hold on at Elnya and 'that I would give the armoured group all possible *Luftwaffe* support if the Elnya salient could thereby be held. Finally I flew to my command post and immediately ordered the concentration of all flying forces in front of the Elnya salient.' A tang of political opportunism is detectable! Was Kesselring acting primarily in the interests of the military situation or adjusting his own position to align with that of the Führer? Was he trying to get Göring out of a jam with Hitler or merely putting himself in a better light with Guderian, another of Hitler's favourites who, at that moment, was being pushed forward by the inner circle of Hitler's young entourage as the most desirable replacement for the failing Army Commander-in-Chief, von Brauchitsch? It is known that the *Luftwaffe* liaison officers were particularly keen that this should be done and it is quite likely that Kesselring was aware of it too and that, as an admirer of Guderian, 'my old friend of *Reichswehr* Ministry days', he would have approved.

On the 5th the Elnya salient was evacuated, but by then the situation had changed again as Guderian, contrary to Halder's wishes, now drove rapidly southward to complete the envelopment of Kiev while Russian attacks flailed dangerously against his flank and rear. All was in flux with the High Command a victim of pressures from all sides. Kesselring, his *Luftflotte* reinforced from other sectors, applied some elements to hold off these Russian attacks while using the rest to help Guderian's advance, throwing his weight in the direction of the true point of local decision and thereby gratifying each faction in turn. Post-battle analysis by the Germans supported the original notion that the main air effort should have attended the drive to the south and deprecated any diversion to Elnya, despite the risks involved. Kesselring's allocation of resources in this crisis were those of the administrator who seeks a solution by compromise in an endeavour to satisfy everybody. That hard, inner stiffening which is essential in bracing the top-class commander to an unbending purpose had yet to ossify within him. Yet nothing of lasting value was decided at Kiev. Russian industry remained safe and Moscow, their capital city, was unthreatened. Far too late the advance on Moscow was at last ordered, and for this venture Kesselring was again cast in the leading airman's role.

With Army Group Centre, reinforced with three of the four panzer groups, committed at last to a unified drive on Moscow, it was logical that the maximum possible air support should also be given to this belated effort – and logical too that von Bock should maintain his affiliation with Kesselring. VIII *Flieger Korps* came back along with still more fighters and bombers from the neighbouring *Luftflotten* I and IV, giving him, in aggregate, half the entire *Luftwaffe* strength in Russia – a total of 1,320 aircraft of which 720 were bombers and 400 were Messerschmitt Bf 109s. The attack opened with routine efficiency on 1 October and the Army swept forward in the same old way as before – until the first snow fell on the 6th, that is. This, the harbinger of rapidly deteriorating weather, not only slowed or even stopped the Army, but often made flying impossible. To make matters worse the Army began to demand of the *Luftwaffe* what it could no longer do for itself; it wanted supplies flown in since no longer could a sufficient quantity be dragged up the mired or rutted roads by wheeled vehicles, and the railhead was still far to the rear. Thus yet another debilitating chore fell upon the *Luftwaffe* as, simultaneously, its dwindling resources began to fade. A crisis of materials supply and production on the home front had suddenly revealed, in August, what had always been threatened if a campaign, that was intended to be short, dragged on. More aircraft were being lost than were being built. Neither the means nor the capacity to rectify that were in sight.

Under these circumstances the likelihood of reaching Moscow evaporated. Before the middle of October, Kesselring was privately convinced that ultimate success would be denied, though he exerted his drive, persuasion and charm to the full in keeping the offensive moving. It was not a case of blind optimistic obstinacy but the product of a studied belief that, all too frequently in history, campaigns had failed solely because the eventual losers had given up prematurely without being aware of their opponent's dire straits. Kesselring always hoped that the enemy was a little more shaken than he was himself. Yet for all the horror of the struggle that was then reaching a fresh nadir in brutishness, as the Russian propaganda machine at last began to make headway in goading the people into a whole-hearted resistance, the war in Russia had still to tap the depths of vicious ferocity that was to characterise the years to come. Kesselring's war in the East was an event of relative disjunction, a detachment in the clear air above the squalor of the front and the bestiality of a real people's war verging on civil war on the ground – with all that meant in terms of human suffering. In personal terms he was engaged in the sky in the sort of knightly combat fought by his pilots. When he landed it was to find comfort at fairly well-appointed headquarters or on some carefully established airfield. From the mud and the blood he was inevitably, by his role, detached, though this is not to say that he shirked danger or was insensitive to the suffering that was being caused as, for example, when a pilot was forced down behind the Russian lines and later found mutilated. Sadly he was to say on one occasion, 'With every stroke of my pen I condemned many young men to death but I simply had insufficient time to concern myself about it . . .'. But a change for him was impending in venue as well as in responsibility.

In September the OKW opinion had been put to Kesselring by Jeschonnek that a stronger German presence was needed in the

Mediterranean, possibly to implement a plan called 'Orient' which had been drafted on Hitler's instructions in June to consider ways of conquering the Middle East through a double envelopment from Russia (after that country had been beaten in, say, August or September), and along the North African coast by an Italian German Army directed through Egypt. Kesselring, it was thought, would be a good choice as Theatre C-in-C as well as Commander of a *Luftflotte* and the idea had been attractive to the German High Command just when it looked as if the Russian campaign might soon be over and they could soon hope to give their full attention to defeating the British again. Instead there was failure in Russia and this, compounded by strong evidence of a British revival in the Mediterranean, meant that remedial attention could no longer be denied that region. The British were sinking so many ships in the Mediterranean that supplies to North Africa were seriously imperilled. An offensive in the Western Desert, aimed at the destruction of the Italian Army and its vital German *Afrika Korps* under the command of Erwin Rommel, was impending and might easily compel the withdrawal of Axis forces from Cyrenaica. Thus a further substantial diversion of German forces to the Mediterranean was deemed unavoidable, for political if not military reasons, in order to keep Italy in the war, but it was expedient that these should be tactfully applied, predominantly by air forces. Hence it was entirely logical to send Kesselring, the best soldier among the airmen and a man of polished manners with experience of diplomacy as well as a good command of the Italian language. The Italians might resent it but, as Count Ciano put it on 10 November, 'Under the circumstances we have no right to complain if Hitler sends Kesselring as commander in the south.'

The orders which consigned him, along with the headquarters of *Luftflotte* II, to Italy, arrived at the end of November as the *Wehrmacht* in Russia was making its final, ineffectual struggles in demoralising conditions of blizzard and deprivation to reach Moscow. Kesselring was undoubtedly sincere when he wrote in his 'Memoirs' that 'however much I might welcome the prospect of a new assignment to sunnier climes, I was sorry to leave von Bock's Army Group'. As it happened the whole German hierarchy was due for a change. Von Bock was soon to give up on grounds of ill-health, so the personal relationship would have been severed in any case, and von Brauchitsch and Guderian, among others, were about to be sacked. By that time, too, the *Luftwaffe* in Russia was exhausted with many units on their way home for enforced rest and refitting.

Only at this moment was the parlous situation of the *Luftwaffe* coming to be revealed. Ernst Udet, one of the wildest of the 'Old Eagles', committed suicide on 18 November. He had been out of his depth in the world of technology and bureaucracy, had failed to foresee the requirements of the future and had not been brought to book by Göring. This was another disastrous consequence of the feuding between Kesselring and Milch in 1937 and now it was for Milch to perform a rescue operation, if he could, to weild increased power as Göring's prestige began to slip into decline. Of Udet, the man who had ruined the *Luftwaffe* of his creation, Kesselring would never speak again. He did not forgive and he deliberately omitted him from his 'Memoirs'. Milch he would later acclaim for his tireless efforts, their mutual anger subsiding as the need to save the *Luftwaffe* and Germany became more apparent. Already it was obvious that Britain, with American aid, was beginning to assume both a technical and a numerical lead. Refuse to recognise the fact though they would, the Germans were on the verge of losing the initiative and were actually being forced into a holding action. Kesselring, nevertheless, left Russia for the Mediterranean after a briefing by Hitler and the Staff in Berlin, filled with the conviction that he was embarked upon yet another campaign of conquest.

This was not just a question of the optimistic nature of the man rising to the surface. It was the attribute of a good commander dedicated to the accomplishment of his task. As he put it himself after the war in his *Commentaries on the North African Campaign*, hereafter referred to as 'Commentaries';

> Pessimists are in a fortunate position. They always predict or prophesy unhappy events. If things turn out well, they will not be mentioned. They will be utterly overlooked and feel themselves lucky. . . . If leading personalities express their opinion, during the events themselves, loudly and stubbornly, the intellectual powers of both leaders and those led are distracted from their labour which should be holding their entire attention. In other words, such men have a damaging influence on overall chances of success. A personality prone to such trends of thought will unconsciously falsify orders. For instance, instead of 'fighting' he will order a sort of 'administrative march' in order to prevent the extermination of his own troops . . . Set-backs and failures to such alarmists are a matter of course; successes are unpleasant proofs of their erroneous opinion'.

With that as his philosophy he took plane for the Mediterranean where Rommel, depressed in spirit and ripe for defeat as the British offensive began to overwhelm his outnumbered troops, awaited.

6

A Glorified
Quartermaster

It had come as a relief to many Germans when Benito Mussolini had withheld from Italy's treaty obligations by abstaining from war on the German side in 1939, for Italy's war making capacity was not rated highly in Berlin. But while it was seemingly of only passing account when the Italian dictator, in search of cheap enrichment, had leapt on to the crest of victory in June of 1940, by the end of the year Italy's chapter of military reverses were the cause of alarm on both sides of the Brenner Pass. A sweet midsummer dream had been rapidly converted into a winter nightmare. The poor showing of the Italian Navy against the British in the Mediterranean, coupled with the rough handling of their army in Africa, when added to the debâcle following the invasion of Greece in November and the eclipse of their technically out-classed air force, had seriously weakened Mussolini's prestige. At the end of the year the Fascist régime, along with the nation's economy, showed signs of collapse. Increasingly Italy became dependent upon Germany for essential raw materials, such as oil, coal and steel, of which Germany did not herself possess enough. Proudly refusing a German offer of air support in the autumn, the Italians were compelled to ask for help in December after their army had been routed by the British in North Africa. A pattern of aid in a state of decline, which was to regulate her relationship with her more powerful Axis partner in the years to come, was thus established.

From beginning to end, Hitler's involvement of Germany in the Mediterranean theatre of war was as unwilling as it was parsimonious. Always, in his view, this was a secondary war zone and invariably he allocated it the barest minimum of resources, usually sending help as props to shore up the collapse of yet another section of a rotting edifice. Paradoxically, however, this remedial policy was frequently stimulated to such an extent by the extrovert personalities he sent to implement it, that the drain upon Axis resources became increasingly enervating. Ambitious men such as Student, von Richthofen, von Arnim and, above all, Erwin Rommel and Albert Kesselring, would, by their demands and activities, attract greater resources to the theatre than Hitler ever intended it should have. When *Flieger Korps* X was sent to Sicily in January 1941 to assist in re-opening the strangled Italian supply lines to North Africa by neutralising the air and sea power exerted by the British from Malta, that was but a minor diversion. But after the Italian Army was routed at Beda Fomm in February and Rommel arrived in Tripolitania with the *Afrika Korps*, a much-expanded commitment was assured, for Rommel would not be content with limited operations. The unresolved Italo-Greek imbroglio, politically linked by the British with the March revolt by the Yugoslavs against too close a subservience to the Germans, was further cause for a wider dispersion of effort. Anxious for the safety of his southern flank during the projected invasion of Russia, Hitler had felt bound to bring the entire Balkans under his direct control with a swiftly executed occupation of both Yugoslavia and Greece in April. But the diversion had not ended there. Simultaneous with the invasion of Greece, Rommel had well exceeded his instructions by sweeping the British out of Cyrenaica and besieging Tobruk, thus initiating the saga of desert battles which were to drain German resources in an area in which Hitler had little interest. Among the most serious blows the Germans sustained at that time was the losses to the èlite *Luftwaffe* paratroops, under Student, who suffered appalling casualties in undertaking the supplemental invasion of Crete. Something more vital even than good men was lost in that Pyrrhic victory; it had been strategically weakening that a formation which might have given complete victory at Smolensk, as Kesselring desired, was unavailable, but far more damaging that the concept of airborne warfare suffered a serious setback and that Hitler was ever afterwards luke-warm to this sort of operation.

It was not the reverses inflicted on Rommel by the British in November 1941 which compelled the ultimate German commitment to the Mediterranean, but the fact that, in the preceeding months, supplies were not getting through to North Africa. The General Staffs had been fully aware throughout the summer that something more had to be done to buttress Italy in this theatre of war, but the rate at which the supply ships were being sunk left no further room for delay. Reinforcements were required but the only way to get them there was the application of positive action to break the British blockade. To do this a man was wanted who might not only inspire but persuade or drive the Italians to pull their weight. It would be of incidental advantage if he managed to exercise restraint on the effervescent

Rommel and reduce the wastage he was causing by his activities.

Erwin Rommel, an arrogant extrovert and single-minded soldier, had been built by Dr Josef Göbbels into one of Germany's propaganda darlings. Tactically brilliant and immensely brave, he had led his men from the front with almost miraculous success. But among his allies and some of his own nationality, he had created an atmosphere which was the antithesis of the important military principle of co-operation. He had bullied and offended the Italians in the same rough manner as he had forfeited the wholehearted collaboration of the *Luftwaffe*'s *Fliegerführer Afrika, Generalmajor* Stefan Frölich, thus circumscribing the assistance which might have been obtained from the 150 German aircraft available. Antagonism between the *Luftwaffe*, on the one hand, and Rommel and the German Army in Africa, was therefore habitual long before Kesselring arrived. One of the reasons, as Kesselring points out in the 'Commentaries', was 'Rommel's opposition to the proven system of air to ground liaison . . . he did not want to part with any means of combat . . . This attitude was completely wrong in principle because no assignment of aeroplanes to corresponding headquarters had been carried out through the liaison detachments.' Rommel tended in most instances, in fact, merely to apply a veto.

Not that the *Luftwaffe* was blameless for the theatre's difficulties, as Kesselring was quick to notice. After the capture of Crete a *Luftwaffe* recommendation had arbitrarily shifted the lines of communication to run naturally from Greece to Benghazi via Crete, thereby denying the Italians adequate means to protect the traffic that traditionally went via Sicily and, thus adjacent to Malta. The Italians, too weak to run convoys without German aid, were virtually denied adequate supplies for their own colony when the Germans concentrated their entire air effort in the Eastern Mediterranean. Nor, of course, could they be aware of the real reason for the ease with which the British intercepted and sank the Axis convoys, when the details of almost every convoy were notified in advance to Allied Intelligence due to their ability to read the Germans' coded radio messages. Until the end, practically every one of Kesselring's intentions would be signalled to the enemy, a state of affairs which would be responsible, indirectly, for sowing the seeds of angry dissent among Germans as well as between Axis allies.

The campaign hinged on supply and, with Cyrenaica in British hands, the key to supply to Tripoli was Malta, as Kesselring grasped from the beginning. But whereas his superiors considered, in their old-fashioned way, that Malta could be neutralised by bombing from a strong *Luftflotte* II transferred from Russia, Kesselring, enriched by his experience of intensive combat, knew this to be misconceived. His instant reaction, scoffed at by Hitler and Göring, was to comment that nothing less than the occupation of Malta would suffice. Rebuffed at the outset of his new assignment, he flew to Rome to meet the German representatives. There, he studied the susceptibilities of his new allies and also formulated a workable strategy backed up by arguments that would persuade *all* his masters.

In his dual appointment as C-in-C South and of *Luftflotte* II, Kesselring arrived in Rome on the 28 November. At once Hitler's notion that the Italians would be prepared to fall under Kesselring's direct command was shattered. The Italian Chief of Staff, Count Ugo Cavallero, positively refused to relinquish control of Italian troops. He was, however, prepared to hand over units of the Air Force whose aircraft, by common consent, were rated as 'flying coffins'; it would be for the *Luftwaffe* to make up for that deficiency, and, as they knew, Bruno Loerzer's highly practised II *Flieger Korps* would soon arrive from Russia. Kesselring recognised that it would be disruptively useless to insist upon overall command even though Hitler had deluded himself that this would be granted by Mussolini. Instead he launched himself at once into a political balancing act, the precarious diplomatic course which was to govern his every subsequent move. On the one hand he mixed placation with goading to stimulate an aggressive frame of mind in the Italians without, at the same time, hurting the feelings of Cavallero and the Italian *Comando Supremo*. On the other he endeavoured to stimulate the Germans simultaneous with his attempts to mitigate their more bellicose outbursts of frustration whenever the Italians adopted an obstructive attitude. Like an impressario training a chorus of prima donnas he tried to manipulate the posturing and relatively ineffectual Italians (of whom, officially, only the King and Mussolini were his superiors) and the dictatorial Hitler and the ambitious Rommel (who sometimes conspired together with or against Kesselring).

In name he was Commander-in-Chief, loaded with the heavy responsibilities and worries that title implied. In practice his authority was weakened, lacking as it did the irrefutable political support and power which such an appointment demanded, denied direct command over the German *Afrika Korps* under Rommel. Any progress he made would be entirely dependent upon his persuasive skill, his charm and his ingenuity. A policy of transparent straightforwardness was unthinkable. His diplomacy would have to be Machiavellian in the land of Machiavelli. Somebody – almost everybody in the end – would get hurt. Kesselring merely had to settle his priorities and, if possible, manoeuvre his way towards an indistinct and distant goal. The Italians must be upheld sufficiently to satisfy their ego and preserve their participation, but the German cause must come first. As

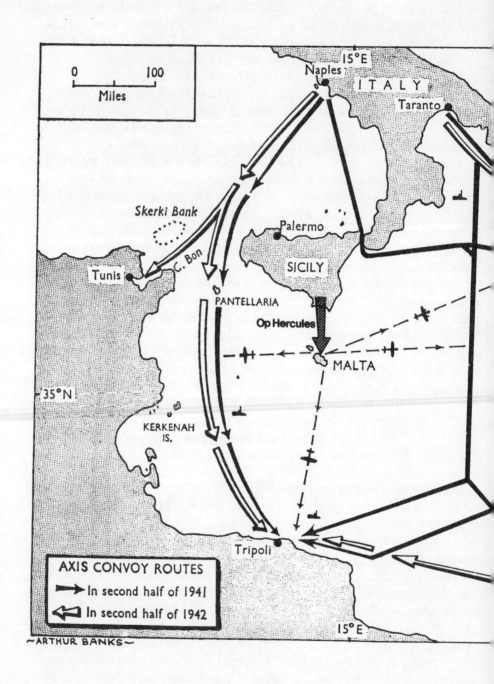

0   100
Miles

15°E

Naples

ITALY

Taranto

Skerki Bank

Palermo

Tunis

C. Bon

SICILY

PANTELLARIA

Op Hercules

MALTA

35°N

KERKENAH
IS.

Tripoli

15°E

AXIS CONVOY ROUTES

→ In second half of 1941

⇐ In second half of 1942

~ARTHUR BANKS~

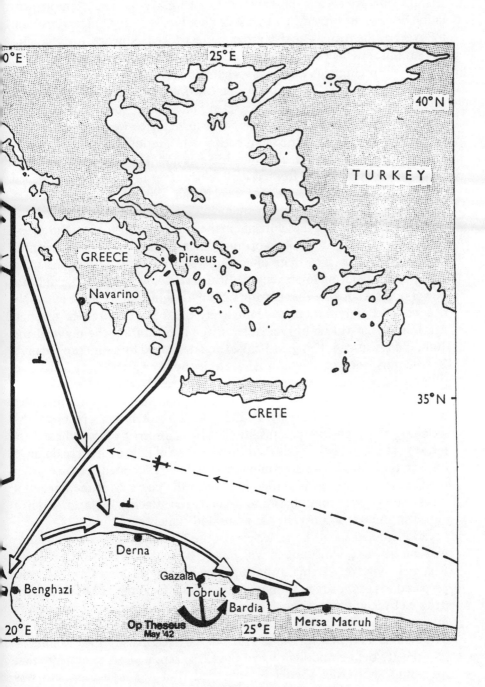

40°N

25°E

TURKEY

GREECE   Piraeus

Navarino

35°N

CRETE

Derna

Gazala

Benghazi   Tobruk

Bardia

20°E   Op Theseus   25°E   Mersa Matruh
        May '42

an individual Kesselring must survive to ensure, if possible, the implementation of German strategy, and a fair deal for his *Luftwaffe* officers and men followed by the Army – in that order of precedence. Nowhere does he actually say this, but his actions leave no doubt as to his intentions early in 1942.

With the preliminary meetings with the Italian *Comando Supremo* and the German attachès in Rome (von Pohl of the *Luftwaffe* and von Rintelen of the Army) behind him, Kesselring set out on a tour of inspection on what, in moments of intensive operations, were to be thrice-weekly flights, in all sorts of weather. They carried him between the headquarters of *Luftflotte* II in Sicily, the various *Luftwaffe* units in Sicily and throughout the length of the North African shore, from Tripoli to wherever the front line happened to be. At last he came face to face with an embattled Rommel on 16 December. It was an unfortunate moment that they chose, for Rommel was plunged in despair and therefore not in the least bit likely to greet the cheerful Kesselring in a mood of co-operative relaxation. On the 15th Rommel had signalled a warning that, 'after four weeks of costly fighting' in unavailingly endeavouring to prevent the British relieving Tobruk, 'the fighting power of the troops . . . is showing signs of flagging, all the more as supply of arms and ammunition has completely dried up. . . . retreat through Mechili-Derna will be unavoidable, at the latest during the night of the 16th, if it is to escape being outflanked and destroyed by a superior enemy'. It was this sort of pessimistic attitude upon which Kesselring had philosophised in the extract from 'Commentaries' given at the end of the previous chapter. But just then neither the Italians nor Kesselring were much interested in philosophy. Politics controlled their deliberations – the weighing of the sensitive practicalities in giving up territory (whether or not it had strategic or tactical value); the revaluation of policies if, in so doing, a crisis in civil morale and determination would be generated at a time when the German Army was in retreat in Russia; the guessing at the impact of news, barely a week old, that America had been attacked by Japan and had joined in the war against the Germans and Italians.

Cavallero had spent the better part of the 16th in conference with Rommel and his staff, a meeting in which, as Cavallero puts it, 'feathers flew'. Rommel, however, seems to have persuaded himself that Cavallero was prepared to permit a retreat, though this was far from the case. The Italian, irritated by Rommel's arbitrary manner, departed to gather reinforcements in the shape of Kesselring, Marshal Bastico (the Governor-General of Tripolitania) and General Gambarra. They arrived in a group at Rommel's HQ shortly before midnight when Cavallero repeated his arguments that the withdrawal order should be cancelled. But although Cavallero was backed up by Kesselring, who pledged action by the only instrument to hand – the fullest possible support by the *Luftwaffe* to help make a stand – Kesselring can scarcely have been serious in underwriting such a risk. More likely he was seeking to bridge the gap between two anxious and angry men and certainly he knew that Rommel had only to stick by his resolves – as stick he did, well knowing that an enemy flanking attack through the desert might soon complete the total envelopment of the Axis army.

Rommel pulled back to Benghazi to evade the net, hindered rather than helped by the *Luftwaffe* which, quite inadvertently, conspired further to unsettle Kesselring's relationship with the *Afrika Korps*. In his 'Memoirs', Siegfried Westphal, Rommel's Ia at that time, records (with captious relish) Kesselring's arrival at the HQ on the 18th, flushed with pleasure, to announce, 'Rommel, I have good news for you! The *Luftwaffe* has repeatedly bombed the British pursuing Group Crüwell . . .' Unhappily at that very moment the duty officer entered with a signal to say that the air attacks had fallen on German troops who were hurt in more ways than one. Rommel demanded that Westphal check that the bomb line, as agreed with the *Luftwaffe*, was correct. At once it was proved that the Army, at least, was not to blame. Kesselring, of course, was very embarrassed and said he would investigate the matter. But lasting harm was done. He had got off to a doubly bad start and generated uncertainty and suspicion. Never could he hope for the same courteous relationship with Rommel as he had enjoyed with von Bock. To make matters look worse for the *Luftwaffe*, the Army, reinforced by 22 new tanks, then gave the British two sharp drubbings on 26 and 29 December, accomplishing their mission without much air support, except, that is, the essential reconnaissance which made so many things plain on the other side of the hill. In retrospect it is difficult to substantiate Kesselring's claim in his 'Memoirs' that 'without the reckless spirit of our airmen . . . Rommel's army would not have been able to halt its retreat in the Sirte'. This was merely an example of his loyalty to the *Luftwaffe*.

Westphal, one of the most accomplished and urbane products of the General Staff and a critical admirer of Rommel, in due course would be among those best placed to judge the comparative merits of Kesselring and Rommel as their frictional relationship developed. But early in 1942, as he recalls, 'My relations with Kesselring were not especially good . . . I sometimes found it necessary to deal with difficulties with the *Luftwaffe* leader [Frölich] who was always amiable and helpful.' Unhappily Frölich abhorred Rommel to the extent that he was bent upon avoiding contact with the army general as much as possible – an unacceptable state of affairs which, along with most other clashes of personality involving Rommel, had somehow to be put right by Kesselring. To this the man who had under-mined Milch's position with Göring addressed himself with characteristic finesse. Appreciating, as he says in the 'Memoirs', that 'Rommel's great reputation, then at its zenith, was an obstacle to the introduction of any change', he set about removing Rommel's props while strengthening his own supporters among those *Luftwaffe* leaders close to the general. To begin with he tried to have Westphal replaced, suggesting to Rommel, as Westphal reports, that the Ia was 'a troublemaker'. Rommel replied that 'I would not think of it and I am happy to have him.' Jeschonnek, however, was perfectly prepared to replace Frölich and happy, moreover, to send his own Chief of Operations, Hoffmann von Waldau, a clever but forthright staff officer who had rarely hesitated to confront Göring as well as Jeschon-nek with unpalatable truths. Göring had relieved him for his temerity. From March onwards he would stand up to Rommel – to the benefit of them all.

Alter the supporting cast though he might, Kesselring had always, on stage, to deal with Rommel himself and here, as Westphal has pointed out to me, difficulties arose simply because of the character differences. The two may have met previously when Rommel was an instructor at the Infan-try School in Dresden in 1932 and Kesselring was enjoying his final spell of regimental duty. They certainly saw each other during the Polish campaign. But there is nothing to suggest that they 'collided' on either occasion. In background and training they were, of course, poles apart since Rommel was a fighting animal *par excellence*, though quite literate as his books and articles on war had shown before the war. To Kesselring men like Rommel fell into the lowest category among the distinguished high-ranking officers of the Second World War: he rated him plainly as 'a leader type without General Staff experience', with the implied inuendo of a pernicious handicap – as indeed it was in Rommel's case, for Kesselring has noted that Rommel 'was very touchy about this'. If there were two qualifications of a higher commander that Rommel lacked it was the ability to grasp the need for co-operation between allies (and supporting arms, too, it may be added) and an oversight amounting to ignorance of the fundamental importance as well as the actuation of logistics. While Rommel would worry, and inter-minably complain about lack of supplies, and Kesselring persuade Rommel to at least pay lip service to these vital factors, it was Rommel, when the bat-tle called (or, as Kesselring has put it in a post-war memoir to the British, 'who would never stop when he won a tactical victory') who abandoned logistical considerations and launched forth on dangerous gambles. In this respect it was the well-educated Kesselring who, almost in isolated splendour, had to provide depth of understanding to North African strategy in order to achieve lasting results, for he received but little support from the Italians or the German High Command either.

Differences in breeding and temperament also helped drive Kesselring and Rommel apart. Rommel, the son of a Württemberg schoolmaster, was anathema to the aristocratic Bavarian (also the son of a schoolmaster). The contrast between the pathologically modest Kesselring and the braggartly Rommel can readily be found by reading Kesselring's 'Memoirs' and Rommel's 'Infantry Attacks' in which the latter takes every opportunity to publicise his deeds of bravery while the former dismisses his altogether. In debate – perhaps confrontation is the more apt word – Rommel would too frequently be forced into acrimony in order to combat or dismiss Kesselring's quieter and more devastatingly marshalled arguments. Both were prone to intrigue but that came a lot less naturally to Rommel than to the staff-trained officer, the General Staff snob. While Rommel seems scarcely to have been willing to discuss any subject other than military matters, Kesselring exuded a breadth of vision and culture which the Württemberger could never match. We learn as much of Kesselring from his comments upon Rommel as we do about Rommel himself. For example, in comments written for the British in 1945, he indulges in irony and exposes his own prejudices: 'To subordinate commanders he [Rommel] was at times insultingly rude. If he had not been a Württemberger one could perhaps have said something to him.' And, 'In spite of his simple nature he put up with publicity men around him', this latter remark being remarkably perspicacious in its discernment.

When free from patching up quarrels and substituting new personalities for old in the command hierarchy, Kesselring bent himself to his principal task of shaping a workable strategy for a theatre of war where, except for a policy of survival, none really existed. Forbidden by Hitler to use the port of Bizerta in Tunisia (which would have solved many problems) because the French armistice was not to be violated, he looked to Malta. Convinced that Malta had to be physically occupied and that bombing by the 400 aircraft of Loerzer's II *Flieger Korps* from Sicily would be inconclusive, he set to work persuading Hitler, Göring and the OKW that an invasion of the island was both feasible and imperative. Realising that a strong Italian involvement, particularly in the commitment of their precious navy to a most hazardous venture, was mandatory, he tackled them primarily having already won the confidence, for the time being, of Cavallero. The negotiations were delayed, however, by Rommel who, reinforced and also aware of a temporary British weakness, had abruptly driven eastward on 21 January, routing the British. Kesselring was informed of this project through *Luftwaffe* channels (though not by Rommel himself) but the Italians were completely taken by surprise and consequently distressed and alarmed. When Cavallero and Kesselring visited Rommel on the 23rd (having delayed in order to see what would happen) Rommel was making full tilt for Benghazi and was not in the least bit ready to accede to Cavallero's request that he restrict the operation to a raid. In tenor and achievement the heated discussion was similar to its forerunner on 16 December except that, in refusing to comply, Rommel exposed his main source of strength by announcing that only a direct order from Hitler would make him change direction. Kesselring contented himself with making diplomatic noises to satisfy Cavallero and the latter, who went away grumbling, took the opportunity to remove XX Italian Corps from Rommel's *Panzerarmee Afrika* on this, the very day it had been put under command of this newly named formation. Cavallero no doubt acted out of fear, not revenge as Rommel asserts, but at the same time he went on talking to Kesselring. A sound relationship had worked up between them, founded perhaps on the esteem of the Italian for the German who, that night, flew him home across the desert in a Storch which was unequipped for night flying, a classic example of Kesselring's supreme confidence in his ability as a pilot as well as willingness to take personal risks.

Kesselring was indeed able to placate Cavallero and revert again to long-term planning with *Comando Supremo*. But Rommel's riposte, which eventually advanced the front line to Gazala and again placed Benghazi and the Derna airfields in German hands, introduced a new dimension. As II *Flieger Korps'* offensive against Malta intensified throughout January it not only placed the island's survival in peril but, to an increasing extent, prevented the British strike forces from harrying Axis convoys to North Africa. Quite soon Rommel's reserves were rebuilt to a level which enabled him, once more, to contemplate taking Tobruk, that essential logistic stepping stone between Benghazi and the Nile.

On 31 December, well aware of the dissent that it would invoke, Kesselring issued his directive for 'the Battle against Malta' giving as its aim the creation of 'a secure connecting route from Italy to North Africa and to attain air and sea control in the area between southern Italy and North Africa'. Vice Admiral Eberhard Weichold, the German naval commander in Italy who headed the liaison team with the Italian Navy, was as anxious as Kesselring to capture Malta and wanted *Luftflotte* II to soften up the island, assault it or at least 'completely neutralise it'.

Kesselring, with the Navy on his side, had now to persuade a doubting Mussolini, through Cavallero and *Comando Supremo*, to sanction the invasion of Malta while, at the same time, pressing a similar case with Hitler through Göring, who was not a bit enthusiastic either. It was a prolonged argument, one which eventually seemed to go Kesselring's way in February when, at a conference between Hitler and Mussolini, approval in principle for the project was given. But the plan was never really settled. Though OKW made the scheme official by enquiring formally of Kesselring as to its feasibility in March and Kesselring replied on the 11th that the Italians intended to capture the island, adding that this would be 'no problem' and 'significantly easier then the seizure of Crete', he was to find Cavallero loaded with doubts a week later, declaring that the assault could not possibly be launched before 1 August, which was far too late. This Kesselring felt compelled to accept with the result that the German Navy became uneasy. OKW therefore pressed Kesselring to obtain an earlier date from Cavallero who agreed, subject to the *Luftwaffe* weakening the island to such an extent that a surprise attack might succeed.

Hitler too, and with good cause, felt uneasy, possibly because it was not his own idea or perhaps because he failed to comprehend fully the workings of air and sea power, or simply at the instance of some intuitive quirk. In effect Hitler, as *Reichschancellor*, was never fully convinced of the political need or, as Supreme Commander, the military propriety of the plan. The tale of Operation 'Hercules', as the invasion was called, is one of vacillation from start to finish. Admiral Raeder, head of the *Kriegsmarin*, felt the need to support Kesselring in order to keep 'Hercules' on course, with Suez as the principal but final objective if all went well. Kesselring worked hard to persuade Rommel as to the need for 'Hercules's' priority over any offensive in Cyrenaica. But it was the *Luftwaffe*'s superlative bombardment of Malta, inflicted with its full verve and skill, which settled the matter – though not entirely to the Axis strategic benefit.

Getting into top gear on 20 March after the previous weeks' preliminaries, a concentrated attack devised by Kesselring, Loerzer and Loerzer's Chief of Staff, Paul Deichmann, laid the foundations of air superiority by destroying many British fighters on their airfields. Successive attempts by British aircraft carriers to fly in more fighters, above all the superior Spitfires, were made abortive by well-timed attacks which caught the fighters on the ground while they were being refuelled after their long flight. Desperately anxious to hold Cavallero to his promise to advance the invasion date if the *Luftwaffe* won a crushing victory, Kesselring prematurely announced to Mussolini and Cavallero on 11 April that 'Malta as a naval base no longer demands consideration'.

But though the air attacks went on and, by 29 April, the British had but a handful of fighters left on the island, both the Italian and German naval staffs were sceptical. In Deichmann's opinion Malta was ripe for conquest, its anti-aircraft fire faltering from shortage of ammunition. He was one of the most trusted of Kesselring's colleagues among the members of the old Imperial Air Force, who had been an observer and therefore not to be numbered as an 'Old Eagle'. In 1934, as a keen supporter of the theories of Douhet and the policy of Wever, he had become the keenest advocate of a strategic air force and the long-range Ural bomber. Since 1940 he had held his present post in the West, as well as in Russia, and had proven himself far-sighted and efficient – a first-class staff officer. His conviction, therefore, was weighty. But the *Luftwaffe* boast that it had put the naval and air bases out of action for the loss of only eleven aircraft was not wholly convincing to the Italians – and the 'losses' did not include high wastage rates.

Rommel needed no persuading to attack: with him it was only a matter of where. The neutralisation of Malta, rebounding to his logistic benefit, also proved the desirability of occupying the island, a need which became all the more essential as it dawned on the Germans that the immense quantities of fuel and bombs being used against Malta and the wastage of over 300 aircraft could only be subtracted from resources that might otherwise be despatched to Cyrenaica and that, with a new major offensive impending in Russia, many of the aircraft left over would soon be taken away. In other words it could only be a matter of time before an unconquered Malta would reassert its pernicious influence. In mid-April Rommel had made a proposal of his own to OKW (without telling Kesselring) to the effect that Malta must be taken prior to an attack on Tobruk which, in turn, must be secured before an advance to the Nile. Haste was essential with risk as its partner. It was well known that the British were preparing a new offensive in the desert which might begin at the end of May: this Rommel had to pre-empt. At a crucial conference at Obersalzberg on 29 April, Hitler, Mussolini, Cavallero and Kesselring reached the final decision to go ahead – but still half-heartedly. Kesselring's extravagant claims that Malta was knocked out reverberated to his disadvantage. When he asked that the invasion date be advanced to 31 May, as Cavallero had said it might if the *Luftwaffe* achieved its aims, Mussolini and Cavallero reversed course on the grounds that the subjugation by air no longer made an invasion necessary at once and that the date as originally proposed, 1 August, was still the only one they could meet. Indisputably Kesselring fought desperately hard for acceptance of his scheme at this conference, endeavouring mainly to staunch the Italians' wilting courage which threatened most to undermine his advocacy. Without them on his side Hitler, OKW and the Navy were justifiably uncertain of the project in the same way as they seriously doubted Kesselring's judgement of land warfare matters – forgetting he had been a soldier far longer than he had been an airman. Yet the final ordering of priorities at Obersalzberg may well have been determined by a weakness inherent in Hitler's psychological yearning for cheap victories at a time when expensive defeats were evident in Russia. Airborne forces had been costly, too, as those under Student, who was preparing to spearhead 'Hercules', had learnt at Crete. Rommel's genius, exaggerated by Josef Göbbels' propaganda ministry, seemed to promise an inexpensive victory, and he therefore stimulated Hitler in a way Kesselring did not. So Operation 'Theseus', the attack on Tobruk, which had been made possible all the sooner by the efforts of Kesselring's *Luftflotte* II, was to take place first and had to be completed by 18 June, followed on 18 July by 'Hercules'. Then would come a reassessment as to whether or not an advance on the Nile could be undertaken. With this compromise Kesselring had to be content, along with an admonition from Hitler, when he pushed his case too hard, 'All right, Kesselring, keep your shirt on. I'm going to do it!'

To support Rommel's offensive against the British in the Gazala Line to the west of Tobruk, Kesselring assembled some 260 aircraft on 26 May having, in the meantime, called off the attack on Malta on the 10th, leaving only 115 aircraft in Sicily to hinder British attempts at recovery. But already the imminence of that recovery had been demonstrated. More Spitfires were flown in from carriers on 9 May, but this time the British ground organisation was equal to the situation by rapidly dispersing the aircraft to shelters and refuelling them so quickly that they were in the air to greet the *Luftwaffe* as it appeared in an attempt to repeat its previous massacre. Also a single ship had slipped in with more anti-aircraft ammunition. Within the next few days the Germans were to lose more aircraft than they had during the 11,500 sorties of the previous five weeks. Yet, on the 10th, as his airmen grappled with Spitfires, Kesselring cheerfully signalled to Hitler: 'Enemy naval and air bases at Malta eliminated.' Of that victory, however, he would write that, in Malta, the *Luftwaffe* found in the RAF a worthy opponent whose fighters' tactics he admired.

To ensure the maximum efficient usage of air effort during 'Theseus', Kesselring moved his headquarters from Sicily to North Africa and took to flying over the battle zone in his own aircraft in order to be constantly informed of the situation and apply his personal influence at the critical moments. Westphal says that 'no other German *Luftwaffe* commander ever came up to Kesselring in his endeavours to help the Army', though he admits having had disagreements with the C-in-C over the recurrent misunderstandings between the two services, recalling an occasion when Kesselring told him that 'The General Staff and the generals were at rock bottom with Hitler. They continually make difficulties . . . The Führer has said that he envies Göring his wonderful *Luftwaffe* commanders. They are always optimistic and take a positive view.' Westphal could not take this and sourly replied, 'On operational matters the gentlemen of the *Luftwaffe* have it easy. They guarantee things which the Army has to fulfil. At 300 km range everything looks simpler from the air.' He adds that Kesselring 'saluted with his marshal's baton, replied, "Herr *Oberst*", and left me standing.' Yet it is likely that Westphal stood higher in the C-in-C's favour than he thought. The Air Ministry History says that Kesselring 'became violent' if roused by criticism of the *Luftwaffe*, though this runs contrary to his son's opinion when he records how readily his father would listen to arguments and how rarely he lost his temper, an assertion he qualifies by saying, 'Of course he knew – like any senior officer – how to resort to the instrument of the simulated, sudden outburst of temper.'

Westphal's assessment of Kesselring's attributes was entirely upheld throughout Operation 'Theseus'. Rommel's initial attack ran into such serious difficulties against the British General Ritchie's Eighth Army that, at one desperate moment, he was on the verge of capitulation. The *Luftwaffe*, on the other hand, won complete air supremacy at the front and systematically played havoc with the British. Kesselring was soon involved in the land battle, at one crucial point, after General Crüwell (then commanding the two Italian infantry corps) had mistakenly landed among the British in his aircraft and been taken prisoner, taking local command. Arriving at the crucial moment at Crüwell's HQ, he was met by von Mellenthin, the Operations Officer, with the request that he take over and make a vital decision. He did so with an amused grin, remarking that it was hardly proper for a field-marshal to take orders from a general. But he was now able to assess Rommel as a commander and appreciate the difficulties of being subordinate to a headquarters 'that issues no orders and cannot be reached'. Yet Kesselring pays tribute to 'the stimulating effect of Rommel's presence on the decisive flank' and records his delight at, later, watching Rommel's 'amazingly expert technique in directing a desert command post'. In the air it was he who was a master and every bit as much at risk, seeking enemy concentrations to strike and personally guiding the waves of bombers and fighters to their targets. Now, too, he demonstrated his innate kindness for those in affliction. Westphal mentions his compassion when he visited him in hospital to commiserate over a wound and to put a Ju 52 at his disposal to fly him from Sicily to Germany.

At the culmination of three weeks' crisis the Germans at last found themselves, due very much to some inept British generalship, in pursuit of a beaten enemy, with Tobruk's familiar perimeter again within striking distance. That this was so, was thanks very much to Kesselring's intervention in correcting an error of Rommel's in connection with the masking of the important Free French 'box' at Bir Hakeim. Rommel had attempted to subjugate the French by aerial bombardment alone, until Kesselring brusquely denounced such waste and said there would be no more bombing until an assault by ground troops was launched. On 9 June this took place and the British line began to collapse. It is a characteristic of certain German accounts that the effects in their favour of air attacks are underrated when they were winning in the desert just as the British, in defeat, overrated them. In matters such as this one attitude rather depends on whose side you happen to be. When their 'tails were up', German soldiers minimised enemy air attacks and naturally preferred to claim all credit for their advances to themselves. The British, slumped in defeat, were prone to collapse under concentrated bombing such as Kesselring threw at them on certain special occasions. Yet these occasions were far from frequent, so tight were the logistic restrictions, so few the airmen and machines.

For the assault on Tobruk on 20 June he could scrape together, from far and wide, only 350 sorties and in so doing took the risk that he would exhaust what small petrol reserves still remained. Prior to the battle he strove for maximum dedication by visiting every unit to talk in person to each crew. No doubt this made a contribution to the quick enemy collapse, but British morale by then was in such a parlous state that artillery fire alone would probably have sufficed. Be that as it may, the port, profusely stocked, fell into German hands within 24 hours. 'Theseus' was triumphantly completed on the 21st and Kesselring could warmly congratulate Rommel, now a *generalfeldmarschall* himself on the strength of it, and with his broadest smile announce, 'Now for Hercules'. He could not have gone farther astray. Rommel, fattened by supplies, was engrossed in a plan to overturn the 'Theseus Hercules' pact and, grasping for personal aggrandisement, by pursuit of the British to Sidi Barrani with an impulse to go all the way to the Nile.

Kesselring says that their meeting on the 21st was very brief 'with no serious discussion about final objectives' and that he made no commitment, as some people have suggested, to an advance on Cairo. Behind his back, however, the issue had virtually been decided – though not by Rommel in the

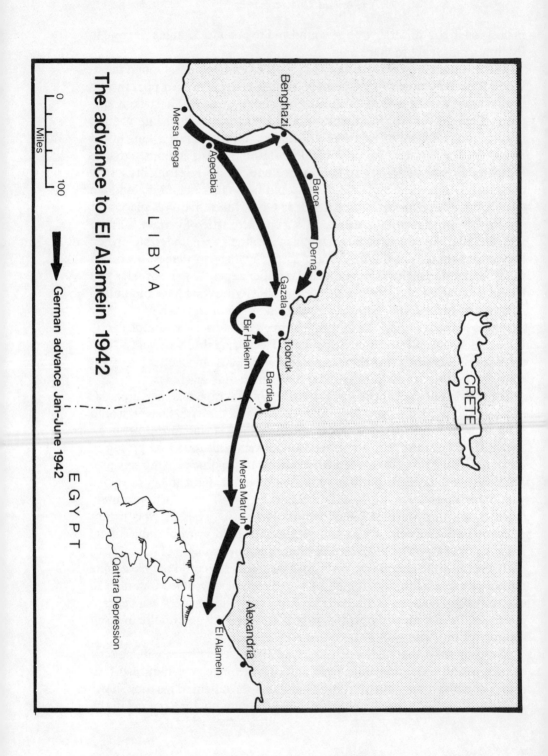

The advance to El Alamein 1942

Miles

0 100

⬇ German advance Jan-June 1942

LIBYA

EGYPT

Mersa Brega

Agedabia

Benghazi

Barce

Derna

Gazala

Bir Hakeim

Tobruk

Bardia

Mersa Matruh

Qattara Depression

Alexandria

El Alamein

CRETE

first instance. When, early in June, the desert battles were poised in crisis, Student, the commander designate for 'Hercules', had been called to Hitler and informed that, although a Malta bridgehead might possibly be won, there was no hope of it being consolidated: the British fleet would intervene and the Italians bolt for their own ports, was the Führer's theme. There is evidence, too, that Göring, fearful of a repetition of the Crete losses, may have injected or reinforced the latent fears in Hitler's mind. Whatever the reason was, Student was forbidden to return to Italy and 'Hercules' was vetoed.

Therefore Rommel merely provided Hitler with a pretext when, on the 22nd, he sent an officer, Dr Ingemar Berndt, who sometimes performed duty as his escort (not as is, sometimes said, as his ADC), to ask for permission to make straight for Cairo, and signalled Mussolini to the same effect, carefully concealing his pleas from Kesselring. It was an adroit move, skilfully executed. Not only did Rommel and Berndt carefully play on the Führer's preference for prestige objectives, such as Cairo, rather than the essential military kind such as Alexandria or the Canal, but in employing Berndt, Rommel sent a plenipotentiary of far greater influence than was normal in a mere lieutenant of the Reserve. For Berndt was an intimate of Dr Göbbels, had previously been an under-secretary in the Propaganda Ministry and had been specially sent to Rommel by the Doctor to act as an observer or reporter to accompany this star performer. Berndt, as Westphal remarks, was a man to avoid, but no doubt he understood better than Rommel the Führer's political inclinations as, together, they also flattered Mussolini by suggesting he should come to North Africa and ride through Cairo on a white horse. Kesselring was therefore wasting his time when he signalled Hitler to request Rommel be halted and for 'Hercules' to be carried out as originally planned. He warned, with abundant and forceful truth, that the *Luftwaffe* was temporarily exhausted and could not give adequate cover for the long-range drive Rommel intended. He said, too, that with Malta already resurgent and supplies at a premium (despite the acquisitions in Tobruk) there would be a logistic breakdown. He called the scheme 'madness'. Hitler brusquely replied with a direct order to give maximum support.

On 26 June, when the Axis armies, weak in armour and already under heavy attack from the British air force, stood poised before Mersa Matruh, Kesselring met Rommel, Cavallero and Bastico at Gambut. They stood at a crossroads of history, on the same day as the armies in Russia took the fatal roads leading to the Caucasus and to Stalingrad. The fate of the Axis as well as Africa was at stake, but the outcome of this, the celebrated meeting of the marshals, was a foregone conclusion. Though Kesselring argued strongly to the last against going on and Cavallero gave him tacit support, the latter, delighted to be rid of 'Hercules' was, in any case, already under instructions from Mussolini to reach for the political advantage – as Kesselring sensed. The decision was Rommel's and he would not draw back from what he recognised as a gamble. Overall loomed Hitler and his belief in Rommel's victory psychosis. General Walther Nehring, who had recently arrived from Russia to take over *Afrika Korps*, and was at the meeting (and who was to sponsor a German Study of the North African Campaign) has confirmed to me Kesselring's objections – and adds the opinion that he was right. This is interesting since the original study (which was the target for Kesselring's critical 'Commentaries') suggests that Kesselring supported the advance on the Nile – sharply denied by Kesselring who states that he then felt '*Comando Supremo*, influenced by Rommel, had departed from the plan of campaign comparatively light-heartedly'. This conflict of opinion concerning Kesselring's attitude and statements during the conference (and in the weeks to come) has at its heart the Africa Army faction's mistrust of Kesselring. They identified themselves with Rommel's contention that Kesselring let them down and perpetrated a travesty of injustice by flagrantly accusing Kesselring of 'criminal optimism' in promising supplies to North Africa without understanding the situation. In practice Kesselring could only do his best, as 'a glorified quartermaster', as he now bitterly called himself, to remedy a situation over which he had been deprived of operational control. His energetic and continuous efforts to move supplies from Europe to the front were foredoomed to failure. He was unaware that every convoy that sailed was notified to the British by 'Ultra' so that only a trickle of supplies got through the British air and sea blockade.

Even so the Germans' peril would have been averted without much harm had the British only stopped the German attack on the defences of Mersa Matruh on 26 June – as they should have done. As dusk fell on the 27th the Germans came to a halt, baffled by a disorganised British Army that remained undefeated in material terms. But at that moment General Auchinleck was engaged in a command reorganisation, having sacked the leader of Eighth Army who had failed at Gazala, and had taken direct command into his own hands. He was too late to save the immediate situation. General Gott, the commander of mobile troops at Mersa Matruh, had already lost heart after two years of almost uninterrupted desert war in which set-backs had been more frequent than triumphs, and prematurely, in face of pressure which was by no means irresistible, withdrew. Had he held on it might well have been fatal for Rommel's chances of advancing to the next defence line which Auchinleck was preparing across the defile of El Alamein. Had the British not given way the difference between Kesselring and Rommel would have been resolved on the spot. The advance would have been halted and Kesselring, no doubt, would have tried to revive 'Hercules'. As it was Rommel shot ahead into a situation that could not have been better set as a trap if it had been contrived, positively inviting the rebuff which Kesselring felt sure must come to an offensive 'with too broad an objective' that was 'therefore wrong and liable to disaster'.

A distinct choice was presented to the Axis forces as they recoiled before the heavy gunfire which poured upon their emaciated columns at El Alamein. They could exist where they stood in a state of semi-immobility induced by the fuel shortage at the end of a long and exposed line, or they could pull back to safety on the Egyptian frontier – as Rommel had originally intended if things went wrong. But Mussolini had arrived with his white horse and could not be kept waiting, and Hitler insisted upon results; so a battle to exhaustion was ordained into July, with Kesselring monotonously intoning the impossibility of alleviating the logistic situation. In July only twenty per cent of the supplies required reached North Africa and the British Air Force, virtually unopposed by an exhausted *Luftwaffe*, tore the Axis lines of communication to pieces. Hitler, who, in the manner of all revolutionaries was the last man on earth to willingly give up a conquest, would not consent to withdrawal. Refusals of this nature were now his creed. Faced with this situation, Kesselring also began to assume the cloak of a gambler, but, unlike Rommel, for calculated reasons. With Malta dangerously reactivated in his rear and most unlikely now to be invaded, the only way to smash the British in the Middle East, when Germany was so heavily committed elsewhere, was to seize the Suez base with its vast supply stocks before the British regained their poise. In the 'Commentaries' he argues that 'a purely defensive solution was not practicable'. To await a British offensive and then counter-attack would be fatal. A German attack, to succeed, would have to come soon, before the British recovered – but that, as Rommel pointed out, depended on his receiving adequate supplies and reinforcements. Rommel and Kesselring contemplated a withdrawal but agreed they must attack providing supplies could be built up sufficiently. That demanded another air offensive against Malta in August.

At this moment Rommel lost heart, telling OKH on 22 August that he was ill and asking that a substitute, preferably Heinz Guderian, should be sent out in his place. Hitler would have none of it. Guderian was *persona non grata*, having been sacked for defiance of orders at the end of 1941. The Führer, however, was agreeable to Kesselring taking over as Supreme

Commander in North Africa with Nehring commanding the Army. At that Rommel decided to feel better, qualifying his change of mind with the reservation that he must soon take a long cure in Germany. Quite obviously the fire which previously charged his energy had been doused. Defeat loomed ahead and he was unwilling to face it when it came.

Angry recriminations among Army Officers, stimulated by Rommel in moments of deepest gloom, stud the story of the Axis attack against the well-prepared British position on Alam Halfa ridge on 30 August. One faction claims that Kesselring 'guaranteed' supplies and Kesselring retorts that 'It is utterly impossible that I should give any such assurances under these circumstances, though I did everything in my power to improve the supply service.' A classic cause of disunity between Army and *Luftwaffe* comes to light over the promise by Cavallero of delivery of 6,000 tons of fuel oil due in two tankers at Tobruk, supplemented by 400 tons daily, *if necessary*, by air, promised by Kesselring. Air supply was at once necessary since the tankers were sunk at sea by an air attack which the *Luftwaffe* was unable to prevent. But the entire 400 tons by air was never in prospect either. Westphal was present when Kesselring made the offer and pointed out that it would require 250 lifts by Ju 52s which, even under ideal conditions without enemy opposition and bad weather, would be impossible. Kesselring lost patience and told Westphal to leave them. From the distance Westphal saw the two marshals shake hands and heard Rommel say 'Splendid!'. The attack was sanctioned on the strength of Kesselring's assurance, but the fuel never reached the front. Rommel felt he had been fooled and never forgave. In fact his driving ambition had *allowed* him to be fooled. At the time, to Kesselring, the failure to deliver that which arrived was incomprehensible – and much did arrive, as Westphal corroborated. Deichmann put his finger on what had happened when he wrote to Kesselring:

> It is an established fact that, when Rommel tried to hold you and OKW responsible for his enforced capitulation owing to fuel shortage, we found out that, in his rear area, fuel was freely issued in any amount to the columns on the road . . . Rommel's attention was drawn to this by teletype message but he replied that he was only interested in the fuel which we flew to his tanks. It was his quartermaster's job to bring the fuel from the rear to the front. Probably a scapegoat for the failure was sought at the time.

Kesselring says that if he had realised this he would have made delivery nearer to the front even at risk to the transport aircraft.

Failure there surely was. The initial German assault, harried from the start, bogged down in soft sand and minefields. Shot at and bombed without let and with little hindrance, the Axis troops wilted and, once more, found no salvation, only death, from the skies. Though a mere handful of aircraft was available to Kesselring, even these were handicapped by lack of fuel. So the British bombers operated much as they chose and Rommel abandoned hope. Indeed it was Kesselring who now did the urging as the soldier gave up. Nevertheless within 48 hours both the Axis air and land forces were compelled to pull back before a solid enemy resistance and due to their own fuel shortage.

Rommel had shot his bolt. Defeat, compounded by ill-health, made it his earnest wish to return to Germany for 'the long cure'. It was, for him, a personal turning point, one that came on the eve of Germany's last victories in Russia and the end of her military dominance. To his credit at this bleak moment, he penned a generous testimonial to Kesselring who had, he wrote, 'considerable strength of will, a first class talent for diplomacy and organisation, and a considerable knowledge of technical matters' – attributes, we might add, which he, in all but the first instance, was deficient. Rommel goes on, 'Kesselring had the *Luftwaffe* and Göring behind him and could thus command sufficient support at the highest level to enable him to tackle questions of high policy in relation to Italy. This suggestion [made on 8 August to Keitel that Kesselring should assume control of Mediterranean shipping with special powers] unfortunately was not acted upon either early enough or in the form in which I wanted it.' In point of fact two of the personalities mentioned above were already in decline. Due to the now blatantly obvious failures by the, *Luftwaffe* as Allied aircraft bombed German cities, Göring was losing favour with Hitler. As for Rommel, he had fallen in prestige too and Kesselring was making progress in having him sent home – even though he deeply admired Rommel's mastery of what he termed 'a poor man's war'. It was not a sacking; just an easing out of Rommel. General Stumme was merely to be his deputy, but undeniably Kesselring was not sorry to see the back of the turbulent Rommel. Of Stumme he would say in the 'Commentaries', that, 'Both troops and staff of the Panzer Army [Afrika] had full confidence in him and they worked well together.'

The initiative now rested with the British and the Americans and it was against them that Kesselring had now to arm himself. Over the horizon threats of a totally different character to were in the offing.

7

Back to Soldiering

It has been suggested by Walter Winterbotham that, 'When all the preconceived ideas of victory by the *Luftwaffe* were finally shattered, Kesselring must have seen little future for his career under a discredited Göring and must have started to look about for some other field for his undoubted talents and qualities of military optimism and Nazi political fervour which Hitler so admired in him.' There is but little evidence to support this sweeping and cynical assertion. The subject of Nazi fervour we will return to later but, as for the rest, Winterbotham's theory seems to be based on a dubious understanding of the real run of events since he is quite wrong when he says in his book that Kesselring arrived in Rome as 'airman turned soldier' in July 1941. There was nothing (even on the *actual* date of the appointment in December) to connect Kesselring's advancement with fading air power, nor was Göring yet discredited. These things would come, but by the time they did any change in Kesselring's circumstances would largely have been created by events that were beyond his control.

The incidence of abortive attacks on Malta convoys in the summer of 1942 did, however, illustrate the advancing eclipse of the *Luftwaffe*. Its air crews performed with the old dash but a noticeable technical and numerical inferiority prevented them from benefiting by their prowess. For example, a convoy of 6 merchantmen, escorted by a battleship, 2 aircraft carriers, 3 cruisers and 17 destroyers, which fought its way through in mid-June against approximately 100 German aircraft, supplemented by a number of less enthusiastic Italians, lost four merchantmen. In April it would have been another story. No longer in August could the *Luftwaffe* press air attacks over the island in face of fierce opposition by Spitfires. That month, when the renewed offensive to neutralise the island was at its height, as cover for the shipment of supplies to Rommel, 700 Axis aircraft (220 of them German) could sink but 2 and damage 2 more of 14 merchantmen – an index of vastly improved British defences as well as of weak performance by the Axis air crews. But the compelling reason for Kesselring, the airman, to become much more Kesselring the soldier, and even the sailor, was force of circumstances. The Germans – though not Hitler as yet – had awoken far too late to the meaning and demands of the Mediterranean struggle. All at once it was recognised as a problem in a different category to anything they had tackled and that it required a special solution. In August a reorganisation, hinted at by Rommel, was put in hand. Tempered by the sensibilities of the Italians (with their lack of enthusiasm for the war) and the fluctuating directives of Hitler and OKW (on those occasions they could spare time from the all-consuming assault on Russia as, steeped in renewed visions of victory, the armies drove deep into the Caucasus and approached the bend in the Volga at Stalingrad) it went some way to satisfy the wishes of Kesselring, its designer.

At last Albert Kesselring was able to assume a mantle fit for a real Commander-in-Chief. The discussions about reorganisation which had begun in August were finally implemented at the beginning of October. Kesselring became responsible for the defence of all German-occupied coastal areas in the Mediterranean with the exception of those sectors under *Panzerarmee Afrika*. Thus he became the only German to control all three Services in joint-command. Therefore he was given a separate staff from that of *Luftflotte* II, taking Deichmann (*Luftwaffe*) as his Chief of Staff for the theatre, Westphal (Army who was still chief of operations to *Panzerarmee Afrika*) to assume, in February 1943, specific responsibility for the African theatre, and Weichold (Navy) as German Naval Commander in Italy, though he came under the Italian Naval command. The relationship with the Italians through *Comando Supremo*, held together by links through the military attachés in Rome, remained as before, leaving each faction with liberty to act with a considerable degree of independence. Mussolini, through *Comando Supremo*, retained his direct control over *Panzerarmee Afrika* and Kesselring his working relationship with Cavallero. At the same time General Alfred Gause was appointed to Rome as Rommel's deputy, to act on his behalf without being under Kesselring's command. Had conditions for misunderstanding and indecision been deliberately sought they could scarcely have been arranged more methodically. Moreover this discordance in command (representing the prevalent atmosphere of mutual mistrust) was an invitation to downfall at a time when the British, French and American allies were combining their resources with consummate unselfishness. In August a new British Commander-in-Chief, Harold Alexander, had arrived in Cairo and command of the Eighth Army in the desert had been taken over by Bernard Montgomery. Back in London, the Anglo-American forces which were charged to open a new front in North Africa that year were placed under the command of Dwight Eisenhower.

While Hitler and his close entourage still dwelt in ecstasy at the magnitude of the deep advances into the Caucasus, those less privileged, who fought for every crumb in the Mediterranean, endured from day to day in the keen anticipation of disaster. Indeed, the main reason for granting Kesselring additional scope was the result of intelligence then available to OKW that foretold enemy landings 'somewhere' in the Mediterranean concurrent with the expected British offensive at El Alamein. An appreciation by Deichmann in September pointed to Greece, Sicily or Italy as the likelier targets. But he also seriously contemplated a breakout, through the Dardanelles, by the Russian Black Sea Fleet. As less likely eventualities were landings in Spain, Southern France, or North Africa, though these were given keen consideration. OKW, according to Deichmann, was shy to reveal its sources of information and did not look favourably on the possibility of a landing in French North Africa since the French were unlikely to collaborate with the British for whom they had held little love since the denouement of 1940. Greece and Crete, which came under C-in-C South East who reported direct to Kesselring, could readily be put into a strong state of defence. Regarding Italy, it was another matter since here the local authorities had to be consulted at every step and at every step they were obstructive, fearing a German take-over. For a start the Italians made it clear that their Fleet would not leave port unless closely escorted by German fighters. At places such as Sicily, Sardinia and Corsica it was thought better to allow local German commanders to strike deals with their Italian opposite numbers. A web of negotiation and intrigue was substituted for the desirable system of firm control through recognised channels of command that was normal in other theatres of war. As far as French North Africa was concerned, no positive defensive measures were taken; not even a contingency plan was produced because OKW forbade it as an intrusion into political affairs. By far the most ominous reason for this prohibition was the physical impossibility of raising worthwhile forces: C-in-C South simply lacked the troops and shipping to undertake counter-action. Kesselring was made aware through his *Luftwaffe* contacts of the discussions between OKW and the Italians on the subject

1 *The Father—Carl Adolf Kesselring*

2 *The Mother—Rosina Kesselring*

3 *The future field-marshal, aged four*

4 *The gunner lieutenant in 1904*

5 *Flight at Metz in 1912, with the famous smile well in evidence*

6 *The staff officer, 1917*

7 Reichswehr *days—probably taken while in the Ministry, 1928*

8 *Building the* Luftwaffe: *an exhausting day with the Chief of Administration as seen by a contemporary cartoonist c. 1935*

9 Right, above *Meeting in Poland: Erwin Rommel stands between Kesselring and his Führer*

10 Right *Kesselring with Göring* (right) *and Milch* (extreme left) *in March 1940*

11 Left *The Field-Marshal, July 1940*

12 *A picture taken by Kesselring, showing a Russian airfield under bombardment*

13 *On the Holy Mountain with Löhr, Göring and Loerzer*

14 *On the Holy Mountain in September 1940 directing the Battle of Britain*

15 *First visit to North Africa*—left to right: *Frölich, Rommel, Kesselring, Crüwell, Gause*

16 Right, above *Desert conference*

17 Right *Planning 'Hercules' and 'Theseus' at Berchtesgaden: Kesselring, Hitler, Mussolini and Keitel*

18 *Tension in Tunis: Kesselring and Walther Nehring* (right)

19 *Battle near Tunis: German tanks and infantry at Tebourba early in December*

20 *At Frascatti with Cavellero* (centre) *and German ambassador, Hans von Mackensen* (right)

21 *Tasting the men's meals in Italy*

22 *With Westphal and von Richthofen directing operations at Anzio*

23 *Command Group in Italy*—left to right: *von Vietinghoff, Kesselring, von Senger and Westphal*

of seizing Gibraltar and sealing off the Mediterranean, but, quite incredibly, was not informed of the outcome; and as for knowledge of enemy intentions he was as badly informed as everybody else on the Axis side.

Axis intelligence sources produced a shower of guesses to cover nearly every contingency. Admiral Canaris, the head of the military *Abwehr*, was roundly accused by Kesselring, with justice, of promoting the war of nerves against the Germans! Canaris's most reliable agents spoke of landings that would come in the eastern Mediterranean. In fact, the only certain eventuality in the German book, though without knowledge of its timing, was the impending British attack at El Alamein. It was a personal calculation by Kesselring, based on the evolving programme of air bombardment, which led him to estimate with plausible accuracy that the blow would fall about the middle of October. But do what he could to prevent it, the well-proven gambits of earlier years no longer prevailed. Malta defended itself brilliantly and Axis convoys for North Africa went on being sunk at a crippling rate. Stumme's army at El Alamein, ensconced in a 'devil's garden' of minefields, realised that its next battle would be the most desperate of all. As for the expected landings elsewhere, a study by Kesselring of the reports supplied by Canaris failed, according to Deichmann, to form any picture. Indeed he concluded (correctly) they were so misleading as to constitute a deliberate plot by the enemy. At last, however, it began to look as if the landing might come in the western Mediterranean since activity at Gibraltar was sharply increased; but still there was no indication as to time and place. Hitler guessed now that the south of France was threatened, as did Kesselring, though the latter also gave serious thought to Corsica as a target while, in practice, tending to let events reveal themselves. It was Mussolini who got it right when, with political intuition, he said it would be French North Africa, but this happy insight everybody else rejected for military reasons. The guessing game reached its zenith early in November, simultaneous with the climax at El Alamein where, since 23 October, a gruelling battle had taken place among the minefields, to the accompaniment of an air and artillery bombardment.

Kesselring had flown to the battle front on the 24th to find tension already at an unusual height. It was not only that the British had made significant penetrations among defences which Rommel, with Kesselring's approval, had laid out, and which Stumme had further strengthened. Stumme himself was missing from a visit to the front and it was Westphal who was conducting the battle. Who would replace

Stumme? The obvious choice was Rommel, but Rommel had yet to recover his health and was still recuperating in Germany. Kesselring makes it quite plain in the 'Commentaries' that he was reluctant to recall Rommel but that he had very little choice other than to do so. For Rommel, the propaganda figure, to be absent would have aroused unacceptable comment on all sides. Arriving via Rome on the evening of the 25th, where he was briefed on the catastrophic supply situation, he once more entered the battle, convinced that 'there were no more laurels to be earned in Africa'.

Braced by Kesselring who, as usual, was trying might and main to inject fresh fuel supplies, only to have them lost at sea, Rommel held on. But by 2 November he knew that the time for withdrawal had come and he began to 'thin out' at the front. Already Montgomery was pushing massed armour through a gap in the defences and *Afrika Korps* had but thirty tanks left to hold them, supported by less than fifty aircraft which were hopelessly outnumbered by immense British formations. The air factor alone was enough to persuade Kesselring that Rommel was right to retreat, but Hitler took the opposite view. On 3 November the Führer ordered Rommel to stand fast, signalling, 'It will not be the first time in history that a strong will has triumphed over the bigger battalions.' Under different circumstances Kesselring might have agreed with the Führer's philosophy, but just then he was at the front, Hitler was not and philosophy had to give way to practicalities. Nevertheless Rommel obeyed and, with indignation, cancelled the retreat, thus stretching the front line to breaking point. It was still holding on the morning of the 4th when Kesselring arrived. Westphal recalls the scene as the C-in-C appeared 'as the rescuing angel'. On the false assumption that it had been Kesselring's reports which had encouraged Hitler's pernicious order (he had yet to be sceptical of Hitler), Rommel pointed at Kesselring and in high emotion cried, 'He has done us all an ill-turn . . .'. Calmly, in his most self-assured manner, Kesselring placated them and, as Westphal says, 'without humming and harring' assumed full responsibility for recommencing the retreat since Hitler's order had been overtaken by events. Kesselring also signalled his decision to Hitler asking for a change of directive. Due to this, adds Westphal, 'we escaped destruction in the nick of time'. The incident, of course, made a deeply unfavourable impression on Kesselring who was constantly monitoring Rommel's performance and had correctly diagnosed the prevailing mood of defeatism at Rommel's HQ. Later Westphal was to hear that Kesselring had sent a signal to Germany stating, quite correctly, 'Rommel and Westphal both overstrained to the highest

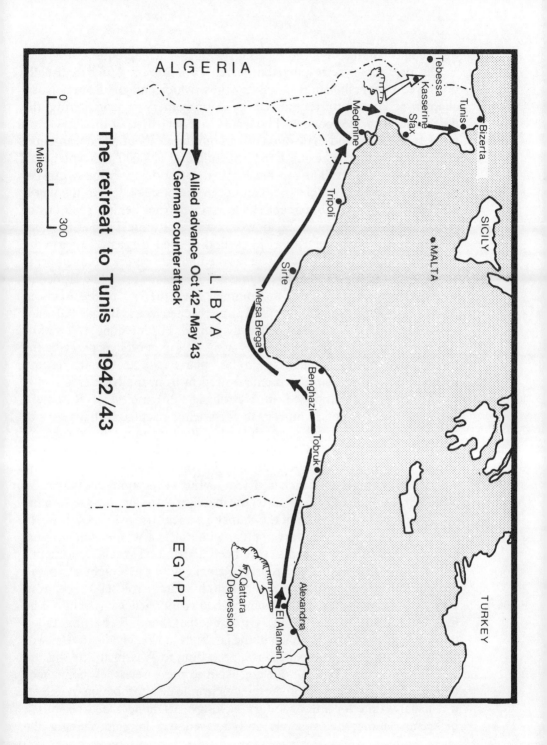

The retreat to Tunis 1942/43

ALGERIA

LIBYA

EGYPT

TURKEY

SICILY

MALTA

Tebessa
Kasserine
Tunis
Bizerta
Sfax
Medenine
Tripoli
Sirte
Mersa Brega
Benghazi
Tobruk
Qattara Depression
Alexandria
El Alamein

Miles
0
300

Allied advance Oct '42–May '43
German counterattack

degree and troublesome (*sauer*). Both require a strong boost.'

The precipitate retreat by the beaten *Panzerarmee Afrika* is usually portrayed in British histories, notably those which eulogise Rommel, as a chapter of opportunities missed by Montgomery in completing the destruction of his opponent. The fact is that very little of the Axis army was left to escape and that which did amounted to about one dozen tanks and a few thousand men out of the 700 tanks and 104,000 men who began the battle in October. The survivors bolted so fast that only the swiftest of runners could have caught them and even the best soldiers in the world will hesitate when an opponent shadow-boxes from behind positions of strong defensive potential. Shadow-box was all Rommel did at first but not for long. Soon, to Kesselring's undisguised disgust, he virtually ceased all opposition. For when he reached Sollum on the 8 November it was to hear that a large Anglo-American amphibious force had landed in French North Africa. This, to Rommel, spelt the end of the Army in Africa. From that moment, until his army reached Mersa Brega, 300 miles to the west on 19 November, he hardly paused. His mission, as he saw it, was to prevent the liquidation of his army. His own officers describe the retreat as 'more or less a route march under slight enemy pressure . . . while reinforcements flowed in from the back area'.

The bitterness expressed in Kesselring's 'Memoirs' at Rommel's independent behaviour (contrary to Kesselring's demands that he try to delay Montgomery's advance in order to win time to establish a bridge-head in Tunisia and prevent the British from occupying forward airfields) is the culmination of six months' frustration. While the withdrawal went on they bickered about almost everything, in particular over the role of the *Luftwaffe* units, the inability of the air crews to support the army and the behaviour of the Ramcke parachutists who, according to Rommel, 'had never been very popular with us because, following normal *Luftwaffe* practice, they had always been demanding special treatment'. When Kesselring wished to decorate Ramcke with the Knight's Cross in recognition of a magnificent desert march which saved 600 men from capture, Rommel refused. But Rommel had abandoned Ramcke just as he left the Italians in the lurch. On the other hand Kesselring failed immediately to inform Rommel of the landings in French North Africa or the Axis counter-measures because, according to Westphal, 'he did not want to worry us. As if we did not listen to the wireless'. When senior commanders have lapsed into a state of chronic disapprobation in defeat, it is usually time for a few salutary sackings. Auchinleck had permitted bickering among his generals and delayed too long in sacking the commander of Eighth Army after the defeat at Gazala, but had himself been sacked by Churchill in time to allow Alexander and Montgomery to take the helm prior to Alam Halfa. And Montgomery had mercilessly sacked men who were tired or who did not inspire his confidence.

Why, then, did not Kesselring sack Rommel at this moment, particularly since, after the war, he was bluntly frank (and rightly so) to assert that it was a mistake to keep Rommel in command? The reasons are complex, but in the simplest of terms can be reduced to the conclusion that it was not in his power to do so. Rommel had been brought to prominence as much by the publicity lavished on him by Josef Göbbels as for the merit of his military achievements. It would have been unthinkable to demand the much-vaunted Desert Fox's dismissal even in the aftermath of defeat. Göbbels had the Führer's ear and, on the grounds of public morale, would defend his hero to the last, as is made quite plain in those extracts of his diaries which have survived. But in any case Kesselring had his hands full with far more threatening and weighty matters at the other end of his vast command. The Allied landing in French North West Africa, for which no provision had been made, was the main charge upon his attention as he found himself plunged into a cauldron of political intrigue, strategic dilemma and tactical improvisation.

It can be fascinating to observe a commander at work through the eyes of his Chief of Staff, particularly if the witness transmits the currents of tensions overloading the staff machine in an atmosphere of uncertainty and drama. This was the case at HQ of C-in-C South at Frascati on the night of 7/8 November. There Paul Deichmann witnessed the state of surprise and the guesswork of the preceding weeks being converted by random reports from a misty vision to a supposition which, as the incoming messages of doom increased in volume and authority, assumed a grim reality. Deichmann recalls Kesselring's reactions that night, remembering the arrival of the first reports from agents telling of shipping without lights passing through the Straits of Gibraltar, then news of shipping off Oran and Algiers, interlaced with a misleading report from an Italian reconnaissance aircraft, until finally a broadcast over the French radio and messages from German aircraft confirmed that landings were in progress at those two places. Later there followed reports of another landing at Casablanca. Already Kesselring had made his first move, telling the German naval commander to send U-boats to intercept the enemy convoys, a request which had to be approved by the Italians – who objected and had to be firmly overruled by Kesselring. Apart from that there was not much he could do at once since, as Deichmann points out (with injured disgust), Oran lay beyond the range of German bombers and torpedo planes. As the chief advocate of the Ural bomber he felt miserable at that moment and this is almost certainly the occasion Kesselring referred to during his evidence at Nürnberg when he remarked, 'the absence of a four-engined bomber became extremely awkward'. Moreover targets at Algiers could only be attacked at night when cloud cover was suitable since the Germans did not have a long-range fighter for escort by day – another deficiency to be laid at Udet's door. It was beyond reason, of course, to expect anything from the Italian Navy which would not have stood a chance against the vast Allied Fleet.

Lacking both a plan and the forces to support strong intervention, the manner in which Kesselring improvised to stabilise the situation and create a strong German bridgehead in Tunisia is all the more remarkable. This, at best, would serve as a base for future offensive action or, at worst, allow Rommel's army to be withdrawn from Tripolitania to Sicily. As usual he was hindered by Hitler, but gradually he obtained his most essential needs. Not until the 9th was he given a free hand in Tunisia and only then with the proviso (soon to be cancelled) that he did not go there himself. In Hitler's mind politics were filed in a different compartment to military matters, and military personalities, at that moment, seemed more unreliable to him than ever. The offensive in Russia was faltering, he had replaced the Army Chief of Staff, Franz Halder, after months of angry recrimination, and he was beginning to look doubtfully upon the indolent Göring. The fact that Hitler seems scarcely to have contemplated exploiting the recognised diplomacy of Kesselring may well have been a product of a current feeling with Keitel and Jodl at OKW that Kesselring was too soft with the Italians. Be that as it may, Hitler's coolness, concomitant with his abrupt dismissal of Kesselring's case for 'Hercules' and the shock he probably suffered as the result of Kesselring's determination to have his way over a retreat from El Alamein, disposes of the suggestion that Kesselring admired the Führer for his military optimism and his Nazi political fervour. On 8 November Kesselring was classified by Hitler as just another recalcitrant general. To Kesselring Hitler remained Supreme Commander, to whom he had sworn an oath of loyalty, whose misconceptions had to be corrected.

That day the imperative need for optimism could not be gainsaid. Deichmann, emulating Rommel, thought that 'The German Italian forces and the African war theatre seemed lost, even if the French could not or did not try to prevent the landing.' Yet Kesselring's improvisations, so different to the well-thought-out, long-sighted constructive methods for which he was celebrated, now conjured up in a flash a new and viable strategy. Regardless of whether the French resisted the Allies or not, he was clear that his aim must be the creation and consolidation of a bridgehead in Tunisia, to push it as far south as possible to make touch with Rommel's army coming back through Cyrenaica and Tripolitania and to thrust as far west as possible to forestall an Allied advance along the coast from Algiers via the port of Bône, while giving air support to the French who were resisting still at Algiers. But whereas, on the 8th, there was still a glimmer of hope that the French would hold out, this was extinguished on the 9th when Admiral Darlan, Deputy to Marshal Pétain, (the head of the Vichy French Government) who happened to be in Algiers at that moment, put an end to the fighting and ranged the French in Algeria on the Allied side. It was this news which convinced Hitler that Kesselring must act with all possible speed and which led him to find and put strong forces (such as made Rommel's mouth water) at his disposal. The problem of how to get them to Tunisia in sufficient time and quantity, arriving, it was hoped, unopposed, had yet to be solved.

On the 9th the Vichy French, under local pressure, gave permission for the *Luftwaffe* to use airfields in Tunisia and Bruno Loerzer landed at Tunis airport, at the head of German squadrons, to negotiate for co-operation with the French Admiral Esteva. To provide a German military presence on the ground, Kesselring's headquarters guard was flown in too, followed by a steady stream of airlifted troops and supplies. Loerzer tried to gain French co-operation, but on the 10th that hope had to be abandoned. Darlan's defection, some inconclusive discussions between Hitler, Count Ciano and Pierre Laval (the Vichy French representative), had convinced Hitler that the French were insincere, compelling him to take a hard line and occupy Vichy France next day, concurrent with the disarming of the French troops in Tunisia. Kesselring hoped to accomplish the operation with the minimum of fuss using the first echelon of a parachute battalion flown in. To some extent they succeeded in keeping the French in parley while his own forces were increased at the vital points. Rather ingenuously he complains in his 'Memoirs' that he might have achieved his aims had not the Italians, against his wishes, flown in a squadron of fighters on the 10th. Possibly this produced local repercussions but the fact remains that German intentions were so blatant that the French were bound to swing to the Allies if only because the Axis had breached the Armistic agreement of 1940. At once the French blocked the harbours and began quietly transferring their army from its barracks into the countryside. Having failed to achieve the total disarmament of the French, it was imperative for the Axis to secure a firm grasp on the main points of entry into Tunisia (Tunis and Bizerta) as a preliminary to further expansion. Fortunately for the Axis, the Anglo-Americans were too busy digesting Algeria and Morocco to move eastward immediately and, in any case, they were justifiably fearful of the *Luftwaffe* should they move beyond the range of adequate fighter cover. A landing undertaken at Bougie on the 11th proved the truth of this when seventy-five per cent of the assault shipping was sunk for the loss of six German aircraft.

In spite of bombing by the RAF from Malta, the Axis built up quickly in Tunisia, the first ships to bring tanks and guns arriving at Bizerta on 12 November. In Tunis, Colonel Martin Harlinghausen, the *Fliegerführer Tunisia*, won Kesselring's approbation by vigorously extending German influence well beyond the city boundaries. At Bizerta, however, an army officer, Colonel Otto Lederer, who had been appointed commander of the bridgehead, was far less ambitious and dallied for fear of provoking a dangerous French reaction. Containing his impatience for the time being, Kesselring permitted Lederer to have his way, though reserving the right to demand an attack on the French if necessary. At the same time he asked for the immediate replacement of Lederer by a more senior and incisive officer, a request which immediately produced a general of considerable reputation and notable ability.

Walther Nehring was one of the tank pioneers who had been Guderian's Chief of Staff in Poland and France, a panzer division commander in Russia and commander of the *Afrika Korps* until he was wounded at Alam Halfa on 31 August. Though still not fully recovered from this wound, he was sent back to Africa, charged with the task of establishing a defensive line at Mersa Brega for occupation by Rommel's retreating army. But on arrival at Rome on the 12th he was diverted to Frascati to receive from Kesselring some extremely precise orders. He was to extend the Tunisian bridgehead to the Algerian frontier, to create room for manoeuvre and remove at once the atmosphere of pessimism exuded by soldiers like Lederer. Nehring was not Kesselring's choice since previously he had acquired reservations about Nehring's luke-warm determination. The latter has told me that, shortly after the fall of Tobruk in June, Kesselring had remarked that, while Rommel always worried he, Nehring, held too many reservations. In the 'Commentaries' Kesselring writes of Nehring, 'I needed a different personality'. To give Nehring's hotch-potch force of a few hundred men a dignity and status far beyond its means, they called it

XC Corps, and Nehring began to play his bluff hand with assurance, beginning, quite literally, with a bang, by surviving a crash on coming in to land at Tunis. While making a tour of inspection, he sacked Lederer for lack of aggression, and (rather like Fink in his omnibus at the beginning of the Battle of Britain in July 1940) commanded with verve from a taxi cab aided by one staff officer using the public telephone system for communication. There is no record as to whether Kesselring was as shocked by this as he had been by Fink's arrangements.

Gradually order and cohesion were imposed. After an attempt by German paratroops to seize the airfield at Souk el Arba on 16 November was frustrated by the drop of British parachutists with a minute or two to spare (no doubt the British were forewarned through 'Ultra') and the French General Barrè, with 10,000 men and a few guns, imposed a screen hindering German patrols as they probed westward, a game of military subterfuge was played with skill by Nehring. By the 19th he had established defended localities controlling the distant approaches to Bizerta and Tunis on a line stretching from the coast to Medjez el Bab, and as far south as Gabes. The British and Americans were bluffing too, by attempting, with little more than a division, to seize the ports. Everything hinged on the competitive rates of build-up by the two sides allied to the determination of Nehring and General Anderson, on the British side, at the battle front. Anderson was prepared to take risks and brought pressure on Nehring. Kesselring, with all his energy thrown into the work of despatching men, equipment and supplies to North Africa as fast as they arrived in Italy, was ruthlessly determined on compliance with his established priorities. On 16 November he finally scotched Rommel's attempt at establishing, through General Gause, a private source of supply. With Hitler's approval he set Gause to work under his personal control, organising the transit of men and material to *all* parts of the theatre – which meant that Rommel's army went to the bottom of the list. Rommel, much against his inclinations, was told by Hitler to hold Mersa Brega with reduced forces. The bulk of the 18,000 men, 159 tanks and 127 guns, along with 13,000 tons of supplies, which found their way to Tunisia by sea and air went to Nehring, as Kesselring insisted it must. Quite unexpectedly, however, Nehring seemed to put the vital bridgehead at risk when, on 25 November, seventeen light American tanks broke through and, with a rush, drove across Djedeida airfield (a mere 10 miles from Tunis) playing havoc among parked German bombers and fighters, to destroy more than 20 along with other installations before withdrawing with the loss of only one tank. The state of shock in Nehring was alarming.

At once he made arrangements to pull back to a close perimeter around Tunis giving up the airfield, and rang up Kesselring 'in a state of understandable excitement and drew the blackest conclusions . . .'. Kesselring was not to be stampeded. Already he had detected signs of reduced momentum in the Allied advance and had concluded that it would only develop cautiously particularly if harassed by an aggressive defensive. He believed, too, that the *Luftwaffe* was playing a vital role in delaying the enemy – as it was. So he sharply told Nehring to cancel the withdrawal and insisted upon a counter attack aimed at the endangered area next day – an attack which, by inflicting heavy losses on the Americans, brought the enemy advance to a halt.

This direct intervention into the battle by Kesselring occurred almost as an incidental at a moment when he was preparing, with meticulous care, for much more rigorous disputations elsewhere. Nevertheless, the discussion he was to have with Hitler was one he could now undertake in an easier state of mind, knowing that Nehring had recovered his composure and that the immediate crisis was over. At last Hitler was on the verge of finding time to diverge from his obsession with the Russian front (where stalemate at Stalingrad was on the eve of being broken by a great Russian counter-offensive) to give deeper thought to a longer term strategy for the Mediterranean. He was pleased to learn that Hitler concurred quite closely with his own opinion that Tunisia took higher priority over Tripolitania, having discounted Mussolini's insistence that Cyrenaica should be retained and Rommel's pleas, in person on 28 November, for total withdrawal from North Africa. To Mussolini Hitler offered a sweetner, the lure of a forthcoming Italian occupation of Tunisia in recompense for Tripolitania. For Rommel there was a sharp rebuke and a lecture on the propriety of standing firm in order to maintain the Army's morale and also the need to hold Tunisia for political reasons – a standard, patronising Hitlerian lecture reserved for generals who exhibited signs of challenging the Führer's authority. As a result of the conference, and overburdened as he was (or, to put it Kesselring's way, 'The Mediterranean did not interest Hitler'), Hitler sent Göring to Italy to sort out the difficulties with the Italians, Rommel and Kesselring. This was bad news for Rommel, for Göring was already well briefed by Kesselring and in no doubt as to the changes which ought to be made. In effect he was convinced that Rommel was a sick and depressed man whose imminent replacement by a leader who believed in victory was essential. Göring's frank remarks, as reported by Rommel in his diary, are almost identical to those used by Kesselring in the 'Commentaries'. Yet there is no possibility that Kesselring, when he wrote the 'Commentaries', could have had access to that diary.

Göring and Rommel travelled to Rome in the former's special train, and the tired and dispirited *generalfeldmarschall* has left us his angry reminiscence of the bombastic *Reichsmarschall* preening himself among his sycophants, the young *Luftwaffe* officers of his entourage. For Rommel things went from bad to worse after they arrived in Rome on 2 December and Kesselring joined them on the train for a preliminary conference before going to meet Mussolini. The C-in-C, as usual on these occasions, was calm and in complete possession of himself and his brief. Brilliant improvisor on the battlefield though Rommel might be, he was a tyro by comparison with Kesselring when it came to bureaucratic and diplomatic in-fighting. Already, at a previous meeting in Tripolitania with Cavallero and Bastico, Kesselring had eradicated one of Rommel's prime debating points by obtaining the Italians' agreement to a further withdrawal from Mersa Brega when Montgomery felt ready to advance again. By now Kesselring had formed an accurate impression of this British general's cautious habits, whose rate of advance ran conveniently at a pace which allowed the Axis enough time to prepare an adequate defence of Tunisia. That being so he was content, in Rome, to reject with finality another favourite proposal of Rommel's – that the retirement should proceed farther north than the existing pre-war French fortifications at Mareth and occupy, instead, the defile at Gabes. The Italians were in no position to concede due to the political deal Mussolini had struck already with Hitler. Rommel thus was isolated and made all the more indignant when Göring and Kesselring insisted on delaying the withdrawal to Mareth as long as possible in order to retain the Tripoli airfields to the last moment. In defeat Rommel could but content himself with the tart comment that 'it was all the same to us where the aircraft which bombed our ports came from'. But the day belonged to Göring and Kesselring.

Mussolini's meeting with Göring merely affirmed the political decisions he had agreed with Hitler. Göring's task was to create a sound basis for future collaboration and, above all, aggressive action. With Kesselring, Rommel, Cavallero, Gause and the others he presided over a conference on 2 December directing it, as the American Official History says, 'in a forceful manner without much regard for Italian susceptibilities'. Everything of moment was covered, including protection of ports against air raids, anti-submarine measures in the Sicilian narrows, the creation of an offensive capability by the Italian Fleet by providing it with much-needed fuel and, above all, the placing of the logistic organisation on a sounder footing under a special plenipotentiary in Rome. Acting with the force and vigour which had originally brought him to power, he toured Naples and Sicily before attending a final conference on 5 December prior to returning to Germany. Majestically he had driven piles into the logistic morass leaving Kesselring, after his departure, to make the arrangements stick. Of one thing Kesselring could feel reassured: he had gained a distinct advantage over Rommel, one which was improved when he obtained agreement from Hitler and OKW to his proposal that a higher staff than that of XC Corps was needed in Tunisia. Colonel General Jürgen von Arnim was to be sent from the Russian front, briefed by Hitler and given command of what was called Fifth Panzer Army with instructions placing him under the Italians who, he was given to understand, 'must not be allowed to sustain another defeat'. Actually he was directly under Kesselring. Von Arnim writes: 'Why I should be called . . . from the middle of an unconcluded battle is still not clear to me. I can only presume that Field-Marshal Kesselring, who knew me from previous years, perhaps recommended me.'

It would have been most unusual if Kesselring had not had a say in von Arnim's selection and quite at variance with the normal conventions. Plain common sense (apart from the protocol that a high commander has to be consulted about his immediate subordinates) rules that the men at the top should be bound by the congruity of the past, allied to a proven ability which makes them suitable candidates for the tasks of the future. Patronage was, and is, an essential aid to selection and promotion in all armed forces, if not in other walks of life. It was as inescapable among the Germans as it was on the Allied side where, for example, Dwight Eisenhower, having failed to take Tunis, needed support from his patron, the U.S. Chief of Staff, George Marshall, to withstand the disappointment and disfavour of President Franklin Roosevelt. Likewise, Harold Alexander, after contemplating the failure of his predecessors (Wavell and Auchinleck) to retain the confidence of Prime Minister Winston Churchill, was at pains to forge a direct link with the Prime Minister and use it to sustain his own position as well as that of his arrogant and tactless subordinate – that ascetic equivalent of Rommel – Bernard Montgomery. And Montgomery, too, often turned for help to his patron, the Chief of the Imperial General Staff, Alan Brooke.

So there is nothing extraordinary about Kesselring's dependence upon Göring, when necessary, or Rommel turning for aid to a sympathetic Hitler. It is interesting again to observe Rommel's application of political guile (so frequently overlooked by his keenest supporters) in employing Göbbels' agent, Ingemar Berndt, to act as his spokesman even when he could have pleaded a case in person. By deputing Berndt to submit to Göring the scheme to withdraw to Gabes as a preliminary to striking at Algiers, Rommel reveals an admission of his own inadequacy in coping with the higher echelons of command and also his dependence upon the indirect political support of Göbbels. Even if, as Rommel writes, Berndt had 'a very persuasive tongue', that is insufficient excuse for his withholding from putting a case in person to Göring, simply because 'sooner or later I would have been bound to speak out, which would have finished any chances I had'. There can be no clearer illustration of Rommel's dialectic inadequacy or indication of his inferiority as a high commander by comparison with Kesselring, who was invariably his own man and always master of every contingency. In the upper realms of command there is but little room for the simple *beau sabreur*. A commander-in-chief has to cope with the all-embracing, vicious problems and practices generated by modern total war and has to face the subversive elements which so easily stain the warrior's shield. Kesselring, for example, had to be cognisant (though he omits it from his 'Memoirs') of a scheme operated by Admiral Canaris and the Military *Abwehr* to involve Arabs of the Destourian movement in acts of sabotage against the Allies. The plan mainly failed but it created the atmosphere of civil war and the unavoidable products of partisan warfare in rear areas, with people shot out of hand and the growth of bestiality and hatred. This was the sort of warfare which Kesselring had come to loath in 1919, which he had been aware of again in its infancy in Russia in 1941 and which, in the future, was to be the bane of his life. But he had to cope with it: it could not be dismissed out of mind and discussion.

Immediately von Arnim arrived with his Chief of Staff designate, Heinz Zeigler, at Frascati on the 7 December 1943, he was swept up in a torrent of briefing from Kesselring. He watched the C-in-C, in his airman's role at his daily conference, deftly arranging priorities and directing attacks on enemy targets before taking a simple snack and going to Rome on the diplomatic round to meet Mussolini and then to Tunisia where he landed next morning – to find that nobody expected him. His arrival and the purpose of his mission, which, in the first instance, was to replace Nehring, came as a complete surprise to the commander of XC Corps. Since wavering at Djedeida, Nehring had conducted himself with staunch determination and had thrown the Allies back on Medjez el Bab. Kesselring denies that he got rid of him 'because his opinions differed from mine'. Nehring, not surprisingly, does not believe this, nor could he accept Kesselring's excuse that he had omitted to tell him because, 'He did not want to worry me'. Yet there is enough evidence to suggest that Kesselring was being perfectly sincere in this anxiety. Westphal, among many on Kesselring's staff, was conscious of his commander's deep, underlying kindness and his predilection for trying to cushion people from pain. When Nehring arrived back in Rome he declined Kesselring's invitation to a talk. So Kesselring went to see him. Nehring remains bitter to this day and it is easy to see why. But again, as Westphal shows, Kesselring was not the man to reject frank advice given in the Prussian manner. At the root of Nehring's dismissal lay Kesselring's disquiet at what he saw as his subordinate's fundamental disagreement with Axis policy. Nehring had declared that it was impossible to hold Tunisia because the Axis was neither strong at sea nor in the air. He had identified himself with Rommel by proposing that the Tunisian bridgehead should merely act as a base through which Rommel could be withdrawn to Sicily. Kesselring had retorted, 'You must put that in writing', adding, 'Abandonment of Africa is out of the question'. Thus, in so far as the confidence of C-in-C South was concerned, Nehring had talked himself out of a job in which he did not believe. He had to go.

If Kesselring could have put half as much effort into combating the Allies as he sometimes seems to have been compelled to put in trying to impose his will upon his own subordinates, Axis resistance in North Africa might have been prolonged longer than it was. Rommel, in possession of permission to withdraw under enemy pressure as it developed, was on his way backwards no sooner than Montgomery attacked at Mersa Brega on 11 December, and by the 21st he was at Sirte, lobbying hard for permission to recommence the retreat as quickly as possible. Von Arnim, in the meantime, embarked upon a strenuous attempt, in the week preceding Christmas, to drive the British out of Medjez el Bab – a costly failure because he had yet to understand mountain warfare. But he, at least for the time being, was carrying out his C-in-C's intentions (with over-ambitious objectives demanded, as von Seeckt used to prescribe) whereas Rommel, thoroughly mistrustful of Kesselring, was indulging in backstairs sabotage while conducting a verbal guerrilla warfare of recrimination against the *Luftwaffe* – to which the airmen retaliated with asperity. Yet Kesselring, by degrees, was gaining the upper hand. Westphal had been sent to command a division in *Afrika Korps* on the 7th and to Germany on sick leave on the 29th, depriving Rommel of his most capable staff officer and loyal ally. The continued retreat by his army progressively diminished Hitler's support. Another mission to Germany by the persuasive Berndt in January revealed this only too clearly when he received a cold shoulder. Rommel told his wife that 'Kesselring had supplanted him in the Führer's favour', but it seems to have been overlooked by Rommel that Berndt was only a lieutenant and Kesselring a field-marshal! With every step nearer Tunisia that Rommel took, the closer came the moment when he would come under tighter control. On 22 January Tripoli was evacuated and by the 28th his men had retired into the Mareth line, shepherded by only the lightest of British forces. Italy's African Empire was finished, Marshal Bastico was on his way home upon the dissolution of his command and the Axis command structure in North Africa was on the eve of radical change. But while Rommel and Bastico were entering the shadows, von Arnim, encouraged by Kesselring, was enjoying a purple patch. Striking without warning on 18 January at the ill-equipped French corps holding the Eastern Dorsal on the southern flank of the bridgehead, he had virtually annihilated the French, stolen the initiative from the Allies (whose logistic position was weak), and by the 25th stood poised and confident with any of a number of alternative courses of offensive action open to him. Logistically deprived though he might be and unwilling as he was to base future offensive operations on the possibility of capturing enemy supplies, he temporarily held the whip-hand.

Nevertheless lack of supply was the rock upon which everything broke and the Axis were no closer to solving their difficulties than ever they had been. An attempt by Göring to establish a 'plenipotentiary for the Mediterranean' was stoutly resisted by Grand Admiral Raeder and Vice-Admiral Weichold who declined to surrender their authority over the sea lanes because they believed it would lead to a complete collapse of supply. Relations between Kesselring and Weichold became so strained that the latter offered his resignation. A grim guerrilla warfare went on between the two men with Kesselring demanding to be given full responsibility along with the tactical control of the motor torpedo boats – a proposal that Weichold rejected with righteous anger. While Kesselring expressed his dissatisfaction with the conduct of operations by the German admirals and threatened to put them all under arrest, Weichold, supported by Raeder (who himself resigned on 30 January after a row with Hitler) objected to Kesselring's interference.

The chill wind from Hitler and the radical alterations to command structure and organisation which blew through every higher German headquarters in Italy and Tunisia throughout January, sprang from a

Führer conference at Rastenberg in East Prussia, attended by Kesselring, between 18 and 22 December and, to a large extent, was generated and conditioned by events at Stalingrad. For on 19 November the Russians had launched an offensive which, on the 23rd, had encompassed the total isolation of the German Sixth Army from its base of supply and begun the long siege which was to drag on into February. Troops which previously were intended for Tunisia had now to go to Russia where a huge disaster was impending. Transport aircraft which might have doubled supplies to North Africa had now to maintain the remaining link with the Stalingrad garrison.

Reverting to his proposition of the previous year, Hitler attempted again to persuade the Italians to allow Kesselring the power of a real Commander-in-Chief over the Italian as well as the German forces. Inevitably Mussolini vetoed it and insisted that the channel of command should continue to pass through *Comando Supremo*. But it was at this conference that a complete withdrawal from Tripolitania was agreed, along with the removal of Bastico, though with the proviso that command of the German-Italian Panzer Army (or First Italian Army as Rommel's force would eventually be called) should be given to an Italian. Hitler's way to obtain *de facto* control without upsetting the Italians was through a formula originally devised by Kesselring; that of close co-operation and discussion between Axis partners – so long as the German partner was more equal than the Italian one. Dominance Kesselring achieved by obtaining Italian agreement to the insertion of a German operations section within *Comando Supremo* in place of the existing liaison officer and then by staffing it with so many men that the original Italian establishment was outnumbered. The pill was sugared by an assurance that the Germans would confine themselves to recommendations and requests only – but that was far from Kesselring's real intention, as soon was to be shown. As an additional attraction, Kesselring supported an Italian suggestion that Rommel should give up command of First Italian Army to make room for an Italian, Marshal Giovanni Messe, when that formation backed into Tunisia – a concession that cost him nothing. Rommel was told on the 26 January 1943 and took his dismissal quite well by admitting to the effects of strain, headaches and sleeplessness while recording his relief at being saved from the role of scapegoat 'for a pack of incompetents'. He was told to hand over as soon as his army had occupied the Mareth position; von Arnim's Fifth Panzer Army, meanwhile, was immediately brought under *Comando Supremo* in accordance with the Rastenberg decisions.

Kesselring could look back on the Rastenberg conference with a feeling of positive achievement even if the results of his endeavours appeared complicated in the extreme. He had managed to rid himself of the unwieldy commitment as commander of German forces in the Balkans, had won approval for his own headquarters to shed its *Luftwaffe* designation and become, instead, a genuine joint services command. He had also reached agreement on the creation of an Army Group Africa headquarters to co-ordinate the activities of First Italian and Fifth Panzer Armies. It was a fine piece of constructive empire building even if it fell short of his primary intention to make Army Group Africa report direct to him, thus by-passing *Comando Supremo*: that was a move Hitler would not yet countenance. In effect, he was to represent Hitler with the Italians, impose the German will over the Italian armed forces command, act as superior officer of all German forces in the Central Mediterranean, and arrange their supply. It was a mammoth, possibly over-centralised, task which would, sometimes at the least convenient moment, demand his presence in more than one place at once. A great deal would depend on his powers of persuasion and the goodwill of both nationalities along with the excellence of his key officers. Temporarily he placed von Arnim in command of Army Group Africa, in addition to his other duties, but the hunt was on for somebody else with greater prestige. He also needed a strong chief of operations at *Comando Supremo* whom he could trust to suppress the dissidence between nationalities and branches of the service, without detriment to German (and his own) interests.

Siegfried Westphal was in hospital in Germany when he was informed that both Kesselring and Rommel wanted him back in Italy immediately to take over what would be 'a quiet job' with C-in-C South in charge of a new section. The Chief of OKW, Field-Marshal Keitel, asked him to become 'responsible adviser' on army matters to Kesselring with terms of reference which Westphal himself drafted. But on his arrival at Rome he detected a distinct coolness when he was sent to an hotel and forbidden to report to Frascati. By then Westphal knew his Field-Marshal and at once went to see him, brushing aside the aides who tried to stand in his way. Kesselring complained that 'nobody told *him* how to employ his officers' and, anyway, who had drafted the order making Westphal the *responsible* adviser? He was distinctly taken aback when Westphal admitted that it was he. This was the turning point in their relationship. Kesselring said that the word 'responsible' had been deleted by Keitel, but now it was up to the pair of them to collaborate fruitfully. And so it was to be. For the next fifteen months they were to form a formidable team, indulging in frank exchanges of view allied to staunch loyalty that bound them to a

collaboration and eventual friendship. Nearly every day they would visit
Mussolini together to impress German policy upon shrinking allies as well
as upon German subordinates and the German hierarchy alike. For the
most part the Italians could be managed; they depended too much upon
German help to withstand for long and Kesselring was at his best in
suppressing Mussolini's excesses. Westphal remembers Kesselring
politely turning down proposals by Mussolini to use hospital ships to
transport fuel and for the employment of poison gas in the way the Italians
had done in Ethiopia in 1935. The Germans, he said, could not be a party
to infringement of the Geneva Convention. Westphal also recalls an
attempt on his own part to convince General Warlimont of OKW of the
need to withdraw some of the best specialists from North Africa before
they were lost in what everybody visualised as the final debâcle on that
continent when Axis forces could prevail no longer. Kesselring could not
lend support to this since it would conflict with the views of Hitler. Both
he and Warlimont, with intimate knowledge of their megalomaniac
Supreme Commander, knew when to be cautious in their own interests.
Kesselring's political antenna, well tuned by the years at the highest
ministerial level, sensed precisely when to signal the changes and when it
was diplomatic to switch off and say 'that one cannot expect of the
Führer'. It was a knack he developed into an art.

The settlement of the appointment of the Army Group Africa
commander proceeded along devious lines, stage by stage, though, from
the beginning, as Kesselring repeats in the 'Commentaries':

> Rommel was the first to come under consideration . . . He had also
> been proposed by me for I believed that this promotion would increase
> his ambition and his efficiency . . . Furthermore I believed that
> Rommel's acknowledged personality would be able to remove possible
> frictions with Messe sooner than anything else. It was not intended to
> control Messe by this measure. German interests were to be safe-
> guarded by the German Chief of Staff attached to Messe. General Bayer-
> lein lived up to expectations . . . [a slight understatement since it was
> weeks before Rommel allowed Messe to issue an order] After the nerve-
> racking retreat an opportunity was to be given Rommel to conclude
> the damaging period of retreats by a successful series of offensives.

Not that Rommel saw it quite like that when his term of command was
further extended on 18 February in order to conduct certain offensives,
but it did set the stage for Kesselring's own advancement as a field
commander.

One supreme accomplishment of generalship that Kesselring displayed in North Africa was a prescient forecasting of his opponents' future moves. He had shown it all along but never so positively as when Nehring had hesitated before Tunis. In mid-January he had taken their measure again by accurately perceiving that General Eisenhower would attempt to prevent the juncture of Rommel's army in Tripolitania with von Arnim's army in Tunisia. This, indeed, was Eisenhower's pet project, a drive to the coast out of central Tunisia aimed at Sfax. So, as a precaution, Kesselring sent the 21st Panzer Division to Sfax early in January in position to counter an Allied move on Gafsa should that take place. Gradually a policy of Axis aggression was formulated. In the process Kesselring imposed his will upon friend and foe alike, through direct orders in the field that paid but cursory respect to the consultative agreements worked out with *Comando Supremo*, and by stealing the initiative from Eisenhower. As he put it in the 'Commentaries,'

OB Süd [C-in-C South] as the senior German officer, was the commander of the army group. At the same time, I was also in a superior position in my capacity as authorised representative of the *Comando Supremo*. There were no open frictions. My directives on the spot were irrevocable orders. My operations section (Army) under *Oberst* Westphal, as the so-called Africa Staff, worked out the orders at Frascati which, for good reasons, were issued under the heading of the *Comando Supremo*. My Chief of Staff *OB Süd*, General Deichmann, states that he experienced certain resistance which must, however, have been unimportant and perhaps only exceeded the usual amount of friction between superiors and subordinates due to the fact that Deichmann was a general staff officer of the *Luftwaffe*. Westphal did not report any particular friction. It would have been improbable anyway as he was *persona grata* with Rommel.

Put that way it looks quite simple, but now there was von Arnim to deal with (who had ideas of his own) and the new Italian Chief of *Comando Supremo*, Vittorio Ambrosio, who replaced Cavallero on 2 February. With Ambrosio Kesselring never achieved the same accord as he had with Cavallero, who was sacked for being servile to the Germans. Ambrosio was not only anti-German but forced to be obtuse and devious in order to satisfy his role as an instrument of defiance of the Germans. A good soldier, popular in his own army, and a patriot too, he opted to stay in Italy to preside over the daily affairs of *Comando Supremo* rather than accompany Kesselring to the battle front at moments of decision. His aim was to seek a way of arranging Italy's salvation. From the start suspicion and rancour, due to the oppressive German presence and Ambrosio's determination to resist it, brooded over all their proceedings. Ambrosio's protests at the large German contingent in *Comando Supremo*, his rejection of the kind of collaboration pact operated by Cavallero and his suggestion that Kesselring should become Army Group commander in Tunisia so as to remove him from Rome, along with a redeployment of troops from the Balkans in order to strengthen the Italian garrisons, were acts which Kesselring regarded as 'treachery' and led him to a symbolic offer of resignation to Mussolini – that was predictably refused. These exchanges were the first serious fissures in the Axis hegemony and prompted Hitler's harbouring of deep suspicions about Italian fidelity.

The opportunity to strike the Allies, while they were temporarily weakened by logistical difficulties, led to the first clash of interests and ambitions between Rommel and von Arnim. Each army commander devised plans that wrote the leading role for himself and gave the other a subsidiary part. Early in February Rommel proposed once more that the bulk of resources should be given to him for a drive against Gafsa which could be directed northwards against the enemy's rear while von Arnim fixed their attention with holding attacks in the mountains. Von Arnim, with a far keener appreciation of the parlous Axis logistic situation, but far less experience of mountain warfare than Rommel, made a counter-proposal for strictly limited attacks by his army at the northern end of the Eastern Dorsal. Kesselring, telling von Arnim to think of the battle and not worry about supplies, rejected both schemes and opted for an integration of them both; not, be it noted, a compromise. He produced the master plan which was to lead to the infamous American debâcle at Kasserine – parallel thrusts by von Arnim with two panzer divisions through the Faid and Maizila Passes directed on Sidi Bou Zid while Rommel, with a so-called *Afrika Korps* battle group, made for Gafsa. The allocation of forces to the two armies took a week's negotiation, and the plan was progressively varied by the gradual acquisition of additional intelligence of the enemy. Kesselring's main role was that of referee, almost, in fact, that of Army Group commander since the Italians steadfastly refused to have Rommel in that role. This was potentially dangerous since Kesselring, due to his other commitments, could not be on the spot all the time. Privately he confided to Rommel that, if the situation developed the way they both hoped, the propitious moment would arrive when everybody would be ready to grant Rommel complete responsibility – but that was a distinction which, like a knight's spurs, had to be won on the battlefield.

The manner in which von Arnim's thrust shattered the 1st U.S. Armored Division at Sidi Bou Zid is notorious and takes precedence in drama and repercussions over Rommel's swift advance on Gafsa. In aggregate, these tactical victories had, by 15 February 1943, engineered the political situation Kesselring and Rommel desired. They could now contemplate the enveloping drive to the north coast as originally postulated by Rommel. Already it was intended that the 21st Panzer Division and the Italian *Centauro* Armoured division should be transferred to Rommel's command from von Arnim's, while 10th Panzer Division exploited westward towards Kasserine. But on the 16th von Arnim threw a spanner in the works by declining to release 21st Panzer Division, saying it was required to clear up the situation around Sbeitla. He then deflected it northwards to destroy the enemy at Fondouk in pursuit of his original aim of attacking the Dorsals, regardless of Kesselring's wishes. Thus Rommel found himself at Gafsa, with a beaten enemy in full retreat before him but only the *Afrika Korps* battle group, reinforced by the low-grade *Centauro* Division, to carry out Kesselring's sabotaged grand design. Unfortunately for Rommel and himself, Kesselring was with Hitler at Rastenberg when the critical moment arrived on the 17th, a day on which Axis units dallied or counter-marched when a superb opportunity was presented by Allied confusion.

Failing to receive co-operation from von Arnim, Rommel signalled Kesselring on the afternoon of the 18th requesting that both 10th and 21st Panzer Divisions should be assigned to him. Kesselring concurred but it was too late to take full advantage of the previous and now lost opportunity. Several hours were required to recall the panzer divisions which von Arnim was in no hurry to relinquish, and even then he was to withhold certain elements from within them in order to participate in his holding attacks further north. Furthermore the orders which Rommel finally received from *Comando Supremo* were ambiguous – an inevitable (and quite common) consequence of the complex staff and communication system in use – and a contradiction in terms of Kesselring's belief in his own absoluteness of command. Kesselring wished Rommel to advance via Tebessa (as did Rommel) plunging far deeper in the enemy rear, though at greater logistic risk, than von Arnim's chosen objective of Le Kef. *Comando Supremo*'s order mentioned both objectives with emphasis on Le Kef and so this gave Rommel a free hand while enabling von Arnim to believe that Kesselring supported him. Each proceeded on the false premises of wishful thinking.

Kesselring, sensing trouble when he got back to Rome, flew to HQ Fifth Panzer Army on the 19th to find that fatal damage was done. Von Arnim had blocked any possibility of throwing a concentrated stroke by all three armoured divisions against Tebessa via Kasserine. He had held back 21st and 10th Panzer Divisions in the hope that an alternative plan of his own would be accepted and allow them to advance on Le Kef via Sbiba and Pichon. This Rommel, in the realisation that any further delay would be fatal in the face of Allied counter-measures, had perforce condoned by abandoning hope of the use of 10th Panzer and by permitting the 21st to attack Sbiba, doing the best he could by sending only the *Afrika Korps* battle group northward towards Thala and the *Centauro* Division in the direction of Tebessa as a flank guard. It was now simply a matter of watching diluted and divergent thrusts reaching like fingers towards the blocking positions established by the enemy at Pichon, Sbiba and Thala which could be broken only by a clenched fist of concentrated divisions. Relatively weak Allied forces prevailed with difficulty against each of the four Axis probes. Had one or other of those probes contained the maximum weight of Axis armour the outcome might have been very different, if not conclusive.

At this dolorous moment there was a closer affinity between Rommel and Kesselring than at any other time in their professional association. On the 20th they met again, this time in the entrance to the Kasserine Pass where American troops maintained but a tenuous hold. Significantly, Rommel did not complain about von Arnim, nor was Kesselring uneasy, but they agreed that a breakout to the north must take place that day. Kesselring departed to see von Arnim once more; to upbraid him for withholding parts of 10th Panzer Division from Rommel (including the powerful Tiger tanks); to insist that he despatch it now and conform to the broad strategic plan, and to say that he would recommend to *Comando Supremo* that Rommel should assume command of those elements of von Arnim's army, including 10th Panzer, which were allocated to the drive at Kasserine. That day the Germans, still with attenuated forces, broke through at Kasserine, scattering the Americans in panic, and pushed a hard-fighting Allied rearguard back upon Thala, 25 miles to the north. But in the approaches to Thala British and American forces made their stand on the 21st and threw back the initial German assault while, to the west, the Italians approaching Tebessa were stopped by the remnants of the 1st U.S. Armored Division.

Only part of 10th Panzer Division was yet in reach of Thala, 21st Panzer Division had stalled at Sbiba and supplies were running low once more.

When Kesselring again flew over to meet Rommel on the afternoon of the 22nd, 'with vague apprehensions', it was to discover that Rommel had already passed to the defensive since he saw no possibility of breaking through with the forces at his disposal. After an hour's discussion, frequently interrupted by telephone calls, Kesselring drew the conclusion that Rommel was depressed and had lost confidence in the operation. Disappointed, he concurred and together the two Field-Marshals turned to consider their next spoiling attack – as to all intents and purposes these offensives were, both in actuality and intent. They decided upon an assault by all three panzer divisions on the British Eighth Army at Medenine where it lay making preparations for the first stage of its advance into Tunisia through the Mareth Line. This may not have been a sharp turning point in the North African campaign (for that was already lost) but it was a crossroads in Kesselring's career. In the aftermath of Kasserine, as the Americans began to demonstrate their sense of pride by a redoubled determination to win battles and expunge the stigma of defeat, he was to find himself engaged against an enemy who rarely again offered soft options. From now on his battles were to be hard, disenchanting and against desperate odds.

The last German offensives, the widespread, badly generalled, abortive assaults by von Arnim with tanks in the mountainous terrain of the north and the exemplary repulse of Rommel at Medenine on 6 March served notice of an end in North Africa that was drawing rapidly in sight. It mattered not that *Comando Supremo* should at last agree on 23 February for Rommel to become Army Group Commander, even though he had wished to decline the job on the grounds of his ill-health, or that his apathetic conduct of the attack at Medenine contributed to defeat there. Nor did it matter too much, except from a prestige point of view, when Rommel secretly left Africa for the last time after Medenine, saying to von Arnim, his successor in command of the Army Group, 'I don't know what I will achieve but I will do everything possible. If our suggestions are again turned down and things come to an end here I will return.' Von Arnim inherited an impossible mission, a defensive battle without hope to which Rommel would not return.

Hope was about the only luxury remaining to the Axis and nobody attempted to inject it more than Kesselring. He had failed to bolster Rommel's morale. From now on he commuted regularly between Tunisia, Rome and Berlin; drumming up promises of support from Hitler and OKW which were rarely honoured; steadying the Italians in their shaky resolve; urging supplies to the front across the increasingly dangerous strip of water which a force of 500 German aircraft, aided by the Italians, could barely make safe for itself; encouraging the commanders in the field with acts of undiluted optimism in which he did not entirely believe but which was part of the performance which any leader must constantly play if he is to do his duty by maintaining the aims thrust upon him. And if sometimes he over-acted and offended the audience by demanding sacrifices which were ridiculous, that can best be defended as a measure of his dedicated sense of mission. At that moment there was no call to reason why since, as yet, the war was not lost. Kesselring may have compromised over details but only very rarely in the matter of principle.

The *Luftwaffe* was fading not only in North Africa but in its abortive and terribly costly effort to supply the trapped garrison at Stalingrad by air and in the damaging battles over Western Europe that were then beginning to over-tax its strength. Gradually those elements that were essential to the conduct of attacks on Allied sea supply lines in the Mediterranean had to be sacrificed. Among the first to go were the torpedo bomber units because the training schools in this particular technique had to be closed from lack of resources. With fewer and fewer air units at his disposal, and Malta so well revictualled since mid-November that it had reassumed its full offensive capability, Kesselring, as C-in-C, had no other option than to concentrate on command and control of surface forces as the only effective weapons left at his disposal. Since the Italian Navy was loath (for excellent nationalist reasons) to commit its major units to battle, the brunt of action fell on the Army. Kesselring's return to soldiering therefore had nothing to do with Winterbotham's aspersions of personal opportunism. In any case, it was several weeks before the Allies found out that Rommel had departed and that it was Kesselring and von Arnim who opposed them.

A clear exposition of Kesselring's strategy and tactics in the aftermath of Medenine can be found in the 'Commentaries' where he wrote:

Logically . . . the inevitable conclusion could not be avoided that the fighting for Tunisia was now only of an episodical character. Did Rommel's desire, therefore, to withdraw to the Enfidaville position [the mountain barrier barring the way into Tunis from the south along the coast road] naturally follow? Such a question deserves a negative answer, in my opinion, because to carry out this decision would have meant an immediate or at least a quick end to the overall operations, whereas, on the other hand, there was at least a hope of delaying the beginning of operations against the European southern front until 1944 by a stubborn fight for Tunisia.

So, in the strategic sphere, Kesselring was entirely in favour of defence in depth to gain time for the winning of whatever advantages might be found elsewhere. It was the same with his tactical views.

'A single position cannot be permanently held against the modern means of attack of ground and air forces', he wrote. 'The most favourable prospects for defence will be found in a defence zone which is sub-divided into several positions. The natural configuration of the terrain in Southern Tunisia offered such a defence zone, the foremost position of which was the Mareth and the hindmost the Akarit. It would have been operationally incorrect to have withdrawn immediately to the latter . . .' – as, of course, Rommel had wished to do when he opted for the Gabes line after he rejected the one at Mareth for being too vulnerable to outflanking. In the next few weeks, events were to prove Kesselring largely right in his judgement though perhaps suspect in his airman's desire to hold on to the airfields in the south.

Already Kesselring had become opposed by the man with whom, for the next two years, he was to fight a duel – General Sir Harold Alexander, who had been appointed commander of 18th Army Group on 19 February controlling the contingents of British, American and French troops whose task it was to clear Tunisia of the Axis by May in readiness to invade Sicily in July. Alexander had co-ordinated the Allied defence against Kesselring's offensive at Kasserine and now was beginning to orchestrate the series of blows that were to be rained on the Axis from one end of the front to the other. While von Arnim would be Alexander's opponent at the front, always it was Kesselring with whom he was really in contest and usually it was Kesselring, even though he benefited from less voluminous and trustworthy intelligence than his opponent, who guessed well what Alexander would do and who stayed one jump ahead in the tactical battle.

As Kesselring feared the most any Allied attack which might split the southern army from that in the north by a drive into 'the deep flank', as he called the direct threat to Tunis, he appreciated that thrusts from the south, though threatening, would not endanger the existence of his two armies. It is reasonable, in the circumstances, to accept Kesselring's defence of his strategy in relation to the main events of the weeks to come. When Montgomery attacked frontally at the Mareth Line, close by the coast on 22 March, he only attempted what Kesselring and von Arnim expected of him, and he was held. And when Montgomery reinforced the subsidiary turning movement to circle the flank of the Mareth position (as

Rommel had known could be done) it was a relatively simple matter for the Germans to establish a lay-back blocking position at El Hamma on the 26th in time to extricate most of their men from the Mareth Line, thus proving Rommel's fears groundless. Likewise the successful defence of Maknassy by Colonel Lang against the main American attack led by George Patton, from 23 March to 7 April, was a feat of arms in good defensive terrain which Kesselring had assessed as entirely feasible. The same could not be said, however, of the poor defence of the Akarit Line (where the Italians fought badly) against the British on 5 April, though even in this instance it could be claimed that the position had imposed sufficient delay to allow fresh defences in rear to be fortified. Nor was Kesselring so very far wrong when he made the assumption that Eighth Army would not, in the meantime, have 'learnt the secrets of a reckless pursuit operation'. The Axis forces, in the main, were able to retire into the mountain stronghold of northern Tunisia without suffering too heavy a loss. These were calculations upon which he could pride himself as a soldier, engaged upon that most difficult of all military operations, the withdrawal under pressure from a strong enemy.

It is during the period of retraction that we see Kesselring develop mightily as a truly great leader in time of adversity. Flashes of genius and miscalculation illuminate the clouds of defeat. For a start he managed to avoid implementing Hitler's insistent orders to carry out still more wasteful spoiling attacks by invoking the wording of an instruction which hinged upon reinforcement of strength which all knew to be impossible. He also managed to have cancelled a Hitler order, prompted prematurely by Rommel, to thin out the Mareth Line. At the same time he promoted a shoal of investigations into ways of increasing supplies by orthodox and unorthodox methods, by the use of ships large and small gathered from a variey of untapped sources, and the employment of Siebel ferries. Such were his persuasive powers with Hitler and Göring that he obtained useful reinforcements of transport aircraft at a time of impoverishment in the aftermath of Stalingrad. He never gave up even as these resources were remorselessly smashed by the vastly superior enemy sea and air forces. The British had done no better in reverse in similar circumstances at Dunkirk and had not the need then to prolong their effort for weeks on end. He wanted 120,000 tons to be brought into Tunisia each month (having told Hitler in January that 60,000 was feasible) and he was lucky to receive 40,000 that month and declining amounts thereafter. That which he achieved with his masters was the result of sheer ability and patience, the reward of endless pains to equip himself with all the arguments – technical, political and strategic – and to present them with persevering calm to a Supreme Commander who was renowned for his brusque dismissal of disagreeable arguments by embattled soldiers. If this was made possible because Kesselring wore a *Luftwaffe* uniform, then the dog-in-the-manger soldiers who tended to despise him would have done well to be thankful for small mercies. Army generals were rarely so successful in their submissions to Hitler.

In battle his skill in arriving at the right moment to give crucial orders was as awe-inspiring in its intuition as that of a Rommel or a Guderian. He stood alongside General Bayerlein when he threw the British back at Mareth, though not always was his personal intervention timely or wise. When von Arnim told Messe to begin the withdrawal from the Mareth position on 24 March, because the British seemed to have seized a dangerously threatening foothold on the German side of the anti-tank ditch, it was Kesselring who came to Messe and encouraged the Italian to execute a counter-attack which he erroneously deemed feasible but which would have been fatal. Not only the absurdity of the order but also the atmosphere this interference by Kesselring created worried von Arnim who, nevertheless, was suffering from the consequences of mistrust over his own behaviour at Kasserine. In demanding that Kesselring should take back his suggestion to Messe, von Arnim asked him to 'refrain from meddling with the command of divisions over the head of army and army group . . . He was undermining confidence in the responsible leadership . . . Only one man could lead the army group. I was not angry about it. If he wanted to do it he ought to come to Africa and I would be only too pleased to step aside! He understood that and reversed his instruction to Messe.'

Less and less, of course, could Kesselring become involved with the detailed direction of operations in Tunisia as the Axis armies took their final stand in the mountains at the end of the headlong retreat from the south. More and more he had to give attention to the forthcoming battles in Europe while von Arnim played out the final drama in Africa. Overriding practically everything else in his mind was the imperative need to keep Italy in the war. Germans who denied this, therefore, as often as not fell into the category of those, like Jodl of OKW, who felt Kesselring was far too pro-Italian. Italians were becoming anathema to OKW where the aims were often confused. In discussions with Hitler on 8 April, Mussolini and Ciano had pleaded for an end to the Russian war so that Germany could turn all her attention to dealing with the Mediterranean situation. It was a self-centred request of sheer desperation without the slightest chance of being granted. Not only was Hitler solely intent on fighting the Russians, and therefore saw the holding of Tunisia as the best way to prevent an invasion of Sicily and Italy (and therefore as a prop to his Russian policy), but the Russians, in the aftermath of Stalingrad, with their victorious armies chasing the Germans from the Caucasus and back to the River Don, were not in the least likely to welcome an armistice. Conquest of the fascist beasts was their aimno Mussolini was reduced to pleading with Kesselring to redouble the attempts to supply the armies in Tunisia, and Kesselring, whose air force was being remorselessly eliminated on the African airfields, besides heavily damaged on the aerodromes of Sardinia and Sicily, could but wearily give assent and himself press von Arnim harder while realising, as an Allied offensive mounted in fury at every corner of the bridgehead, that it would only be a matter of days before all was over. On the 18 and 26 April no less than fifty Ju 52s and twenty-seven of the gigantic Me 323 transport aircraft were shot down. Nobody could say that the *Luftwaffe* was not making sacrifices.

Nor, for that matter, could it be said that the German admirals dragged their feet any longer, even when they were practically powerless to squeeze many more sacrifices out of the Italians. Admiral Karl Dönitz had taken over from Raeder at the end of January and he, faithful to Hitler, was determined to spare nothing in trying to upply Tunisia. In February he had sent Rear-Admiral Friedrich Ruge to Italy to examine the supply situation and then had put him in charge of the German supply traffic. Ruge did his best but the task was hopeless. The Italians refused to sail any more destroyers or cruisers in such dangerous waters and the smaller surface craft could but bring in a trickle of supplies. It was Kesselring who turned down a last, desperate suggestion that U-boats be employed to bring in a trickle of petrol on the grounds that for such a small amount of fuel it was not worth risking valuable boats. Ruge, who met Kesselring every two or three days, formed a more favourable impression of the C-in-C than had Weichold and Raeder. He has told me that, although Kesselring did not know too much of naval matters, 'I don't remember any particular difficulties in getting him to agree to the measures I thought necessary', and goes on in a personal assessment of Kesselring: 'He was dedicated to keep away from everything that looked like politics. For him, Hitler had come into his position legally, and he, Kesselring, therefore had to execute his orders . . . I liked him because he was a decent man . . . I respected him as C-in-C, but I was not overawed by him. In my opinion men like Raeder and Rommel were superior to him.'

On the 17 April Kesselring made a last visit to Tunisia – a fairly uneventful one from the flying point of view, not a bit like the occasion when he had been shot at (and missed) by his own anti-aircraft guns at Tunis as he was coming in to land, an event which earned a stern rebuke for the gunners for having missed so easy a target! Grimly, with von Arnim, he contemplated the multi-pronged Allied threat, the withdrawals which had already been made and the rapid deterioration of equipment and supply. Exhortation was the only palliative left. Von Arnim would soon ask him to stay away realising only too well that Kesselring must concentrate on the battles to come, not the one that was lost. All Kesselring could do was concentrate his persuasion on the Italians, pointing out to Ambrosio, on 26 April, that a lull in the Allied attacks at that moment did not mean the attacks had been defeated. Worse was in store, as he knew, and could not be denied since the mobile reserves were exhausted. He could only pass the ball to the Italian court by suggesting ways they might better employ their shipping to carry across reinforcements and supplies – knowing full well that this was quite unlikely to be met and guessing that the Italians valued their fleet for its bargaining power should they have need to talk terms of surrender with the Allies.

Every man, every aeroplane, every tank and every gun was needed to defend the homeland now that the battles of expansion had been reversed into a protracted rearguard action. Belatedly Kesselring now joined those who tried, against Hitler's veto, to withdraw key men and specialists from North Africa. Only a few were saved, however, Westphal's initial and timely plan having been rejected. When the end came, it was so swift that many excellent men had to be abandoned, von Arnim among them, on 12 May. An immense sadness enveloped Kesselring as the curtain came down on the North African tragedy, and with it a resolve to avoid similar mistakes in the future. Reflecting upon the lost campaign to Karl-Albert Mügge and, in particular, on the orders he had been forced to give against his better judgement by Hitler, he said 'Never again will I put my name to such orders.' Time would show if he could abide by this resolve but clearly he was better equipped to carry it through than many of his contemporaries. Evaluating Kesselring's performance at moments of stress, Mügge writes: 'He would explain his orders clearly without the chance of misunderstanding, and never dealt lightly with matters. He was never abrupt, as were others, always in control of himself, and addressed people as "Herr" – which was most unusual in the German Army. Never did he mind interruptions: even after strenuous duties he would listen patiently to reports.'

In the days to come these virtues would be tested to the limit.

8

Sicily and the
Road to Cassibile

There have been a number of great commanders in history who, in the aftermath of suffering a serious defeat, have managed to retain their appointment despite the recrimination of critics and rivals. It is to be hoped the survivors usually owed their good fortune to talent and an inner will such as made them stand morally above their contemporaries, although there are several recorded examples of survival being prolonged due to irreplacability, nepotism or even some quirk of fate. It is a measure of Kesselring's stature as well as his standing with Hitler and the OKW hierarchy (despite their underlying doubts) that he stayed in office, overriding the denigration heaped upon him after the surrender in Tunisia. There seems to have been no serious attempt to replace him at once, although Westphal informs us that, in April, Göring rang up Kesselring boastfully to declare 'only cowards are running the Mediterranean war and that if Hitler were to give him command for just one day, he, Göring, would give effective orders'. It was Göring who heartily congratulated Kesselring at that time for his courage in making 100 operational flights over the Mediterranean. And it was Göring, Hitler's heir apparent, who, after the surrender, slandered Kesselring, up to then his model of 'the modern thinking general', as the *Luftwaffe*'s 'State Enemy No 1'. Yet Hitler sent a telegram to Kesselring on 12 May congratulating him on his fortunate escape from being forced down in air combat the previous day, an incident which is just one of the five he admitted to, but of which there is no other record.

At this time, of course, Kesselring had got into the habit of facing Hitler in conference and asking, with tantalising irony, 'When will the *Luftwaffe* arrive?' Göring was indeed in trouble and no doubt had tried to make Kesselring into a scapegoat. A most damaging spy ring (the celebrated *Rote Kapelle*) had been uncovered and found to have a cell flourishing in the Air Ministry. In addition there were the heavy air raids, which regularly penetrated Germany's inner defences, and Göring's recent failure to honour his pledge to supply Stalingrad by air, a failure that had been repeated in Tunisia. Göring was on the way down: Erhard Milch stood as high as ever in Hitler's favour. Moreover Milch, whose energies were now almost entirely concentrated on an attempt to re-establish the *Luftwaffe*'s power by bringing new types of aircraft into service besides raising production, was bent on persuading Hitler that a new C-in-C of the *Luftwaffe* was needed and that Germany must conserve her strength by desisting from major offensives in 1943. In neither case did he succeed since Hitler had overshot the point of reason, and, as an example of the dreams he conjured up in his imagination, told Mussolini in April that the sheer cost in lives to the Russians in seeking to reconquer their lost territory would bleed them to death.

Though Milch maintained his hostility towards Kesselring (as well as for Jeschonnek for whom, as *Luftwaffe* Chief of Staff, the load was becoming intolerable) there is every reason to believe that Kesselring had dismissed their rivalry as an irrelevance of the past. After the war he was to pay a generous tribute to Milch which Milch would reciprocate. In May 1943 Kesselring was far too preoccupied with the war, recementing the alliance upon which the defence of Germany's southern flank depended in an environment of international intrigue and deceit such as put his previous departmental affray with Milch in the shade. The decline of the *Luftwaffe* as a military factor also devalued its political standing. No longer was Göring's air force first among equals of the favoured Nazi-orientated organisations. Heinrich Himmler's *Schutz Staffeln*, the dreaded SS, had overtaken it in influence and meaning because it represented a combined political and military presence which infiltrated almost every organ of state and spread its tentacles throughout the occupied countries. Fortunately for Kesselring and Rommel, the Italian political presence in North Africa had shielded them in the past from surveillance by the SS and Gestapo, just as the nature of that under-populated country spared them the horrors of fighting in urban districts. The desert fighting had been comparatively clean, chiefly between men with only the faintest taint of partisan bestiality in them among the indigenous peoples. There were few advocates for and hardly an instance of terror bombing for its own sake. But as the battle front moved close to southern Europe again it posed the nemesis of total war over civilians, ostensibly friendly ones at that, with an associated intensification of the moral problems.

Long before Tunis fell, Kesselring and Hitler had learnt to be aware of the hot pot brewing in Italy and each had evolved his own way of tackling the political problems involved. But while Hitler fumed, decried Kesselring's diplomatic acumen, and made sweeping plans from a distance, Kesselring out-faced the Italians in everyday transactions and had to contain himself under direct provocation. Throughout April, Ambrosio had been angrily obstructive whenever the Germans tried to put 'ginger' into the defence preparations of the off-shore islands, which everybody realised must soon be the targets for raids and invasion. Yet, although evidence from von Rintelen in Rome, and from other intelligence sources, revealed discontent among the Italians, there was nothing to expose their real intentions since, in fact, they remained unsure of their own destiny themselves. Many Italian officers, plus discontented Fascists, were ready to dispose of Mussolini, as were the anti-Fascists for their own advantage. On nothing else, however, could they unite and so nobody could go to the consititutional monarch, Victor Emmanual III (with whom Kesselring had a working if rather formal relationship), to propose a practicable formula for change.

The friendly relationships which Kesselring fostered with the Italians, and on which he prides himself with monotonous repetition in his 'Memoirs', was largely a chimera. Many Italians, undoubtedly, were charmed by Kesselring and had great personal respect for his culture and humanity, but the fact remained that he was a German at the head of a nation's forces which were steadily subjugating their country. Hitler saw it another way. To him Kesselring was a dupe among 'those born traitors down there', forgetting, as so often did Kesselring himself when he accused the Italians of treachery, that patriotism cannot be traitorous. The Italians simply put their country before the Axis and looked for a salvation that excluded the Germans. In the meantime it is scarcely surprising that they dissembled, or that the King adopted a neutral pose, or that Kesselring should disapprove of Hitler's rough handling of them. Nevertheless, Kesselring's repetition of the treachery charge after the war is one more clear illustration of his strict observance of loyalties that had been formally undertaken and is central to an understanding of his own behaviour in relation to oaths of fealty and codes of behaviour.

There is no more expressive passage of the relationship between Kesselring and Hitler than that which occurred in their resolution of the Italian dilemma. At one political extreme stood Hitler, the demagogue of limited education and culture, whose initial gains had been obtained by coercion of the crudest kind applied to diplomats of the old school in the days of apparent German military supremacy. Once he had become reduced in circumstances, his persuasive powers also fell into decline so that he could no longer bully, let alone persuade, even his closest ally Benito Mussolini to bend to his will. At the other extreme schemed Kesselring, the product of a sophisticated society whose manners had been polished at the tables of Prince Rupprecht and Hans von Seeckt and whose sensitivity and extensive training made him *persona grata* among the class of diplomat Hitler's gracelessness had offended. Lacking the means of irresistible coercion, Kesselring nevertheless possessed the inculcate power to have his way by intellectual application and charm. The pernicious adversity which drove Hitler into a shell, extracted the highest resolve and ingenuity from Kesselring in terms of constructive negotiating ability dextrously mixed with firmness and humanity. On the one hand the Italians were to deal with a racketeer and on the other a patrician; and though Hitler was subject to a barrage of complaints about Kesselring, something in his intuitive psychology seems to have prevented him from a complete withdrawal of support.

Excessive emphasis has been placed upon the true effect of the anti-Kesselring campaign. It existed at the highest level but was also strongly offset. For example, despite Göring's denigration of Kesselring in post-Tunisian days, he did not deny the Mediterranean theatre its fair share of available resources as well as the services of good men. The appointment of Wolfram von Richthofen to command *Luftflotte* II may well have been intended by Göring as a foil to Kesselring's prospects but, turned to good account, von Richthofen was the best of the army support airmen. And the appointment of the ace, Adolf Galland – ostensibly to restore the morale and equipment of the *Luftwaffe* in the Mediterranean – though unwelcome to Kesselring who preferred his predecessor and feared Galland's avowed intent to strip the Mediterranean of fighter aircraft in order to reinforce the defences of Germany, was hardly malignant.

Throughout June and the better part of July, Kesselring felt safely able to put more emphasis on defence against the Allies than into the political balancing act with the Italians, although for much of the time his deliberations were about one and the same thing. It was enough, just then, to know that contingency plans for the disarmament of the Italians had been in existence at OKW since 1941, but disturbing to become aware that an old challenger was working a way back into Hitler's favour. Throughout May, Erwin Rommel had been consulted by Hitler and OKW and, at Rastenberg on the 24 May, when in the process of being appointed adviser on the Mediterranean theatre (a crude challenge to Kesselring's position), had taken part in a frank exchange of views. Hitler had confided in Rommel that though Germany's war production, now in the hands of the highly capable Albert Speer, was expanding fast, it was hardly likely that she could keep pace with the rest of the world ranged against her. Therefore, since the U-boats were being destroyed at an alarming rate, he feared there was little chance of winning the war. Kesselring thought so too, at this time (as he testified at Nürnberg), though whether he based this conclusion on special information or simply by calculation, founded on the wide range of information which came to him from many sources, is not clear. Nor was this the sort of subject he discussed with Hitler. The pulverising demonstrations by Allied air power in its attacks upon the German industrial base and cities (which far out-weighed anything that had been delivered at the height of *Luftwaffe* power), and the capitulation of the islands of Pantellaria and Lampedusa to the overwhelming raids in June, may well have had a disproportionate effect upon his airman's judgement as well as shattering any expectation that there might have been of the Italians fighting strongly for their homeland. Certainly when it came to prescribing the tactics against an Allied amphibious invasion, he insisted upon stationing counter-attack forces close to the beaches so that they could make a quick response unhindered by air attack – a policy which, less than a year later, was to be Rommel's model in laying out the defences of Normandy. From a study of past Allied tactics, Kesselring had concluded also that the enemy would not attempt to come ashore outside the range of shore-based fighter aircraft – an assumption which sounds rather remiss, in the light of past experience, to have excluded serious consideration of carrier-borne aircraft being employed. Nevertheless this assumption usefully reduced the number of potential landing places to a handful and led him to put Sicily top of the danger list.

Those, like Westphal, who hold that Kesselring tended to be a 'compromiser', have only to study his conduct of the Sicilian campaign to have that contention rejected. Consistent with his conviction of the sanctity of defence in depth, he aimed to defend Italy from toe to hip, clean contrary to the expressed opinion of Rommel that such a strategy was too vulnerable to amphibious landings behind the Axis lines. Kesselring believed that prior information would give sufficient time to react to each Allied move, but he based his plan on the hope of continued Italian co-operation. Although OKW, top-heavy with army officers, supported the soldier Rommel against the *Luftwaffe* field-marshal, it was

Kesselring who imposed his views on his subordinates after hearing their objections. He intended to hold Sicily and would not hear of abandoning Italy as far north as the Northern Apennines. Nor would he agree with von Richthofen who believed Sardinia was the next Allied objective. But having given his orders he had still to fight for their application against those who persistently endeavoured to circumvent them and undermine his authority. Rommel, egged on by Jodl at OKW, prepared a scheme of his own for holding in the north; and von Richthofen busily reinforced Sardinia, going direct to Göring for aid if he was balked and receiving encouragement from the *Reichsmarschall* whose jealousy of the C-in-C South was apparent. Hitler, it is true, gave Kesselring spasmodic support; he liked commanders who were not chronically full of woe; emotionally, however, he leant towards the engaging Rommel whose well-considered distrust of the Italians matched his own.

Despite every sort of opposition from colleagues, quite apart from thorough enemy bombing of his lines of communication and airfields, Kesselring managed to have assembled by 10 July in Sicily, twelve Italian divisions (mostly static) braced by two mobile German divisions. In so doing he accomplished a quite remarkable feat of solo diplomacy in overcoming Italian obstruction which stemmed from their own terrible dilemma. On the one hand, along with the desire to remain masters in their own provinces, they wished to disperse the Germans in limited numbers to those regions of little political importance. On the other, in the realisation that they were practically defenceless and that an armistice was nowhere in prospect, they needed the presence of Germans stationed at the most sensitive strategic places. For their part the Germans had to retain the ability to disarm the Italians (if necessary) and seize control of the country without sacrificing their army in the south should the Allies, with Italian support, take possession of Rome and the communications connecting the north to the south. Logistics and the sheer difficulty under heavy air bombardment of maintaining sizeable forces in Sicily had their impact, but it was politics and diplomacy which governed the flow of military reinforcement.

The German reinforcement of Italy was limited, of course, by the requirements of other fronts. A major offensive against the Russian salient at Kursk was in preparation, its timing in doubt, but its demand on armoured troops and aircraft greedy. In any case Hitler felt convinced that the Allies would invade the Balkans rather than Italy, an eventuality Germany could ill afford since vital raw materials came from there and a link-up with the Russians was always to be resisted. Several formations, therefore, were sent there. On the 4 May (just prior to the end in Africa) Kesselring made an initial offer of one German division to Mussolini at a meeting in which he ruthlessly dispelled the Italian dictator's false hope that the Allies might not invade his country. Two days later Kesselring saw Mussolini again and raised the German offer to three divisions, but this was accepted sourly by Ambrosio with the request that they be spread far and wide – one to Sicily, another to Sardinia and the third on the mainland. But when, next day, Hitler raised the German offer to five divisions he effectually called the Italian bluff and thereby confirmed his suspicions. The offer was refused and Ambrosio's political intentions stood revealed, even though they were partly concealed by a request from Mussolini to Hitler for the immediate supply of 300 tanks, fifty anti-aircraft batteries and aircraft for fifty fighter squadrons to re-equip the Italian units which, in truth, were rendered useless by their own out-moded weapons.

Convinced that the Italians were on the verge of defection, Hitler called in Rommel and, with the eager encouragement of Jodl, hatched a plan to create a new Army Group (B) of thirteen to fourteen divisions designed to enter northern Italy when the time was ripe. This arrangement was kept secret from Kesselring, though it is certain that he learned of it by way of the reliable *Luftwaffe* channels. He merely persevered with his own diplomacy and, at an exhaustive discussion with the Italians on the 22nd, persuaded them to accept four German divisions besides getting them to agree to the introduction of XIV Panzer Corps under Hans Hube to Italy. Then, on 1 June, the eve of the fall of Pantellaria, Ambrosio presented him with a request to increase the number of German divisions by one because he now had to put the protection of Italy against the Allies ahead of defence against a take-over by the Germans since so little progress was being made in removing Mussolini – an essential preliminary to making armistice overtures to the Allies. So Kesselring, by adroit diplomacy, had inserted Hitler's five divisions which originally had so abruptly been declined by Mussolini. With this achievement in his pocket he at once went to see Hitler to obtain authority to propose still more equipment to the Italians, if only they would ask for it, and also the offer of yet another division should it be needed.

Once more Ambrosio, under pressure from his generals, tried to divert a panzer division to Sardinia, and again was firmly rebuffed by Kesselring with sound tactical reasons. By now he had Ambrosio's measure as fear of the Allies began to tell on the Italians. On the 17th Ambrosio not only accepted the sixth division but asked even for a seventh, a request that was met with alacrity, particularly since the two divisions in question would be subtracted from those already allocated to Rommel. But when, four days later, Mussolini came forward with yet another ambitious request for German equipment, including 2,000 aircraft, it only went to emphasise the Italian's ignorance of the true German situation. For on 3 July the *Luftwaffe*, for example, could put up only 975 aircraft in the Central Mediterranean, after a truly prodigious effort. Nevertheless the infusion of new formations put a gloss on the strategic picture for Kesselring. On the eve of the Allied invasion of Sicily there were twelve Italian and two mobile German divisions in Sicily, plus three more divisions on the mainland and two more on their way. Moreover Kesselring had once more eclipsed Rommel whose scheme to occupy the north had fallen into abeyance; or as the U.S. Official History justifiably states: 'Kesselring was Hitler's representative on all questions concerning the conduct of the war in the central and western Mediterranean areas.' It was a mere formality that the Germans still came under *Comando Supremo*. Kesselring ruled and, with the forces at his disposal and on the assumption of a reasonable combat performance by the Italians, believed he could protect the whole of Italy.

When the Allies invaded the south-eastern corner of Sicily (Operation 'Husky') on 10 July they tackled opponents whose dispositions matched the tactical concepts of the C-in-C South. Kesselring had been correct in calculating that the attack would fall where it did but he could not entirely dismiss the possibility of a landing in the western part of the island too. So, although he had positioned the bulk of the two German mobile divisions in the east to bolster the static Italians' coastal formations, he had placed two-thirds of 15th Panzer Grenadier Division in the west. Therefore, since the German formations in the south-east did make a spirited counter-attack against the American troops of General Patton's Seventh Army at Gela on the 10th and 11th and fought their way to within sight of the landing zone, it can reasonably be asserted that the entire German and Italian mobile force, used concentrated and in time, might actually have flung the Americans back into the sea. It was, however, the sheer weight of naval gunfire backed up by some determined counter-action by the U.S. infantry, supported by their anti-tank guns, which brought the gallant German and Italian attack to a halt, and so it is doubtful if the introduction of a few additional German reserves would have tipped the scale. Moreover the Italians elsewhere (and soon, too, on this front) were beginning to give up in droves, demolishing Kesselring's hopes that they might fight better at home than abroad.

Kesselring's part in launching the counter-attacks was dynamic – a lot too energetic for many senior commanders in the field who found the *generalfeldmarschall's* orders coming over their heads from long range at Rome. The motivation of this intrusion was over-insurance due to a breakdown in communication with General Guzzoni's Sixth Italian Army on the island and Kesselring's premature conclusion from initial reports that the Italians were collapsing everywhere. Intent upon crushing the enemy infantry before artillery and many tanks could come ashore, he employed direct German channels of communication to German formations demanding they attack without awaiting Italian instructions. Guzzoni, in fact, was attempting to do precisely what Kesselring had always desired and there was little confusion since everybody was working to the same basic plan. Kesselring, indeed, though somewhat put out when Guzzoni correctly brought in 15th Panzer Grenadier Division from the west to stiffen the counter-attack (complaining that its removal took the only mobile striking force from that area) quickly adjusted himself to the situation once it became apparent that the west was not threatened. Not until the 12th did Kesselring arrive in Sicily to confer with Guzzoni and Frido von Senger und Etterlin, the senior German officer attached to Sixth Army. This was a regrettable delay since only on the spot could he form an accurate picture of a situation which, up to then, had been distorted for him by imprecise reporting from *Luftflotte* II. On this, the day that the leading elements of the 1st Parachute Division began to arrive by air in the island, Kesselring came to appreciate at last that the chances of throwing the enemy out were remote, and that any further reinforcement of the island might well be converted into a disaster of Tunisian magnitude.

On 13 July Montgomery's Eighth Army was beginning to make quicker progress on the right flank towards Catania and Enna, and this loosened opposition to Patton's Seventh Army which began also to extend its bridgehead in an advance which rapidly began to gain momentum in a north-westerly direction. Kesselring, whose optimism was sufficient on the 15th to convince him that a bridgehead covering Messina and the Straits might be held, had the decision taken out of his hands within a matter of days by the sort of 'staff manoeuvre' at which he was himself so expert. On 15 July Alfred Jodl at OKW concluded that further defence of the island was impossible and that now was the time to place control of the Mediterranean operations on an entirely different footing. The offensive at Kursk, blunted by the Russian defence, had been called off on the 13th in order to provide reinforcements for the Mediterranean. Jodl suggested that this *volte face* justified new management. Jointly with Rommel he proposed that the Axis forces in Italy should come under one commander – a competent German, one called Erwin Rommel – and that the air forces should be given to von Richthofen. The emphasis was on the word 'competent', thus by cryptic inference squeezing Kesselring out of a job. Hitler did not at once accept this scheme. Although he conceded that Sicily was as good as lost he still kept faith in Mussolini and he did not think that Rommel (whom he now sent on an inspection of Greece) would be acceptable to the Italians. What none of them had fully comprehended, however, was the frailty of Mussolini's tenure of office.

Agitation among responsible dissident Italian politicians for the dissolution of the Axis came to a head once it became apparent how badly the Army was fighting, a discontent which found its keenest expression in their determination to remove Mussolini from power. For this weakening of Mussolini Kesselring was almost as much responsible, in the short term, as any other man, since the Duce's position had been further undermined by the concessions that had been wrung from him by the C-in-C South. But when Mussolini told Ambrosio on 20 July that the termination of the Axis Treaty was desirable he merely hastened his downfall because Ambrosio did not believe him. *Comando Supremo*, encouraged by the King, now began to prepare a *coup d'état* in conjunction with anti-Fascists, and did so with such secrecy and thoroughness that neither Mussolini nor the Germans had the slightest hint of what was in train until its accomplishment on 25 July 1943. On the 24th, in fact, Mussolini, at a meeting with Kesselring and Westphal, had referred to Count Grandi, boasting 'He is faithful to me'. But it was Grandi who, next day, led the Fascist Council, at its first meeting in three years, to dismiss and arrest the Duce, replacing him by Marshal Badoglio. Although Kesselring heard of this within a few minutes of the event, Hans von Mackensen, the German Ambassador, was much slower in sending a comprehensive report to Berlin. Therefore Hitler was unaware of all that had happened until the next day and Kesselring lacked instructions.

Though taken completely by surprise, the German reaction was neither tardy nor chicken-hearted. Regardless of Badoglio's announcement that the Italians would continue the war at the German side, Hitler felt sure this was only a sham. The frenetic discussions at his conferences during this period, therefore, are at the root of much that was negative as well as that which was positive. On the negative side there was his predilection for interfering in details at the lower levels of command, a habit that had grown out of scepticism of generals' abilities but which was partly, of course, the cause of men in Kesselring's exalted position being compelled to intervene at those same levels in order to keep in step with the Führer or to correct what had been put wrong. On the positive side were the political decisions leading to military moves even if, on the political side, all was guesswork. Each side sought secretly to outwit the other – the Italians trying to disentangle themselves with least harm from the German toils; the Germans attempting to keep the Italians fighting on their side while securing their own position in Italy; the Allies straining to complete the conquest of Sicily prior to making the next leap forward into Italy, though, at the same time, endeavouring (with some success) to delude the Germans into believing that Sardinia, Corsica or the Balkans were next on the lists for invasion.

It is a tribute to Kesselring's perception and dominating ability that, in the weeks to come, he could steer a consistent course through a maze of contradictions and emerge at the centre with his integrity and aims virtually intact. At first he is to be seen treading delicately among the various plans that were hastily improvised on the remnants of Rommel's original intervention scheme for the north. Next he was deflecting Hitler's impetuous desire to seize Rome, kidnap the King and Badoglio and recapture and reinstate Mussolini, a venture for which Kesselring was to supply the troops. Westphal recalls his commander's bitterness at this suggestion when he said 'One gives one's whole life as an officer and man of honour until it suddenly turns out that one is only the captain of robbers.' Saying he could not spare the men or vehicles, and working in close conjunction with the Diplomatic Corps, Kesselring frustrated Hitler's scheme and avoided damage to the German name until wiser councils prevailed. As a result he sacrificed any good opinion Hitler may have had of his political acumen. German forces in Rome were to be reinforced by 2nd Parachute Division flown in from France. The mountain passes, particularly the Brenner and those into Yugoslavia, were to be taken over from the Italians before they could strengthen the garrisons. German troops in Sicily, Sardinia and Corsica were eventually to be withdrawn, the garrison in Sicily first to be steered back into a bridgehead covering Messina prior to their evacuation by sea to Calabria. Once the German forces were united on the mainland and extracted from the south, Rommel was to take supreme command because, in Hitler's opinion at that moment of tension, 'Field-Marshal Kesselring hasn't got the reputation. We'll publish that the moment we move in – Field-Marshal Rommel.' Glamour took precedence over genius. The old delusion of Rommel magic overrode the excellence of Kesselring's qualifications.

But Kesselring kept ahead of them all, employing the dialogue with Badoglio to bind the Axis together – a policy which those in Rastenberg came to approve when, gradually, Kesselring sold them his opinion that the Fascists were finished through lack of support from a people who were utterly weary of war and deprivation. Nothing would be lost by keeping in touch with the Italians, he suggested. Crude military intervention at Rome would immediately initiate a confrontation that would cut communications with the south and also overstretch the German forces. On the 28th the over-excited hierarchy in Germany came to understand the wisdom of Kesselring's reasoning. They abandoned the kidnapping plans in favour of a typical example of the Kesselring type of indirect approach – the implacable infiltration of German units among key localities throughout the country. Some Germans actually thought the Italians might remain loyal – as reports from the diplomatic corps and Admiral Canaris's *Abwehr* said they would – but there they were wrong since peace feelers were out already. At the same time a plan called 'Axis' (*Achse*) was drawn up (distributed by hand or verbally to those concerned) which made provision for the take-over of Italy – a project which Kesselring pronounced feasible despite a prospective Allied intervention and the threat of a build-up of Italian troops in the sensitive military and political areas, such as Rome. Simultaneously Rommel in the north began to put pressure on the Italians to allow Germans to take over the Brenner Pass, Kesselring held parleys with Ambrosio in Rome and the latter got very heated while Kesselring, by degrees, manoeuvred the Italian into accepting his view that, surely, old comrades should work together. To von Rintelen's suggestion that he should resign rather than condone the occupation of Italy, Kesselring turned a deaf ear. Eventually, 'by seduction, not rape', as the U.S. Official History puts it, the Brenner Pass fell peacefully into German hands. At once a flood of German troops was poured into Italy, though Hitler shrewdly excluded Rommel from among them in case he provoked additional Italian wrath. Once more the smooth diplomacy of Kesselring had put him one up on his coarser rival.

On 27 July he had begun planning the evacuation of Sicily – an order that was not issued in writing until 2 August but which was ready for instant improvisation in July 'if the Italians should break the alliance with Germany' as he informed his generals. Over them he had mastery; his whole demeanour was that of complete self-assurance with scarcely a sign of the strain under which he was working. Everything depended upon domination of the Messina Straits and a controlled retirement to the

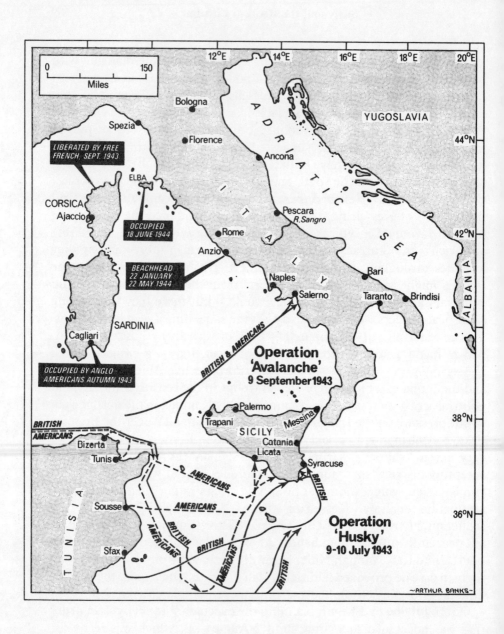

0 ——— 150
Miles

12°E 14°E 16°E 18°E 20°E

Bologna

Spezia

LIBERATED BY FREE FRENCH, SEPT. 1943

ELBA

CORSICA
Ajaccio

OCCUPIED 18 JUNE 1944

BEACHHEAD 22 JANUARY 22 MAY 1944

SARDINIA

Cagliari

OCCUPIED BY ANGLO-AMERICANS AUTUMN 1943

Florence

Ancona

I T A L Y

Rome

Anzio

Naples

Salerno

Pescara
R.Sangro

Bari

Taranto Brindisi

A D R I A T I C   S E A

YUGOSLAVIA

44°N

42°N

BRITISH & AMERICANS

Operation 'Avalanche'
9 September 1943

Palermo

Trapani

SICILY

Messina

Catania
Licata

Syracuse

38°N

BRITISH
AMERICANS

Bizerta

Tunis

AMERICANS

AMERICANS

Sousse

AMERICANS

BRITISH

BRITISH

AMERICANS

Sfax

T U N I S I A

BRITISH

BRITISH

Operation 'Husky'
9-10 July 1943

36°N

~ARTHUR BANKS~

A L B A N I A

embarkation points. The land-phased withdrawal to Messina under the direction of Guzzoni, von Senger und Etterlin and Hube was worked out in detail as a classic in the art of denial of ground to an advancing enemy by inferior forces employing demolitions and mines to inflict the maximum delay with minimum cost at every defensible position. These things the Army arranged to Kesselring's complete satisfaction. But it is another example of his post-war loyalty to save old comrades from calumny, that he wrote in the 'Memoirs' how von Richthofen also performed to his complete satisfaction when, initially, this was not the case. Westphal recalls one of Kesselring's 'great hours' during the planning stage of the evacuation when von Richthofen fervently resisted Kesselring's demand for XIV Panzer Corps to be given maximum protection against air attack during the evacuation, 'even if our Flak artillery were to sustain heavy losses'. Westphal was alone with the two *Luftwaffe* marshals when von Richthofen, so worked up that tears came to his eyes, pleaded for the order to be rescinded, and records his admiration for Kesselring's firm attitude in insisting on his instructions being obeyed. When Kesselring, without waiting for Hitler's final approval, authorised the operation on 8 August, he had placed over 500 anti-aircraft and coastal guns under the command of Ernst Baade, and converted the ports and the five by two mile strip of water into the most fiercely defended zone of air and sea space in the world. Axis torpedo boats and submarines, backed by artillery, deterred Allied naval attack while the sky above was filled with gunfire. This was the work of Kesselring the Gunner overriding the scruples of Kesselring the Airman. Only by night could the Allies fly with a reasonable chance of survival at the lower altitudes while by day they were forced above 23,000 feet in order to escape the gunfire: in neither case were the chances of aircraft obtaining hits on small targets sufficient to prevent movement. Beforehand the British Air Marshal Coningham admitted that 'this intense flak could clip the wings of daylight attack . . . and only a physical barrier, such as the navy can provide, would be effective'. . . . This the Allied navy could not provide since the seaward defences were far too strong. So the Allied air forces were compelled to attack easier targets in the hope of disrupting the withdrawal indirectly by damaging the communications in Italy, wrecking the Axis air forces at their bases, and applying psychological pressure to the disheartened Italian populace.

The triumph of the evacuation, in which the enemy were out-witted by a clean break from contact on land behind the mine and demolition barrier, is succinctly proven by the statistics. By the last night of the evacuation (the 17th) Kesselring could report that 60,000 Germans and

75,000 Italians had been brought out along with nearly all their surviving heavy equipment such as tanks and guns. It was typical of the man's ingrained modesty that he abstained from boasting about this masterpiece, one of the most remarkable withdrawals under intense pressure from a hostile shore in history, and that he toned down Hube's laudatory communique. The credit largely belongs to him despite the claims of those subordinates who were usually so quick to criticise him when things seemed to go wrong, but who now were swift to lay claim to praise for themselves. It was Kesselring who had authorised the plan, which Rommel had declared to be impossible, and he who had thoroughly imposed his will on the planners, above all on von Richthofen.

In any case the ephemeral triumph was at once overshadowed by terrible news from Germany. Hamburg had recently suffered its immolation from pulverising Allied air attacks, American bombers had struck deep and by day into Germany to bomb the ball-bearings factory at Schweinfurt, and the rocket experimental establishment at Peenemunde had been blasted by RAF bombers on the night of the 17th. On the 18th Kesselring was to hear that Jeschonnek, the Chief of *Luftwaffe* Staff, had committed suicide. He had realised in July that his old subordinate was failing and that he had threatened suicide but, with the crisis in Sicily at its height, there was nothing he could do about it. Göring was profoundly disturbed since it had been made plain by the dead man that he blamed the *Reichsmarschall* for what had gone wrong, and Kesselring was forbidden by somebody to attend the funeral. Whoever did so might have saved his breath. Kesselring was present and it was for Göring to tell him the cause of death and, also, that Jeschonnek had suggested in a memorandum that there should be a change in the command of the *Luftwaffe*. That was food for thought. Who might be brought into consideration for the job? What would Göring do? Kesselring, of course, had even less time for internal *Luftwaffe* politics than he had when Milch previously started manoeuvring against Göring, but it was obviously on the cards that he might once more find himself back at the centre of *Luftwaffe* affairs. Meanwhile the war went on.

Kesselring divined that Sicily was no more a victory for the Germans than Dunkirk had been for the British. Unremitting adversity lay ahead, as a series of heavy raids on Italian industrial cities, which provoked protest strikes (that some took as the commencement of insurgency against the Italian government), underlined the unreliability of their ally. Yet the schism in Germany's Italian strategy between Kesselring, who wished to stand as far south as possible (while prepared to give up the toe and heel of the country under enemy pressure), and those like Jodl and Rommel, who desired only to hold the north, was irreconcilable. It led to bitterness on Kesselring's part in complaining that the forces in the north were wasted, even though, on 17 August, Hitler made a gesture in his direction by creating a new army, the Tenth, under an incisive panzer leader, Heinrich von Vietinghoff, to control the two German Panzer Corps (XIV and LXXVI) in central and southern Italy, with direct responsibility to Kesselring. At the same time Hitler told von Vietinghoff that, once a withdrawal to central Italy had been made, Kesselring would go and Rommel take over. Kesselring, in the meantime, was to seize Rome and, if Mussolini could be found and rescued, return the discredited Duce to the seat of power.

Germany's military operations in Italy were like isolated rocks surrounded by a quicksand of intrigue and uncertainty. Concomitant with the self-seeking Rommel's plot to undermine Kesselring's position, was played the charade at frequent meetings between the Italians and Germans over their future collaboration. For example, while Jodl, Rommel, Kesselring and von Rintelen were angrily negotiating with General Roatta (Chief of Staff of the Italian Army) at Bologna on 15 August*, General Guiseppe Castellano was in Madrid representing Marshal Badoglio on a peace mission to the Allies of which Roatta was totally unaware. Kesselring still preferred a small measure of Italian co-operation to their outright hostility, but with von Vietinghoff on the 20th he laid plans to free the mobile German troops in the south from Italian command. At the same time he activated the Tenth Army. This day, too (unknown even to the informed Italians in Rome), Castellano reached agreement in principle with the Allies in Lisbon, on the basis, as it evolved in the coming days, of Italian withdrawal from the Axis and their future collaboration with the Allies against the Germans after an armistice. This was to be announced (if Italian desires were permitted) prior to an Allied landing in Italy. Though the Allies would neither provide a guarantee as to the time of the announcement nor divulge their plans, they were committed to a subsidiary invasion in the toe of Italy by Eighth Army and, subsequently, a major landing at Salerno.

In guessing at Allied intentions, Kesselring was just as far adrift as he had been over French North Africa during the previous November. Sardinia, he thought, must be the objective but this time OKW were dead right and ordered Kesselring, when he visited Hitler on the 22nd (at about

*A meeting to which, quite incredibly, Kesselring was not at first invited, with the result that he tendered his resignation only to have it refused by Hitler.

the time of Jeschonnek's funeral) that he was not to reinforce Sardinia but concentrate on the defence of Salerno and Naples. Salerno was, indeed, the objective of the Allies' Operation 'Avalanche'. Tension mounted in Italian Government circles as the Germans tightened their grip on the vital points and essential lines of communication. The Italians protested but did not dare make a provocative move in case it compromised the armistice negotiations as these entered their next round under Castellano at Cassibile, in Sicily, on the 31st. Previously, on the 28th, Kesselring had become convinced, at last, from reports of Allied preparations in the ports of Sicily and North Africa, that the mainland was the enemy's destination. On the 29th he decided against defending Calabria, and on the 30th may well have abandoned hope of Italian fidelity. Simultaneously the final adjustments to Operation 'Axis' were delivered, saying that the neutralisation of the Italians was to be accomplished by allowing those who remained loyal to the Germans to go on fighting at their side; the rest were to be disarmed and invited to go home. But the 'gradualness' of Kesselring's precautionary methods had little appeal to those at Rastenberg who thought solely in terms of dramatic blows struck in the revolutionary manner. Fearful that the 'Italophiles' (as Kesselring and von Rintelen were called by Hitler, Keitel and Jodl) would let them down, they decided, on 1 September, to replace von Rintelen.

On that day the Italians accepted the armistice terms and during the next began the highly secretive distribution of instructions to senior commanders on their duties when the announcement was made. It would not come into effect before the Allied invasion, which was set for the 3rd when Eighth Army would begin the diversionary landing in Calabria. So the Italian generals had to present a co-operative front to the Germans even though they knew of the commitment to join the enemy. But at last the Germans had a much clearer idea of enemy military intentions and at once began their withdrawal from Calabria, casting anxious glances over their shoulder in consternation at what might happen should the Allies come ashore further north. This was no peace-time, route march kind of withdrawal such as Rommel had executed in Africa, but a tightly controlled retreat on the Sicillian model in which every conceivable delay was imposed in a hundred defiles upon an opponent who advanced with cautious deliberation at little more than three miles a day on average.

Then on 8 September, in a flash, the whole situation exploded.

9

Against Rommel

At Frascati in the early hours of 8 September tension was heightening as cumulative air reports of enemy shipping movements began to harden speculation into concrete conclusions. The first sighting of a convoy heading northward from Bizerta on the 7th made it look as if over 100 ships, heavily escorted by battleships and aircraft carriers, were on course either for Salerno, Naples or the coast north of Rome. Kesselring spent the morning of the 8th studying the reports and preparing for a meeting with Roatta, at the latter's request, in Rome. Shortly before noon he spoke to von Vietinghoff on the telephone to order a hastening of the withdrawal from Calabria and at the same time he put all troops in the central sector on top alert. A few minutes later near-by anti-aircraft guns went into action as the prelude to a rain of bombs on the headquarters, an attack which continued for a whole hour, and had the desired effect of severely damaging the installations, cutting all communications (with the exception of one telephone line) and killing or wounding about a hundred Germans. In the near-by town it was the unfortunate Italian civilians who received the brunt of the attack – a calamity which Kesselring, in his 'Memoirs', converts into propaganda as an accusation against the Italian leaders who, he thought, were forewarned and therefore should bear responsibility for unnecessary loss of life. This was a groundless charge since the Italian Government had been kept totally unaware of the Anglo-American landing plans. Their shock, therefore, was as deep as that of the Germans; everybody had suffered from the classical results of an attempted pin-point attack by aircraft which had resulted in typical bomb scatter – a phenomenon Kesselring must surely have recognised at once from previous experience.

Crawling from beneath the rubble, an outwardly calm C-in-C South issued revised orders. He would now remain at headquarters while

Westphal kept the appointment with Roatta. Von Vietinghoff was instructed to strengthen the region around Rome, where the landings were now thought imminent because Italian troops were seen to be taking exceptional precautions there. Improvisation there had to be due to the lack of a detailed contingency plan which had been impossible to arrange due to the shortage of time, and the inadvisability of making one with Italian participation. Then Jodl called to ask if they had heard a broadcast by Eisenhower announcing the Italian surrender, a question which, when relayed to Roatta via Westphal, produced a blank Italian denial. But the very obstructiveness of Italian troops at their road blocks and the wild enthusiasm of people in the streets told their own story. There was immense relief among a war-weary nation that it might be free of fighting; but also there was surprise at so sudden an ending without warning.

Without pause Kesselring activated Plan 'Axis' and concentrated on securing Rome and its environs with Student's XI *Fleigerkorps*. The utmost speed was essential to capitalise on the Italians' shock to prevent their collaboration with the approaching Allied invasion and destroy their Government. There is evidence to suggest that, although Kesselring put on a bold front, he was, for once, unusually pessimistic. Those at Rastenberg, in fact, immediately wrote off Kesselring along with his command. For a while, von Vietinghoff was left to his own devices, to decide for himself whether it was right to defend the coast or tackle the Italians instead. A signal he received from Kesselring that evening set the tone when it read, 'Italian troops will be asked to continue the fight on our side by appeals to their honour. Those who refuse are to be ruthlessly disarmed. No mercy must be shown the traitors. Long live the Führer!' – but that did not resolve the dilemma.

The Italians, as it happened, were more shaken than the Germans as well as divided among themselves in the upper echelons of command, the only place where Badoglio's intentions were fully known. Although a lightning attempt by Kesselring to seize Roatta and the Army Staff failed, the Germans held the initiative and by bluff and subterfuge were able to obtain the surrender of many troops along with their weapons, equipment and supplies – von Vietinghoff's men in Calabria enjoying notable success in this respect. The King and his Government were on the run and incapable of asserting control; the people were susceptible to rumour and the slightest display of German force. The five or six divisions belonging to Giacomo Carboni's corps, centred on Rome, looked a tougher nut, however. Its units offered quite stiff resistance at first, probably because its leaders were in high hope of immediate relief from an Allied parachute and sea landing within their lines that had been requested during the armistice negotiations. Unfortunately for them it was called off at the last moment because of their own unpreparedness, while, to the Germans, the launching of the major Allied assault at Salerno on the morning of the 9th made it plain that nothing was to be feared in the vicinity of the capital. Even so, Kesselring for once was unsure and doubted the feasibility of subjugating the Carboni Corps. Westphal, who had witnessed the Italian reaction to the armistice in the streets, thought otherwise, and became convinced that if the original spirit of the Axis instruction were applied by persuasion something might come of it. He says that he obtained Kesselring's permission for full freedom of action (along with the blame if things went wrong) while his commander remained in the background, and that it was he who made the initial contact through an old colleague in the Italian Army. There are several versions of how the Italian officer was handled, the most likely one seeming to show that the initiative came from the Germans.* Be that as it may, Kesselring, Student and Westphal opened discussions with an Italian delegation on the evening of the 9th by which time the Allies at Salerno had established a strong lodgement against light German resistance. There was hard bargaining in Rome but in the upshot a tentative agreement was reached whereby the Germans would recognise Rome as an open city in which they would be allowed to keep open their Embassy and maintain communication centres; the Italian troops would lay down their arms and be allowed, subsequently, to work for Germans; and Italian troops would maintain order in the city. Kesselring warned the Italians that unless these terms were rapidly accepted he would demolish the aquaducts and bomb the city. Amid turmoil, but with a clear realisation of the hopelessness of their situation, the Italians argued over the terms all night. One of their factions said the Germans could not be trusted, another would state categorically that the German officers involved were men of honour, and that a personal assurance from Kesselring was sufficient. When the plenipotentiaries returned to Frascati on the morning of the 10th, it was plain that the landing at Salerno represented the main Allied effort and that the Italian people and soldiers no longer had heart for renewed hostilities, particularly against the formidable Germans who pressed in hard around them. Sensing his advantage, Kesselring, through Westphal, stepped up his requirements, demanding what virtually amounted to capitulation. It would effect an economy of force for him that Rome should remain an

*This account is largely based upon the version printed in the Official U.S. History by A. Garland as amplified by Westphal's recently published 'Memoirs'.

open city and would be secured by military police alone, and a shrewd move to send home the disarmed Italians. Heavy pressure was applied by Kesselring who made a personal entry to the conference room at the psychological moment to insist that, unless the agreement was signed and delivered by 1600 hours, the bombardment of Rome would begin – a deadline that was allowed to slip by thirty minutes after a day's procrastination and which had not been acted upon when the Italians signed at 1630.

Italian morale collapsed utterly. Kesselring and Westphal had won another truly remarkable diplomatic victory with the minimum of force. The latter transmits the relief felt by both sides, but then records his disgust at the reaction of their own side.

'If we thought we had done the right thing we could not have been more wrong. OKW criticised C-in-C South for not taking prisoner the whole of Carboni's corps. A telegram from the commander of Army Group B was strange in that Field-Marshal Rommel rebuked his old comrade for similar reasons as if to say he, Kesselring, had grossly failed in his duty.'

And yet, it was Rommel who had miscalculated by adopting an unnecessarily hard line in northern Italy. Forsaking any pretence at negotiation with the Italians, he ruthlessly took prisoner and transported to Germany those who would not at once join with the Germans, and thereby incited an antagonism which was to reverberate into the future. Those Italians who were not captured cached their arms or fled with them into the hills. When the partisan war later broke out on a large scale it was in the north that it was most severe, where Rommel had failed to collect arms, rather than in the centre and south, where Kesselring and Westphal had persuaded the Italians to hand them in. These were the penalties to be paid for obeying OKW to the letter, as did Rommel, rather than dissembling, as did Kesselring.

Had it not been for the schism in the German high command in Italy in the period immediately following the surrender, even better results than Kesselring actually achieved might have been possible. By the night of the 9th when the situation at Rome swayed in the balance, von Vietinghoff, with one division, had managed to contain an Allied landing by elements of more than three Allied divisions supported by massed bombing and naval gunfire. In the days to come, when brought up to six divisions to include those brought back from the south, he would offer the Allies the stiffest fight for a bridgehead they had yet experienced. Indeed, but for the distraction at Rome, von Vietinghoff's reaction could have been quicker and more violent at the outset and blessed with far-reaching results. If Kesselring's request to OKW for two panzer divisions immediately to be relinquished by Rommel's Army Group B, 450 miles to the north, had been satisfied, the final outcome might have been very different to what it was. But OKW stuck to the letter of Jodl's order that 'the most urgent problem is to get the Tenth Army and the *Luftwaffe* out of southern Italy', and refused Kesselring's latest attempt at reversing that policy. Once more Kesselring was made to struggle in order to demonstrate with minimal forces the correctness of his judgement.

Each local success strengthened his hand. On the 9th, as the Italian Fleet sailed to surrender to the Allies, it was attacked by von Richthofen's aircraft, the battleship *Roma* sunk by a guided bomb and the *Italia* seriously damaged. On the 12th the celebrated kidnapping of Mussolini by Otto Skorzeny enabled the Germans to restore a fascist regime to rule their zone of Italy and thus to relieve themselves of total responsibility for its administration. Likewise the evacuation of the island of Sardinia, which was authorised on the 8th, and of Corsica on the 12th, would produce an economy of force without seriously weakening an already perilous strategic situation. The phased withdrawal from Sardinia through Corsica, and thence across the narrow strip of water to the mainland via Elba, was another feather in Kesselring's soldier's cap as well as a diplomatic success. Far from opposing the Germans, the Italians gave assistance with the extensive programme of demolitions preceding the retirement to Bonifacio. It was different on Corsica since there the French guerrillas who infested the hills were being reinforced by Free French Forces. These, to the Italians, posed a greater threat than the Germans, so they were quite co-operative, keeping such bickering as took place to themselves. Senger und Etterlin, who had been placed in charge, found it difficult, at first, to reconcile Kesselring's orders, brought by Westphal, with the realities of the situation, but Senger, of course, imbibed the characteristic army scepticism of Kesselring's soldiering ability, as he makes quite plain in his book, *Neither Fear nor Hope*. But he also could be generous as well as patronising and records with admiration Kesselring's arrival on 19 September. 'Kesselring, who never shirked danger,' he wrote, '. . . issued his own directives for the further evacuation', one which, as the British Official History says, 'was carried out with customary German efficiency'. Together, by 5 October, they managed to extract nearly 18,000 men, over 3,200 vehicles and more than 5,000 tons of stores for the loss of 55 aircraft (mainly bombed on airfields) and 17,000 tons of shipping.

Meanwhile von Vietinghoff had thrown a ring around the enemy beach-head at Salerno where, on ground of tortuous nature admirably suited to defence, confusion reigned supreme. Amid sand-dunes, streams, cornfields and groves against a backcloth of steep hills in which the Germans skilfully fortified themselves, a soldier's battle raged with which neither Generals Alexander and Clark, on the Allied side, nor Kesselring and von Vietinghoff, on the German, could come wholly to terms. Deprived of up-to-date or adequate information they could but plan with inspirational guesswork and hopefully feed in reinforcements to attain numerical superiority. Everything hinged on the rate of build-up and for this race the Germans were by far the better organised. While the *Luftwaffe*, by producing 450 sorties in two days (about one-tenth of the Allied effort), was compelled, in accordance with Kesselring's firm directives, to give priority to strikes against shipping to hamper the convoys at sea, the German artillery and mortars made things so unpleasant on the beaches that the movement of British and American men and stores at times came almost to a stop. Allied air attacks and the terrible naval gunfire also made life very unpleasant for the Germans, but in no way prevented the rapid concentration of nearly six divisions at Salerno within a few days. Relieved of the Italian threat at Rome, and by providing only one strong Battle Group to oppose Montgomery's Eighth Army as it cautiously felt its way through the jungle of demolitions and booby traps blocking every route out of Calabria, Kesselring executed a classic strategic manoeuvre by pitting almost his entire force against a key enemy position which he knew to be inadequately defended. Five days after its start, on the 14th, this major Allied invasion faced a situation against the Germans such as had never been experienced before or (except for one subsequent action by Kesselring) they would ever know again: they were on the verge of being driven, neck and crop, into the sea.

Kesselring and von Vietinghoff correctly read the battle's plot when, on the morning of the 13th, they jointly pronounced their confidence in its outcome. It mattered not that Hitler and OKW on the 12th had already ordained, with Kesselring's connivance, that a retirement from the easily outflanked Salerno position must eventually come, or that their corps commanders were complaining bitterly about enemy counter-attacks and the naval gunfire. None of these things seriously hampered the build-up of German reserves, prevented the work of their artillery or stopped the infiltration of their infantry among the enemy lodgement. Kesselring, furthermore, was heartened by intercepts of Allied radio messages which eloquently told of their discomfiture – though not of the contingency plan of evacuation then being made by Clark. From experience, and not from the hackneyed optimism so frequently ascribed by their junior generals, the Germans recognised an impending enemy collapse when they saw one. With his own subsequent withdrawal firmly in mind, Kesselring encouraged von Vietinghoff to deliver the culminating attack that would shake the Allies to their roots. But when, three days later, against naval gunfire which at last became overbearing, von Vietinghoff had to admit his inability quite to finish the job, there was no recrimination on Kesselring's part. Von Vietinghoff, he knew, had done his best and now was the time to implement the plan he had hatched on the same day as the Italians threw in the sponge at Rome.

The setback at Salerno might well have been fatally damaging to Kesselring in relation to the tug-of-war with Rommel since, unfortunately for him, the reputation of one of Rommel's keenest advocates also suffered. Josef Göbbels' propaganda machine had leapt on the premature claim of victory and had trumpeted it to the heavens. In consequence the eventual retraction was painful for Göbbels who complained bitterly in his diary on 19 September that 'What the army did at Salerno is an outstanding scandal. The exuberant reports of victory emanated from our supreme command in the south – almost directly from Kesselring.' Göbbels was a fierce critic and dangerous enemy of the army generals with whom he included Kesselring. He excluded Rommel, of course, 'one of our most popular generals. We could well use a few more such big shots.' Early in 1942 he had attempted to persuade the *Wehrmacht* liaison officer with the Propaganda Ministry 'to tell me the names of all officers in the OKW and OKH who are guilty of fostering defeats . . . The Führer has called for such a report from me so that he may take proper measures.' But on the 24th, when Göbbels asked Hitler for his opinion on 'our marshals' he discovered that 'His opinion of Albert Kesselring's military abilities is higher than my own.' Certainly it looks as if he was not fully in the Führer's confidence when it came to military matters since it was the Führer's order of 12 September, anticipating eventual retreat, which had governed Kesselring's conduct of the Battle of Salerno.

It is not to be suggested that the defence of Salerno was superfluous or the decision to withdraw was contrary to Kesselring's original intentions. Had the Allies suffered a calamity on the beaches they might well have been deterred from similar ventures in the future, in which case their whole amphibious strategy would have been discredited. Of immediate effect, however, was the advantage of winning time to save the bulk of their forces in the south, to evade the Allied landings at Taranto on the heel of Italy and to swing back and shorten their line, snapping into place a

garter clasped tight from side to side of the country's narrow leg. If, at the
same time, Kesselring was to discover in von Vietinghoff a calm, natural
man of kindred spirit, a commander who abhorred the admission of defeat
and who, on many occasions, had the happy knack of falling in with his
C-in-C's wishes, that was a bonus. Salerno was the first of Kesselring's
land battles in which he rarely intervened below the prescribed level of
command, a sure sign of his satisfaction with an immediate
subordinate – though this was by no means a concession that was to
become a habit.

Hitler's directive for the Italian front, issued on 12 September 1943,
was a document which confirmed the divorce between Kesselring's and
Rommel's separate commands; it placed them both under his personal
command, through OKW, and thus eliminated the ambiguity as to which
of the two was superior officer to the other. But it was not a final solution.
There is even uncertainty if it was entirely the Führer's own production,
rendered at the hands of the OKW staff, for Kesselring says in his
'Memoirs' that he had already, on 10 September, plotted the lines of
defence to which his armies should withdraw, a task he accomplished
simultaneously with enforcing Carboni's capitulation. It would have
certainly been quite out of character and a breach of procedure had he not
at once settled down in the aftermath of the Italian debâcle to shape a
revised strategy and transmit those views to Hitler. The essence of
Kesselring's technique of insinuation was to inject his own ideas at the
earliest moment into the minds of others so as to make it appear that it was
they who had thought of them first. He hoped to persuade Hitler to
modify his demands for a total withdrawal into the sort of delaying defence
he deemed entirely practicable. While Hitler still was strongly in favour of
retiring well to the north of Rome, his advisers (with the exception of the
Rommel faction) for the first time now began to perceive the logic of
Kesselring's belief that a scorched earth policy linked with gradual
withdrawal through successive lines of defence might prevail. They also
came to accept that the danger of being cut off by amphibious attacks in
rear might well be an exaggeration. The action at Salerno had acted both as
a feasibility study and an incentive. As the days went by and events began
to move the way Kesselring had foretold, Hitler came to listen more
attentively to the *Luftwaffe* field-marshal. Kesselring had readily
executed the withdrawal from Salerno that began on the 16th since this
complied with the earlier scheme of abandonment up to the northern
Apennines where Rommel, his divisions neither offered nor asked for by
Hitler or even Kesselring after the first refusal, impatiently waited. On the

17th, however, Hitler edged half a step closer to Kesselring when he told him to retard the withdrawal and hold as long as possible at the next main line of resistance along the River Garigliano (the Bernhardt Line). Hopes of preventing the enemy from taking Rome were rising as it became noticeable that a pursuit in mountainous country that crosses the grain of river and ridge is a laborious undertaking, particularly when the defenders use every delaying device, as did the Germans with professional zeal.

At successive meetings Kesselring described to Hitler the full meaning of his strategy which not only offered a genuine saving of seven or eight divisions, compared with Rommel's scheme, but guaranteed to prevent the enemy reaching Rommel's proposed line for the next six or nine months. The debate began at a convenient moment for Kesselring since Rommel was temporarily out of touch, tucked into a hospital bed with appendicitis for which he underwent an operation on the 19th. For a few days his place was taken by von Vietinghoff and thus Kesselring obtained an unopposed hearing at Rastenberg. On the 30th, three days after Foggia had fallen, Hitler staged a debate between the rivals (with Rommel still a little weak) to seek a judgement of Solomon, it may be assumed – perhaps even as a dialectic diversion from the heavier, insuperable problems piling in from all directions. This confrontation was dominated in temper by the well-known philosophical characteristics of the two contenders. While Kesselring rejected any chance of re-conquering Italy and Sicily, as Hitler at one time advocated, he exuded hopes and was not in the least bit gloomy, as was Rommel. Guilefully he agreed with Hitler that Foggia might possibly be retaken by counter-attack – an eventuality in which he can have had no genuine faith. Yet although Hitler was impressed by Kesselring, he deferred an answer for four days, by which time Naples had fallen and any hope of retaking Foggia had permanently vanished. Perhaps this upset Hitler, for on the 4th he proposed a compromise based on the original divisive organisation. Rommel would stay in the north but Kesselring could persevere in the south, in order to prove his point. He must show that he could execute the prolonged defence of the Bernhardt Line which was then under construction from the mouth of the River Garigliano, on the west coast, to the River Sangro on the east, backed by the formidable mountain chain with peaks whose names were to become legendary in the military annals of the Germans, British, Americans and French. As a practical token of goodwill Kesselring was given two more divisions from Rommel's group.

For Kesselring a great deal more than the defence of Italy now rested upon the plain matter of holding ground. He was fighting, quite blatantly, for his appointment. So even if Hitler, when he procrastinated, had not intended this to be a genuine trial by ambition, he could hardly have injected a more compelling incentive. The pressure Kesselring now brought to bear upon his subordinates was colossal as he moved tirelessly from place to place, driving, urging and cajoling in his determination to exact every morsel of work and ingenuity from weary men and to make the best of the relatively limited resources at his disposal. He had to convert the rickety and disaffected Italian administration to his beck and call while maintaining law and order throughout the country. He had also to construct a labyrinth of tunnels and emplacements guarding key points along the 90-mile Bernhardt Line and win time for its construction by a stiff delaying action through some twenty miles of terrain separating it from the River Volturno, where the Allies launched their assault on 12 October. That Kesselring managed to achieve his aim is all the more remarkable in the light of the attitudes adopted by some of his colleagues. Von Senger und Etterlin, who took over XIV Panzer Corps on the Volturno on the 8th, discovered that his Chief of Staff, von Bonin, was a dedicated adherent of Rommel and vociferous in his denigrating of Kesselring's ideas. Von Senger's appointment by Kesselring to some extent neutralised this carping as well as introducing a leader whose prowess and loyalty were beyond reproach. Determination on von Senger's part and the onset of extremely wet weather to mire the ground, hampered the Allies. Their crossing of the Volturno made slow progress and gave von Vietinghoff just sufficient time to make ready along the Garigliano.

The cost to the Germans in stretched nerves and utter weariness was not to be overlooked, however. Von Vietinghoff, struggling on the one hand to suppress a barrage of complaints from his corps commanders (which, in acrimony and defeatism, at times rivalled that of the British when they had been under pressure from Rommel in the desert) managed well to restrain the Allied advance and yet satisfy Kesselring, who was constantly overlooking his shoulders. Often he gave encouragement but also he fired in a barrage of suggestions laced with criticism when things went awry. One feels sympathy for von Vietinghoff as his last weary troops reached safety over the Garigliano at its mouth on the 4th and the C-in-C complained at the precipitate haste of the final stages of the manoeuvre. 'One cannot fight and build defences at the same time; they don't fully understand that at the top', von Vietinghoff expostulated, and requested to be sent on sick leave. At that Kesselring took charge of Tenth Army himself for forty-four hours prior to the arrival of the relief, Joachim

Lemelsen. This storm in a tea-cup, the natural product of frayed nerves, and Kesselring's granting of leave, must be recognised as a mark of understanding, not of disapproval, for he was entirely content to welcome back von Vietinghoff at the end of the year after he had recovered. Here, as on so many other occasions (including the imbroglio with Rommel), Kesselring demonstrated his acute insight into the effects of tension and a willingness, not shared by all great commanders, to take remedial action in time. He had much for which to be grateful to von Vietinghoff who, with impeccable skill, had accomplished a fine delaying action under heavy enemy pressure and brought his forces to safety, intact. Von Vietinghoff had confounded the enemy, who were assuming they would be in Rome for Christmas, and guaranteed his inexhaustible C-in-C's job. For on or about 25 October (the exact date is by no means certain) Hitler had decided at last to send Rommel elsewhere and to give Kesselring the overall command in Italy rather than despatch him to Norway.

There has been considerable speculation as to why Hitler changed his mind over Kesselring and Rommel, to which there cannot be a positive answer. Probably it was a very simple one of merit. At last the Führer, probably in agreement with Jodl, had come to realise that Kesselring was the better overall commander. Sufficiently impressed on 4 October to give Kesselring an opportunity to defend Rome, Hitler returned to the subject once more on the 17th when it was already evident that, on the terrain between the Volturno and Garigliano, Kesselring was keeping his word. Hitler gave Rommel one more chance. Would he be prepared to execute Kesselring's strategy? Rommel frankly replied that he could not assume that responsibility. Notwithstanding, Hitler permitted Rommel's appointment as originally intended and a draft order was prepared. But in the meantime he re-examined the case and then began to stall, prompted, it would seem, by Jodl whose opinion had undergone a transformation. On the 19th a member of Rommel's staff who had been told that the order of appointment had been approved was telephoned by Jodl to say, with heavy overtones, that, 'It is possible that the Führer's view . . . has undergone a fundamental change.' The order had not been signed after all. Westphal recalls Jodl's change of heart and his praise for Kesselring's handling of the Italian crisis in saying he had done better than Rommel. (Later still Jodl was to admit that he had misjudged Kesselring.) Therefore when Kesselring was called once more to see Hitler on the 25th, the outcome was probably little more than a formality. Supposition had been superseded by reality. Filled with confidence and enthusiasm he was able, quite effortlessly, finally, to convince Hitler of the justification for his proposals. On 5 November the Führer told Rommel he was to take up an appointment in France instead, and that the supreme command in Italy would devolve on Kesselring over a new Army Group C incorporating all German forces in the theatre on 21 November. At the last moment, despite several weeks too long deferred, Hitler had reached a conclusion which, much later under different circumstances, he was to explain when praising the achievements of Kesselring: '. . . it is my opinion that military leadership without optimism is not possible'.

Had there not been the delay in unifying command in Italy under one man there can be no saying what the outcome of the Salerno battle and, therefore, what the future course of the war might have been. If the total resources then available south of the Alps had been placed under Kesselring it is very likely he would have contained the Italians more economically and thus been enabled to deploy far stronger forces against the bridgehead. As it was the British and American soldiers who thus gained respite in an hour of acute peril have Hitler, Jodl and Rommel to thank for their salvation. Yet, damaging to German prospects as was Hitler's prolonged delay in making a final choice between Kesselring and Rommel, there can be no impugning his motives in giving exhaustive consideration to a vital matter. Moreover, if Kesselring had failed (and not from want of trying) to convince Hitler as to his suitability, the responsibility is partly his. Perhaps he had sounded a little too clever and had not succeeded in projecting the sort of charisma Hitler preferred in favoured commanders such as Guderian, Sepp Dietrich of the SS and Rommel. As for Rommel, he cannot be absolved from the charge of putting self-interest before the needs of the situation. *Prima facie*, he indulged in defamation of his rival in order to gratify his own ambition as well as to exorcise the grudge he had borne Kesselring since El Alamein. This is not to decry the integrity of Rommel's military assessment of the situation, which was valid. But sometimes it is necessary to draw into perspective the characters of men who have been accorded emblematic status at the expense of others. Let a few words from von Senger put Kesselring's motives in still clearer relief: '. . . I knew that his optimism and belief in the Führer was not motivated by ambition, but sprang from his innermost conviction'.

10

The Consul

The departure of Rommel and the stabilisation of the front along the Bernhardt Line (the one event marking a lasting change in Hitler's attitude, the other an opportunity to consolidate his power in Italy) inaugurated a new, if short, phase in Kesselring's career. At last he could feel secure in the Supreme Commander's favour and therefore was able to enjoy greater autonomy than any other German commander at any time of the war. While the status of his domain was of lesser importance than many others and there was to be no remittance of Hitlerian interference in operations, Kesselring, through his appointment to the joint position of C-in-C Army Group C and C-in-C South West on 21 November 1943, acquired far more extensive responsibilities than those of a field commander. By the nature of its dependence on the Germans, the Fascist so-called Socialist Republic, set up under the discredited Mussolini, had little prestige and therefore Kesselring became *de facto* ruler of the better part of Italy – a consul in almost everything except name and title.

It was a rickety kingdom which he administered (to say rule would be to go too far) from his headquarters at Monte Soratte, a realm whose frontiers were threatened at all points, either from Alexander's armies pressing hard against the Garigliano and Sangro rivers, or by a landing somewhere along the lengthy coastline, or from within by partisan forces based either in Yugoslavia or of the indigenous kind who were beginning to appear in small bands in the hills and in the urban districts. For some time, too, large parties of ex-prisoners of war, who had been released or had escaped when the Italians surrendered, roamed the countryside and these occasionally combined with the partisan bands. In fair weather, and even sometimes in foul, the air space above was the unchallenged dominion of swarms of enemy aircraft which bombed and strafed to their hearts' delight – sometimes 3,000 fighter-bomber sorties a day were counted. So the lines of communication were being cut repeatedly while movement by road, rail or sea, except by night, was perilous in the extreme. A populace that fomented with underground political activity, stirred up by the anti-fascist parties, brought upon itself a rickety civil administration which could barely function on its own and therefore depended upon the Germans for food – an obligation which Kesselring willingly accepted and implemented, when possible, by the employment of military transport. This was but one of his services to the Italians though it must not be overlooked that something of the kind was essential as a palliative to civil discontent. The skilful administrator who had reorganised the German Army's services and put the *Luftwaffe* on a sound footing, now directed his immense experience to sustaining a nation in order to secure his base areas. Soon there was hardly a German commissary who did not know that it was extremely difficult to pull the wool over the eyes of a C-in-C whose understanding of the tricks of their trade excelled their own. The black market he was compelled to tolerate otherwise, as Westphal points out, the Italians would have starved. He also did his best to protect property and the country's artistic treasures from the worst of the war's ravages although, inevitably, his civilising influence could only be partially effective. Not only would the Allies exact their share of damage but the guerrillas, grappling with the denizens of Himmler's SS who fought to counter their activities in the rearward zones, were bound to take a fearful toll that was both materially and morally destructive. Civil war of a nature he recalled from his experiences in 1919, and which he knew to be rampant in Russia and throughout the Balkans, under Communist control, threatened him.

In accordance with established German policy, the SS presence in Italy was expanded at every opportunity. Under the command of *Obergruppenführer* Karl Wolff it assumed responsibility for the security of the Italian interior, including air defence and the fight against the Partisans though not within the area occupied by the Army. There were, too, several agencies at work in the country whose primary allegiance was direct to departmental heads in Germany, instead of to the C-in-C. The Reich Foreign Labour Service's job was to transport workers to Germany, its purchasing agents employed to pick the country clean for the benefit of the German economy. Nor was the SS, intent on predominance in all spheres, content with its exclusion from the army zone. Westphal recalls a meeting between Wolff and Kesselring at which the former had suggested that the SS should take over every administrative function in addition to its police duties. 'I consider this an ideal solution', said Kesselring. 'Don't you agree Chief?' Westphal, who recognised the dangers of the SS with as much clarity as any General Staff Officer, was not to be seduced, as Kesselring, on the face of it, seems to have been, by the virtues of achieving a theoretically neat and tidy administration. Nor was he beguiled by Wolff, who to Kesselring, appeared a 'mild man'. Westphal objected vehemently, and in due course ranged the other army commanders behind him in rejecting the SS proposition.

In point of fact it is more than likely that, on this occasion as on others, Westphal failed to understand Kesselring's style of diplomacy or the irony of his remarks. Kesselring's apparent concurrence might well have been his way of exposing the flaws in Wolff's proposal, one that the SS leader was not entitled to make and which he would have been unable to implement to the full extent. But if, indeed, Kesselring was in ignorance of the true aims and methods of the SS, he was soon to be disabused. It was Himmler's subsequent barbarous intentions which converted Kesselring into an opponent, albeit in the characteristically muted way that he usually pursued when dealing with really dangerous antagonists. A proposal by Himmler in April to evacuate the population of Rome, at a time when partisan warfare was on the upsurge, was refused by Kesselring with indignation since it would cause starvation for millions of people. No doubt he heard from Westphal of the SS officer who, upon being told of the suggestion's rejection, burst out, 'You wait until after the war. Then we will deal with the General Staff.' But this did not deter Kesselring from resisting Himmler with increasing determination and deft skill. When Herbert Kappler of the Gestapo wished, on Himmler's orders, to arrest 800 Jews, Kesselring, as he said at his trial, had no authority to cancel the order but he nevertheless prevented it by the simplest form of resistance. 'We did not detail any troops for this order . . . and therefore this order was not carried out and he could not arrest these people.'

Reminded at almost every duty moment of the abundance of war's horrors, the staff at Monte Soratte did what it could to make this an oasis of culture. Though twenty-four hours never seemed long enough for a Kesselring day, he tried to make time for civilising functions, for dinner parties to which were invited (prior to the Italian debâcle) not only the members of his own staff but visiting dignatories, such as diplomats, officials and officers from adjacent headquarters and the front. Later only officers were invited and the party ended at the finish of the meal. It was all so like similar functions held by the revered Prince Rupprecht in 1918, of whom Kesselring was to write in his 'Memoirs', 'the Crown Prince dominated the conversation. Whether the topic was politics, art, geography, history or statescraft, he had a mastery of it. Whether he had the same grasp of military matters it was difficult to judge as any allusion to them was carefully avoided.' It is permissible to surmise that this was Kesselring's wry way of penning an allusion to his own erudition, either as raconteur or as soldier. The value of personal relationships and the virtue of kindnesses were paramount to him in so much that he put people first if he could. For example, it was his habit to take a more uncomfortable seat in an aeroplane so that one of his physically handicapped officers might travel more comfortably.

Governing his every moment was the task confronting him. From that he never sought to escape. According to Dietrich Beelitz, his Ia, 'About 8 o'clock in the morning the Field-Marshal received the daily reports and worked in general until midnight with a short break at lunch time. On at least three days a week, and sometimes more, the Field-Marshal went to visit units at the front . . . at dawn.' Westphal in fact complains that his master enjoyed rather too much becoming involved in detail in the daily conferences where so many people gathered to give their reports. There, he thought, the C-in-C was prone to give decisions too quickly without the benefit of repose for that extra ten minutes' thought for which he would have had time if he had been alone with his Chief of Staff. Westphal was once to remind his C-in-C that he had been engaged, after all, as Chief of Staff, not as a secretary, to which Kesselring had sadly rejoined, 'Ah well, you know. Often I would like to swap places with you and do the things you won't let me do.' Later, on his own admission, he was to say, 'I was not a superior officer who was easy to get on with – but popularity is rarely the handmaiden of command.'

In public Kesselring took care to emphasise the bipartisan nature of his appointment. The blue dress of the *Luftwaffe* he often discarded in favour of a khaki uniform of his own design, an apparel which assuaged the feelings of soldiers who had lost faith in an air force that was not only quite incapable of protecting them from attack but, as 1944 went by, could no longer acquire much in the way of warning or information about the enemy. For seventy per cent of his time the C-in-C went visiting the headquarters of each division in turn, encouraging the men under training, assessing their fighting spirit and endeavouring to make his command self-sufficient by harmonising consumption with the limited resources to be obtained from Germany. Sick men had to be brought back into the line as fighting soldiers, scattered units welded into fresh divisions. An empire of schools to train men in the special requirements of the theatre sprang up alongside depots, hospitals and

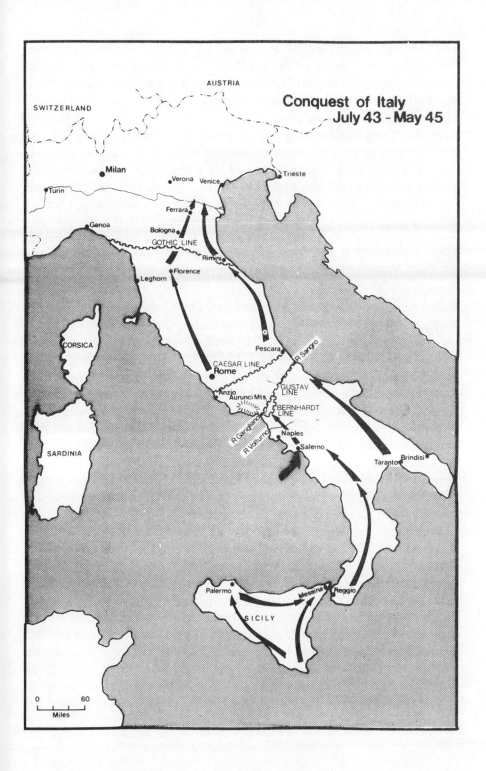

Conquest of Italy
July 43 - May 45

AUSTRIA

SWITZERLAND

Milan

Turin

Verona Venice

Trieste

Ferrara

Genoa

Bologna

GOTHIC LINE

Rimini

Leghorn Florence

CORSICA

Pescara

R Sangro

CAESAR LINE
Rome

Anzio

GUSTAV
LINE

Aurunci Mts.

BERNHARDT
LINE

SARDINIA

R Garigliano

R Volturno

Naples

Salerno

Taranto Brindisi

Palermo

Messina Reggio

SICILY

0   60
├──┼──┤
   Miles

rest centres which dwelt among a population whose burgeoning insurgency was being encouraged by Communists and multifarious resistance groups, aided and abetted by enemy agents. Not that the threat from sabotage was very serious in itself though Kesselring, like anybody else with an eye for men's morale, was deeply conscious of the sense of insecurity that could be invoked by a pernicious underground warfare and keenly aware of the psychological damage inflicted by stabs in the back.

Action at the front absorbed most of his attention, of course, since here the threat to his realm was sustained and here the ultimate collapse might come, almost unannounced, if he were to make or allow a single serious error of judgement. One slip and a strong defensive position might give way and destroy this southern buttress to Hitlerian strategy. It was his task to maintain the front at bearable cost in a campaign which had become attritional, fought across ground that was largely favourable to the defenders against a foe who, unbeknown to the Germans, was also handicapped by a deficiency of resources. Due to the deflection of Allied men and machines to other fronts, it was their task to indulge in a tactically absurd campaign with a view to diverting German troops from France where the main invasion would be launched in 1944. But it was Kesselring's determination to fight for every defensible line in Italy which made their holding operation so prohibitively expensive and therefore a dubious, wasteful kind of diversion. But for the fact that he denied his subordinates a completely free hand, their innate tactical skill might have been exploited to giving ground too readily. As it was, from each of Harold Alexander's moves, there was exacted a price the Allies could ill afford.

In the field Kesselring may well have taken chances by attempting to delay some withdrawal too long, but with Hitler he took no risks at all and unremittingly schemed to balance tactical demands with the tactful requirements of the situation – as an incident on 13 November demonstrates. When Lemelsen, whose front at San Pietro was under severe stress from the Americans, asked permission to withdraw, Kesselring had acquiesced, subject to Hitler's concurrence, adding: 'I will permit you to do anything that you convince me is right.' But no sooner had permission been received and the evacuation begun than the Führer changed his mind 'for political reasons'. 'This,' said Kesselring with embarrassed resignation to Lemelsen, 'is most unpleasant,' to which his subordinate had rejoined, with plaintive understatement, 'I do not like it either!'

The round of preliminary engagements prior to the confrontation at Cassino, of which the affair at San Pietro was just one, took the form of battles between outposts in a tussle for the outlying defences of the Bernhardt Line that abutted the main Gustav Line in the hills looming above the Rivers Garigliano and Moro. This phase was not, as Kesselring deluded the Allies to believe, a struggle for the main position itself. Two main axes of advance were offered to the Allies. Mark Clark's Fifth Army would try, on the left, to enter the Liri Valley after eliminating the bastion of Monte Cassino – after, that is, it had forced the Mignano Gap. Montgomery's Eighth Army on the right was to blast a hole through the lines held by LXXVI Panzer Corps guarding the Adriatic coast on the north bank of the River Sangro and was then to advance towards Rome through the Apennines. Lemelsen's task, carefully monitored by Kesselring, was to maintain just sufficient forces in each sector to impose delay long enough to allow reserves to be switched against major attacks, from one side of Italy to the other, along lines of communication that were constantly subject to interdiction.

Eighth Army's assault across the Sangro on 24 November had been foreseen by Kesselring who had long ago taken Montgomery's measure. Remembering the Western Front in 1917 and 1918, and with recent experience of North Africa, he had every wish to avoid a deep embroilment and to save his men from being pounded by intensive artillery fire and condemned to sweat it out in deep shelters. The adverse effect on morale of this kind of thing he knew too well and feared. So he trusted the heavy mined ground, as well as the customary frictions of war (allied to British caution), to delay the enemy and instructed Lemelsen in the supreme art of timing a withdrawal at exactly the right moment after a stiff penalty had been exacted from the attackers. Edging backwards from crest to crest, a battle of limited movement was imposed upon both sides in appalling weather with a steady rate of attrition to which Montgomery contributed with the uninspired obstinacy of his methods. At the end of a week, with British casualties at 2,000 and higher than those of the Germans, the line stood unbroken. Though Lemelsen complained bitterly and foretold the worst, Kesselring coolly kept him to the aim, and insisted upon the corps commander, Traugott Herr, making do with his own resources. For with the shrewd insight of the born commander that he was, Kesselring had judged the situation to perfection. He no more conceded the likelihood of a breakthrough than should the over-ambitious Montgomery himself, and yet read his opponent's mind exactly when he remarked to Lemelsen, 'It is true we do not want to defend Ortona decisively, but the English have made it appear as important as Rome', and – perhaps in recollection of Verdun and Vimy Ridge – 'It costs so much blood that it cannot be justified', but 'you can do nothing when things develop in this manner; it is only too bad . . . the world press makes so much of it.'

Much the same sort of prestige offensive was under way on the opposite side of the peninsula where Clark aspired to conquer the Eternal City. Here the practical limitations imposed by ground, climate and the small resources at his disposal were outweighed by ambition. Clark's attempts to open up the Mignano Gap with the associated assaults, rebuffs and fresh assaults on Monte Camino, Monte La Difensa, Monte Maggiore and Monte Lungo, produced only the slowest of progress because, as it belatedly dawned on the Allies, sheer fire power was no more likely to take mountain peaks here than it had in North Africa. Infantry manpower was essential in seizing ground that was greedy for men, and the Allies, on that front, had only five divisions to the Germans' seven – a quite inadequate balance for such an offensive, as Kesselring well understood. Already, on 4 December, and long before the Mignano Gap was finally penetrated on the 17th to give the Allies their first sight of the Gustav Line looming above the valleys of the Gari and Rapido Rivers, Kesselring judged that Rome was safe and his promise to Hitler kept.

Contrary to his behaviour with regard to other fronts, Hitler was now committed to positional warfare in Italy and the abandonment of the traditional policy of costly counter-attack whenever some minor feature was lost. And even if Hitler had not acquired complete respect for the C-in-C South West, his opponents most certainly had. Throughout the last quarter of the year they had read his signals and monitored his orders, besides interrogating prisoners and experiencing, with dismay, the frustration of butting their heads against a tough but flexible shield. The British Official History, reflecting contemporary Intelligence assessments, pays Kesselring a generous compliment as 'a formidable commander'. Gone were the sly comments of which one spoke disparagingly of his 'blarney'. In their place appeared marks of respect for a soldier of 'strong mind in assessing tactical facts, a deep understanding of tactical detail, an unfaltering spirit and a stern hold on his troops. For while quick to encourage and to praise, he was as quick to condemn and to castigate any commander or any troops whom he judged to have fallen short of a very high standard.' To the Allies, in other words, he was quite as much a handful as Rommel once had been.

To some among the Germans, Kesselring's exemplary performance warranted his employment in a more important sphere than that of a secondary theatre of war. Since 1941, Rudolf Schmundt, the Führer's chief military assistant and, by 1943, head of the Personnel Office, had been at work trying to replace certain 'entrenched' members of the High Command with officers who had recent experience of combat. In 1941 he had been among those who tried to make Guderian Commander-in-Chief of the Army in place of von Brauchitsch at a time when Guderian was endeavouring to persuade Hitler to replace Keitel as head of OKW. Instead Hitler had taken over as C-in-C himself, in addition to the job of Supreme Commander, and soon afterwards had sacked Guderian. Early in 1943, however, Guderian, at Schmundt's insistence, had been reinstated as Inspector General of Armoured Forces and towards the end of the year Schmundt, very likely in collaboration with Guderian and others, began fresh moves to oust Keitel, who was but a yes-man of the Führer. On the evidence of Albert Speer, who was a confidant of them all, Schmundt preferred Kesselring for the post, a sure indication of the esteem in which the C-in-C South West was held. Two important factors put a stop to this intrigue, however. Kesselring, it was said, could not be spared from Italy where he had become indispensable and, added Hitler, he could not do without Keitel. Keitel, he said, was so obliging. No doubt it was a lucky break for Kesselring in the long run, but on the other hand it was another clear indication of the reputation he had earned.

By the middle of January the scene had been set for what was to be, perhaps, the greatest tactical test he was ever to undergo. Everywhere his troops had retired into the Gustav Line having abandoned, to the satisfaction of von Senger, the vulnerable sectors of the Bernhardt Line. But if Kesselring reckoned, as he did, upon a period of relative calm, this expectation was soon to be violently shattered.

As long ago as 8 November, General Eisenhower had initiated planning under Alexander for an amphibious landing south of Rome that would trap the Germans holding the Gustav Line. The beaches of Anzio had been selected as the most suitable place though nothing was to be attempted until Clark's Fifth Army was ready to assault across the Garigliano on a wide front, conditions which were not achieved until Kesselring chose to back into the fortified mountains behind the Garigliano and Rapido Rivers. Of the Allied plan, as it evolved, the Germans knew nothing and so they could hardly have guessed at the clash of aims between Alexander, who placed the prior emphasis on the landing to erect a barrier across the German communications, deep inland, and of Clark, who saw the landings only as a distraction from the main thrust by his armies into the commanding heights on either side of the Liri approach route. By 17 January, when all was ready, von Vietinghoff was back in command of Tenth Army and could operate in the comfortable assurance that he was well insured by a reserve of two divisions belonging to I Parachute Corps, situated adjacent to Rome, plus a newly formed Fourteenth Army (Eberhard von Mackensen) that was under training in Northern Italy. Surprise there might be in time and place but hardly in terms of disproportionate numbers.

When the British X Corps launched its attack across the lower reaches of the Garigliano on 17 January it certainly did achieve surprise and, moreover, a far deeper penetration of the German defences than either von Vietinghoff or von Senger felt acceptable. The Germans had put too much trust in mines, had too few troops in that sector and were off balance. Therefore, as is commonplace on such occasions, Kesselring became the immediate target for their screams asking for the immediate commitment of reserves – the two divisions at Rome in this case. Von Senger, in order to save time, telephoned his personal request to Kesselring direct, by-passing von Vietinghoff. As so frequently in the past, Kesselring was dependent, in the absence of sound intelligence, upon the inspired reasoning alone of that 'strong mind in assessing tactical facts'. Convinced that the main direction of the Allies was pointed up the Liri Valley and, as he said to von Vietinghoff, 'we are now facing the greatest crisis yet encountered', he initially dismissed the British attack as a subsidiary diversion, prior to the main assault. This he correctly visualised as being likely to come over the Rapido, to the south of Cassino. As to the wisdom of retaining the two divisions at Rome as an anti-invasion force, any qualms in that respect had already been dissipated; although radio intelligence and air reconnaissance had disclosed signs of Allied preparations, Admiral Canaris had once more volunteered a categorical denial that any such thing was in prospect. So Kesselring had merely to decide whether or not the British attack was a major diversion or part of a full-blooded offensive, and whether or not his subordinates at the front were overestimating the danger. On the morning of the 18th he concluded that, at least, it was a serious threat and, without further hesitation, sent the two reserve divisions to that front, thereby stripping himself of an immediate reserve and temporarily exposing Rome. Alarming though the repercussions were to be, this was not the unreasonable gamble that some commentators, in hindsight, have made it out. The German defences along the Rapido and on the heights above Cassino, dominated as they were by the Benedictine monastery and by the higher peaks beyond, were not, as events disclosed, wholly secure. When the 36th American Division crossed the Rapido on the 20th and suffered a massacre on the river banks, its lack of support by flanking British formations (and therefore its failure) was in large part due to the impact of the two reserve German divisions against the British. Nor was Kesselring wholly unprepared for a seaborne invasion since a plan called 'Richard' made provision for elements from every disengaged formation to be sent to the threatened point at the shortest notice. Of vital importance to his assessment was a confirmed impression of his opponents' ineptitude, a disrespect that accrued not in the least from denigration of their courage or combat ability, nor from a lack of organising genius or shortage of material – all of which previously had been demonstrated as in abundant supply. It was simply that he perceived* an ingrained rigidity and reluctance among Allied generals to take risks, as exemplified by their tendency to play safe when, by incurring relatively high initial casualties and taking a calculated gamble, they could, in the longer run, have won a cheaper overall victory. Finally, and this cannot be overstated, Kesselring must have trusted in some measure to luck, knowing that all the Great Captains in history had possessed this blessing to a greater or lesser extent, guessing, perhaps, that this alone would compensate for this material and numerical inferiority. Good fortune was also on his side that January when, again, he was shot down, his aeroplane finishing up in a pond to his amusement at appearing, on a visit to von Vietinghoff, coated in slime. News of this came as a surprise to Westphal who first heard of it from Jodl who rang up for confirmation of a British claim over the radio.

He certainly needed all the luck in the world on 22 January, even though, by then, the two divisions from Rome had done their bit in checking a X British Corps attack at Sant'Ambrogio on the 20th and thus deprived the ill-fated 36th U.S. Division of success. But Rome lay unguarded, the beaches at Anzio almost unwatched. Moreover the C-in-C himself was caught napping, lulled into a false sense of security until he heard the landing had actually taken place at dawn.

It was 0300 hours, an hour after the first troops came ashore behind a noisy naval bombardment in the dark, before Kesselring heard the first report of the virtually unopposed landing, and another three hours before he had mustered sufficient information to appraise the event for what it was – a full-scale invasion. Westphal says that his commander's first impression was one of anger – probably, one suggests, at being made to look foolish. His reactions, however, displayed an exemplary grasp of the situation allied to a cool deliberation which takes the breath away. For a

*Amply corroborated by contemporary records and not just by those opinions he gave after the war.

start von Vietinghoff received a shock when he called that evening to ask, as a matter of course, for the immediate abandonment of the Gustav Line and to be told quite positively that nothing of the sort would be permitted. This was the play of a gambler because at that moment Kesselring fully expected the enemy to cut the two main supply routes within the next forty-eight hours. At the same time he was on the verge of recognising once more that fatal hesitancy in the Allied advance. By last light they had come two miles inland but already were digging in. Already, too, the leading German troops, converging on Anzio from all over Italy (as well as France and Yugoslavia), were being guided towards the most vulnerable points to fill the wider gaps until a screen of infantry, backed by anti-aircraft guns, were ready to deter, if not stop, the next Allied advance. It was like April 1917 at Arras all over again except that now it was he who played Rupprecht in the drama. When the enemy advance began again it was more in the nature of patrolling activity than a full-blooded drive stretching out for objectives deep in the German rear; and so, at once, Kesselring's tentative recognition of enemy inertia was confirmed as a fact upon which subsequent plans could be based. By the evening of the 23rd a determined German line barred the way to the Alban Hills with all manner of diverse units from different formations rubbing shoulders with each other – controlled, at first, by General Mälzer, the Rome Garrison Commandant, next by HQ 1 Parachute Corps, and eventually by von Mackensen's Fourteenth Army brought down from the north. Kesselring then felt safe to tell von Vietinghoff that he 'believed the danger of a large-scale expansion of the beach-head was no longer imminent'. Experience and luck had been his salvation indeed.

The failure of the Allied generals to take advantage of an unrivalled opportunity to shatter the carefully prepared Gustav Line and, probably, to destroy a large part of von Vietinghoff's army, throws into sharp relief the underlying differences between Kesselring's style of generalship and that of his opponents. Neither the Allied Army Group Commander, Alexander, nor the Army Commander, Clark, put strong pressure on the Anzio assault commander, John Lucas, to press fast and furiously inland – a manoeuvre which Westphal estimated would have been irresistible on the 23rd. All three Allied generals, with the spectre of Salerno fresh in their memories, were determined, before all else, to establish a solidly defended beach-head from which they could not be bundled into the sea. Though Clark would speak and send messages to Lucas, calling for aggression, he declined, until it was far too late, to impose a sense of urgency upon a subordinate. Had Kesselring been in

Clark's place there is little doubt that Lucas would have been made to move inland or invited to make way for his successor. While it was true that the Germans subscribed to the same conventions of sanctity of a commander's position as did the Americans, they were never enslaved by it – Kesselring least of all, as Nehring, for example, had discovered in rather similar circumstances. But Kesselring, let it be emphasised, had at this time only Germans to consider whereas Alexander, Clark and Lucas had to make allowance for the susceptibilities of Allies – just as had Kesselring in the days when he, too, was accused of being an Italophile and too cautious. In the aftermath it was the British General Maitland Wilson who put his finger on the root of Allied adversity and, by implication, awarded Kesselring the palm for superior generalship when he ascribed the failure to a 'Salerno complex'. In other words, the jolt administered by the German counter-offensive at Salerno had reverberated in their favour at Anzio. It says even more for Kesselring's superior determination that, although taken by surprise, he and von Mackensen were, by the end of the month, sufficiently restored to contemplate an immediate counter-offensive of dimensions large enough to encourage them to hope for the expulsion of the invaders – a project which was forestalled by a mere forty-eight hours by a long-delayed Allied offensive on 30th January. Only now did the beach-head erupt with the intensive combat that ought to have been in evidence from the start. But with both sides now present in almost equal strength, their offensives could but lead to minor, though costly, realignments of the front, neither having the strength to make decisive gains.

This is not the place to describe in detail the battles for the Gustav Line. These have received full coverage on the pages of many books devoted to their exposition. Here there is space alone to draw attention to a few crucial episodes in the drama that enfolded the Italian front throughout the remainder of the year and to explain Kesselring's part in its major episodes. As both he and Hitler had agreed, a gradual retreat the length of Italy was unavoidable. It was mainly a matter of spinning it out, fighting for every yard for as long as possible. Already, by the beginning of February, Kesselring had kept his promise to deny access to the northern Apennines for six months. Every battle won at the Sangro, at Cassino and at Anzio, added laurels to his crown. But attached to each chaplet was the blight of a destruction which weighed heavily upon his conscience.

The civilised instincts within Kesselring, his appreciation of beautiful things and sympathy with the glories of the past, engendered a bitter irony in that fate thrust upon him responsibility for destruction in Italy, the home of a culture he deeply admired. Who can say what horrors and damage might have been avoided had Rommel succeeded in imposing his strategy upon that of Kesselring? Far fewer churches and ancient buildings might have been destroyed where they happened to stand on ground of excellent defensive character, and almost certainly the monastery rearing above Cassino would have escaped serious harm. Paradoxical factors such as these can only rarely influence a commander in the choice of the ground he must defend but, once the duty to do so is made plain, some commanders do all in their power to mitigate the effects. That Kesselring bore this aesthetic duty in mind is unchallengeable, even though his other motives over subsequently preserving Rome, Florence and Bologna from violation may well have been those of political, administrative and military expediency.* In the case of the Benedictine monastery at Cassino there was the narrowest margin of choice. Because it stood at the pinnacle of a key point in the strongest of defensive positions, it provided the most vital observation post overlooking a vast plain over which the Allies had to come if they chose to approach Rome via the Liri Valley. From the outset both the Germans and the Allies were conscious of its aesthetic, emotional and, let there be no shirking it, propaganda value. Neither side wished to harm the place; above all they did not want to be saddled with the censure for doing so. But the Germans could no more exclude it from their defences than the Allies could be expected to resist the temptation to occupy it themselves. These things the leaders of both sides had recognised long before Hitler took the decision, in mid-November, to incorporate the hill in the Gustav Line. A month previously the Germans had persuaded the monks to permit the removal of the art and literary treasures to greater safety in Rome. They explained that damage to the building's main fabric was almost inevitable – indeed it had already been struck, accidentally, by Allied bombs on 10 October. HQ Tenth Army had been the first to grasp firmly the nettle when they asked Kesselring on 7 December for a ruling on the probity of occupying the building itself, to which Kesselring had replied in practically the only way he could – that he had informed the Roman Catholic Church that his men *would not enter the precincts*. Tenth Army's instructions to von Senger repeated the prohibition but added: 'This means only that the building alone is to be spared.'

*Kesselring's policy in regard to the desolation and preservation of the countryside is clearly revealed in an order to Tenth Army, dated 20 September 1943, in which the removal of valuable industrial machinery is demanded along with the thorough demolition of all communications, power plants, water and food supplies as well as docks. Historic buildings, museums, churches, monasteries and hospitals were to be spared, however.

Joint efforts by French and American troops nearly took the monastery in the first week of February, while the violent grapple on the slopes of Monastery Hill and the adjoining peaks set the style for even fiercer battles to come. But because the brave Americans of 34th and 36th Divisions were stopped just short of the culminating objectives by the gallant and dedicated German parachutists, at the crucial moment when the Allied offensive at Anzio had come to an end, Kesselring found himself in the enviable position of being able to claim that he had contained the enemy without withdrawing troops from the Gustav Line. It did not require Hitler's urging to convince him that Cassino and the monastery could, and therefore must, be held. Moreover the tactical reverse which had been inflicted upon his opponents also wrecked their strategy. Since the Allies were committed to offensive action in Italy in order to prevent the Germans reinforcing their other fronts, fresh, less well prepared direct assaults, in which brute force took precedence over subtlety, had to be launched quickly elsewhere. The monastery was to be eliminated by fire power, regardless of the lesson of history as to the improbability of this method shifting determined defenders. Lacking too was a properly co-ordinated plan since the application to the task of 250 bombers, supplemented by heavy artillery fire, on 15 February would be unrelated to an *immediate* assault on the ruins. By the time the New Zealand and Indian infantry did climb towards it on the 17th the Germans had occupied the rubble and were better placed than ever to inflict a costly repulse. Meanwhile the propagandists were enjoying a field day, each side heaping calumny on the other with the Germans making good use of a superior case until, almost as usual, they overstepped the mark. Post-war analysis has exonerated Kesselring from blame for this act of desecration and he makes a valid military point when he says of a bombardment, of which the sole purpose was destruction, that it was 'prejudicial to the subsequent conduct of the battle'.

This episode, nevertheless, assumed relative unimportance beside two cataclysimic events in March – the outcome of von Mackensen's offensive to eliminate the Anzio beach-head and the first major incident in the simmering partisan war, each of which changed Kesselring's destiny. At Anzio the abortive Allied offensive of early February seemed to create promising conditions for a major counter-attack which would depend upon providing enough good troops and correctly timing the assault when the weather was so bad that enemy fire power might be nullified. This Kesselring proposed but, unfortunately for the Germans, their Führer's sudden willingness to send valuable resources to a secondary theatre of war as a reversal of strategy, carried with it his insistence upon dictating the methods employed. When Hitler jumped to the conclusion that a victory at Anzio might delay, if not deter, the forthcoming Allied invasion of North West Europe, he sent armoured vehicles, aircraft and the élite Infantry *Lehr* Regiment straight from Germany. The everyday task of the latter was demonstrating theoretical assault techniques, but only half its complement was battle-experienced and none of the men were acclimatised to Italy. Hitler also gave detailed instructions for the tactics to be employed, prescribing an assault on a narrow front supported by the sort of artillery barrage he remembered so well from the trenches during the First World War. A bad plan; insufficient artillery ammunition; spasmodic air support by a reinforced *Luftwaffe* component that still could raise only 160 sorties per day at peak and had but twenty-five of the up-to-date FW 190 fighters; and the crushing artillery fire returned by the enemy, condemned the Germans to disaster. Initial penetrations by the experienced 4th Parachute Division could not be exploited and the *Lehr* Regiment crumbled under fire – though Kesselring makes far too much of this debâcle, presumably to foist upon Hitler a share of the blame even though he, Kesselring, accepted it for himself as the penalty for not resisting Hitler's intervention.

As the offensive finally died away, subsequent to a staunch revival early in March, Germany's incapacity to continue the war much longer stood revealed. When Hitler breached precedent after the battle by calling fifteen relatively junior officers to his headquarters for interrogation, it was possible he was looking for information but more likely that he was also searching for a scapegoat. Kesselring responded with the classic defence, getting in the first word by sending Westphal to Hitler on 6 March. Westphal in his 'Memoirs' claims that he went at his own request to expound the subject of Germany's inherent weakness, and that Kesselring prevaricated at this suggestion by preferring a memorandum – a course which Westphal knew would be foredoomed since the paper would simply find its way into a filing cabinet. He says Kesselring then fell back on his next line of defence, pleading that 'Hitler had such terrible worries and it was unfair to ask to see him'. When Westphal prevailed and eventually had a long audience with the Führer, he was accused of being the man who criticised the brave soldiers. In his 'Memoirs' he gives the impression of having failed to put over the point of the need to end the war, though in his contributions to the post-war American studies there emerges a rather different angle in that, on his return to Italy on the 8th, he was 'elated with the praise received and the understanding reached' that another attack at Anzio was out of the question for the time being. As the American Official History pointedly remarks, 'Kesselring had counted on Hitler's understanding'. Moreover he was already planning additional defensive systems behind the Gustav Line, well knowing that the current lull would not be of long duration and that impending withdrawal was a certainty.

It is necessary to re-explore the relationship between Kesselring and Hitler at this point since it may well have advanced a stage further as the result of Anzio. His marked reluctance to engage in a headlong collision with Hitler needs explanation even though it is common sense for any subordinate to avoid being constantly at loggerheads with his superior officer. For a start, of course, it is arguable that Kesselring did burke the issue. More likely is it that he, as usual, sought to gain his ends by indirect dialectic infiltration and most unlikely that he stood back out of cowardice or excessive adulation of Hitler. Undoubtedly he retained some of his original gratitude and residual loyalty for a man who, ten years before, had been Germany's saviour from chaos. Most Germans still did feel that way at that time. One is led to the conclusion that, although Kesselring knew perfectly well that Germany was going irretrievably downhill, there was nothing within his power to arrest that descent. It can be said that, from the periphery of the Italian theatre, he was ill-placed to delve in affairs at the centre – even had he the time to do so which, as a commander engaged upon an exacting task, seems most unlikely. Therefore he adopted the only course open by sticking fast to his duty and trying to preserve whatever assets remained in the Micawberish hope that a few scraps that survived might later be incorporated one day into the foundations of a reconstructed nation. This was the philosophy of those many prominent men within the hierarchy who persevered rather than resigned and who rejected a *putsch* aimed at Hitler and the Nazi regime, recognising in the *putsch* a reversion to the detested anarchy of the past. Alongside his contemporaries, however, Kesselring was almost unique. Whereas they could rarely bend the Führer to their wishes, he could wheedle disproportionate facilities for his own use by playing on the dictator's confidence with far greater skill than had Rommel in the aftermath of the fall of Tobruk in 1942. For in February 1944 Kesselring had caused a sudden turnabout in German strategy by playing on Hitler's sentiments in inviting him to gamble. And by so doing he also played into the Allies' hands by directing strength from the primary fronts to a secondary one.

The outbreak of partisan warfare also created a diversion, besides reviving his raw memories of revulsion at past excesses of 1919 and 1920, and the implications of these things becoming associated with civil war. A warning note sounded loud and clear when he returned from the front on the evening of 23 March, tired but uplifted after spending an anxious day near Cassino where the latest Allied attempt to take Monastery Hill was beginning to fade away in the face of another superb display of determination by the *Luftwaffe*'s parachute troops. He was met by Westphal with the news that a bomb, detonated by insurgents in the Via Rasella in Rome, had killed thirty-two German SS policemen along with eight Italian civilians and wounded about sixty-eight (the figures are those given at Kesselring's court-martial at Venice in 1947). Kesselring was shaken and at once feared that this was the signal for the collapse of a truce he had concluded with the partisans and a renewal of the assault at Anzio to coincide with the offensive at Cassino. Tired as he was, he insisted upon time on his own for thought, well knowing that the incident might be the signal for the end of the truce he had arranged with the Italians and that an inevitable escalation of violence bordering on civil war must follow any repressions he committed. It seems that he was aware that a Communist-controlled Patriotic Action Group was behind the incident, and this must have influenced his judgement, but he at once temporised when Westphal informed him that the primary reaction from Hitler was to order the shooting of hostages in the ratio of fifty for every dead German. Throughout the day Beelitz and Westphal had been endeavouring to mitigate the scale of retribution that was at first proposed. A plan by Mälzer to blow up houses they vetoed and gradually the ratio of executions was reduced from fifty to thirty and finally ten to one in accordance with the statutory figure laid down by Keitel for all such outrages and which had long ago been publicised on posters. But although Kesselring was by no means averse to some form of retribution (as emerged at his trial) legally he was not *responsible* for what took place. The execution order came straight from Hitler, via Jodl, to the local SD chief Herbert Kappler (who as a member of Himmler's Gestapo was decidedly not under Kesselring's command even though he operated within the Army's zone of responsibility). It was Kappler whose SD men carried out the shooting in the Ardeatine Caves of 335 Italians and Jews who were already lingering in local jails, doomed to a man, according to what Kappler told Kesselring in distinctly misleading terms. Indeed, it was this information which, to some extent, salved Kesselring's conscience – he might have felt even better justified had he known that the chief organiser of the guilty group was among those despatched. It seems, however, that he was unaware of the presence of Jews Kappler had seized to make up the requisite number.

After the war Kesselring was to write at length about the ethics and effects of partisan warfare, describing it as a gross breach of international law, a subject to which his attention was to be increasingly drawn after April when preparations for yet another Allied offensive began gradually to appear along with the outbreak of the guerrilla warfare he had feared. The underground war was to wax and wane in direct relation to the measure of success gained by the Allied armies in their prosecution of orthodox combat and provide background to everything in which he was engaged from that moment along with the rapid decline in the conduct of the struggle to which nearly all the participants were committed. Soon, too, it would become merged with the long-standing partisan civil war in Yugoslavia. But the ethics neither he nor anybody else would resolve, by writing, any more than the man who placed that bomb would win the war. In the end nobody was wholly innocent, but the vanquished would foot the bill.

11

Reputations at Stake

When Harold Alexander threw the co-ordinated weight of his Fifth and Eighth Armies against the Gustav Line on 11 May and broke the German resistance, he may have achieved far more than he had thought possible. For, carefully though he had concealed his preparations and assiduously though he schemed to mislead Kesselring, the hope that he would find his opponent totally beguiled must have outraged credulity. Though Kesselring was constrained to say to von Vietinghoff on the 11th, as the latter and von Senger departed to Germany for leave and a course of instruction in ideology, 'I feel we have done all that is humanly possible', he probably sensed in himself the peril in which his armies stood though, certainly, without comprehending the magnitude of the threat. An impotent *Luftwaffe* which could neither gather adequate information nor strike at the enemy, had reduced him to the state of a blind man groping for guidance. The sheer impracticability of identifying enemy formations at the front rendered comprehensive synthesis impossible. Of radio intercepts, of course, there was a plethora deliberately supplied by the Allies to satisfy Kesselring's known addiction to this source of intelligence and framed so as to simulate another amphibious landing somewhere along the Tyrrhenean coast. Kesselring fell for the ruse and detached three high-quality divisions to guard the beaches near Leghorn against an invasion which, had he known it, was quite out of the question since nearly all the available enemy landing craft had been transferred to Britain for use in the impending invasion of Normandy in June. Anxiously Kesselring yearned for prisoners to help reveal the location of enemy assault divisions as they entered the line. He and his subordinates, as the Canadian Official History puts it, 'demanded, ordered and pleaded for the taking of prisoners'. But few came their way and those who did gave little assistance. The arrival at the front of the Poles, the Canadians and the

French, whom the Germans most feared as the best Allied assault troops, was shrouded in mystery.

So, on 11 May, there seemed little danger. Not only were von Vietinghoff, von Senger and the latter's Chief of Staff absent, but Westphal was in hospital recovering from an operation. Kesselring's divisions, moreover, were ill-deployed since, in addition to the three diverted to Leghorn, five belonging to Fourteenth Army, plus two in reserve, were set to watch only four Allied divisions at Anzio and only nine held the Gustav Line against the fifteen Alexander had deployed with a massive preponderance of fire power. Weakest of all were the Aurunci Mountains, which were to be assailed by the French; they were far too thinly held.

There is not the slightest evidence that Kesselring or anybody on his staff seriously suspected at any time that their signals were being translated by 'Ultra'. When Alexander's attacks fell upon lightly guarded sectors or at the weak joints dividing formations, it was assumed that the enemy had gained this information from conventional sources of the kind that the Germans themselves had employed for so long and so well. They simply could not bring themselves to credit the enemy with the ability to read Enigma or to possess an intelligence system that was superior to their own. Tragically for them, it was their own commander, whenever he felt compelled to send long explanatory signals to Hitler (as so often was essential in order to win his way) who gave the most away. Each of Kesselring's long-range radio messages was overheard and gleefully intercepted by his opponents. Only when he restricted communication to letters, telephone calls and personal contacts was it secure.

By the time the absent German senior officers had returned to their posts (the British diligently picking up the signal telling von Vietinghoff to come back) the disruption of the Gustav Line was complete and Kesselring had embarked upon a reluctant retreat that was to last five months. In the ensuing days they were to be ruled by his niggardly unwillingness to give up ground. Each crisis would divulge some fresh insight into Kesselring's steadily evolving prowess as a commander, allied to a quite inflexible dedication of purpose. Driving him on was the inherent professionalism that had governed his entire career, while at the back of his mind there lurked the realisation that whatever he might be allowed to achieve for his country would depend upon maintaining his reputation with Hitler from whom all power emanated. It was this which shaped his course and not, as Westphal has suggested, that the virtue of hanging on to Rome had taken a hold on Kesselring's determination.

This battle, so far as he was concerned, opened in the same way as the invasion at Salerno, with the delivery by the enemy of several hundred tons of bombs on his own headquarters and that of Tenth Army, with serious damage to the communication installations of the latter and an unsteadying effect upon the occupants. Not that there are indications of unsteadiness on Kesselring's part, ignorant though he was of a situation in flux that led to the next crisis on the evening of the 15th. Although his soldiers had fought with exemplary courage, and not a little local success in many places, they were being overborne by an enemy whose strength and objectives he had no time to appraise. On the 14th Kesselring complained bitterly to von Vietinghoff that 'It is an intolerable condition when a division remains in the dark for one and a half days about the events in its sector'. By then, however, he was becoming mistily aware that the French were infiltrating deep into the Aurunci Mountains and that the British and Canadians were through the Gustav Line and driving up the Liri Valley. With prior approval from OKW it became but a formality to ask von Vietinghoff on the 15th if withdrawal to the next bound – the Senger or Dora Line (once known as the Hitler Line) – was necessary and for von Vietinghoff to say that it was, adding that Cassino must also be abandoned. But though there was no hesitation in giving the order it was not Kesselring's intention to allow divisions *carte blanche*. When the 94th, hard pressed by the Americans on the coast, was told by its commander to 'scatter' and make for the rear, Kesselring caustically told Fritz Wentzell, von Vietinghoff's Chief of Staff, 'I can tell you frankly, I can't call anything like that tactics.'

Spring rain came to his aid as the enemy drew near to the Senger Line. Repeated complaints by von Mackensen when it became necessary to begin stripping the Anzio defences in order to reinforce von Vietinghoff (one of whose divisions, the 71st, was down to 100 infantry) began to test his patience and arouse his ire when the departure of those reinforcements was delayed. Sometimes, it is true, von Vietinghoff was denied prompt help because the information Kesselring worked on arrived too late, but the failure of 29th Panzer Division to appear on time on the 20th was – shades of von Arnim in Tunisia – entirely due to von Mackensen withholding its departure. Tersely though Kesselring in his 'Memoirs' would declare how 'I could sympathise with his reluctance to part with his reserves but in this phase of the battle I could not admit his arguments . . .', already he was contemplating a drastic enforcement of discipline. Nor, unhappily, were the soldiers consistently attaining the exacting standards he expected of them. When the 90th Panzer Grenadier

Division fought with exemplary brilliance Kesselring said, with emotion, to von Vietinghoff, 'one could cry with admiration'. He added, with reference to 26th Panzer Division after a bad lapse, 'in the case of others with rage!' Yet, the British arriving at the Senger Line, which they hoped to take on the run, hit the old German intransigence in defence, expressed in a miserly unwillingness to give ground. Heavy rains and the enforced need for the enemy to pause to mount a renewed, full-scale assault once more won valuable time for Kesselring, while von Vietinghoff completed a relatively tidy retreat, clean contrary to the expectations of von Senger who had foretold doom. The time had arrived for Alexander to break out from the Anzio beach-head, an operation which was launched on 22 May against von Mackensen's weakened Fourteenth Army in an assault that did not at first make much ground and cost the Americans appalling losses both in men and machines. A day later the Canadians in Eighth Army cracked the Senger Line and poured up the Liri Valley with the French keeping pace on their left and the Americans forging along the coastal road. Once more the Allies were abetted by Hitler who, on the 24th, steadfastly declined to allow more than 'a step-by-step withdrawal', preferring, in fact, with the consent of Army Group, that no retreat should be made at all without his consent. This placed Kesselring in a dreadful predicament, for having failed to overcome Hitler's obduracy in advance he had now, in sympathetic consultation with von Vietinghoff, to save his men by subterfuge despite the Führer's instructions. To von Vietinghoff on the 20th Kesselring said (not for the first time) 'It is the Führer's explicit order and also my belief that we must bleed the enemy to exhaustion by hard fighting. You have always been optimistic; why has your attitude changed now?' In his turn von Vietinghoff passed on Kesselring's orders with exemplary firmness.

Regardless of their deplorable situation in 1944, the main body of the German nation and their leaders stood firmly behind their Führer; his word was law. Some there might be who plotted his overthrow but those in high office gambled with their lives if they challenged him openly. Commands such as Kesselring repeatedly gave in this mode would, by their reiteration, cement his authority while Hitler was in power. All came to understand and accept that his loyalty to the Führer, by oath, was absolute. So the belief in his Nazi leanings became embodied in a legend. Not that this would have been sufficiently convincing to secure the respect he received from strong-minded and able subordinates at the time they realised that, while he was determined to see the Führer's will was done, he was fighting with every atom of ingenuity to obtain exemptions from

Hitler's misplaced directives to save them from the Führer's follies. If, after the war, von Vietinghoff was to write, 'Field-Marshal Kesselring tended to over-estimate their [the reserves] achievement and also their potentialities regarding time and space because of his scanty experience in the immediate leadership of ground troops. Furthermore he loved the rigid defence', then it can only be stated that he was ignorant of the facts, deficient in understanding of the problem and probably merely joining the chorus of those biased officers who were in ignorance of Kesselring's very considerable previous involvement in defensive operations in two wars. To do von Vietinghoff justice, however, he does go on to admit that it was impossible for him to assess the influence that OKW might have had on Kesselring's conduct of the battle. How could he know from a superior officer who kept his own counsel?

On this occasion it was the enemy who again saved them all. The rupture of the Anzio perimeter on the 25th (the day Westphal had finally to relinquish Chief of Staff due to his health) gave Clark the opportunity to make for Valmontone and place himself astride the Tenth Army's lines of communication. Instead he put the immortality of his reputation first and made for Rome – to be blocked temporarily by von Mackensen on the slopes of the Alban Hills with the intention of allowing von Vietinghoff to come back in safety to the next delaying position – the Caesar Line. A reprieve, prised out of Hitler by Jodl on Kesselring's behalf in the nick of time, enabled von Vietinghoff to evade the immediate danger and also gave his men the opportunity to prepare a number of minor delaying positions in the approaches to the Caesar Line in compliance with Kesselring's tart reminder that Hitler's concession was not an excuse to 'reach it as soon as possible'. The enemy, he said, must still be made to fight for every foot – but for only a few days, as Kesselring must surely have expected. For at each stop-line the issue was resolved not so much by assault as by the battering of a thousand guns which the enemy could deploy and supply with an endless stock of ammunition quite unchecked by the *Luftwaffe*.

The Caesar Line was not, therefore, a position of the enduring kind but its survival might have been prolonged had von Mackensen managed to hold the Alban Hills, as Kesselring wished him to do in order to allow Tenth Army more time to escape. But von Mackensen insisted upon deploying his main strength in the open country of the coastal sector, leaving a quite inadequate guard in the hills which, as Kesselring remarks, could have been held by a battalion at first. The men fought well but a widening gap opened up between Tenth and Fourteenth Army which von

Senger's XIV Panzer Corps, brought back too late by Kesselring, was unable to fill. The Americans drove through the Alban Hills, the Eternal City beckoning them from the distance. Desperately Kesselring pressed von Mackensen to react positively to a threat whose direction was all too apparent, but von Mackensen was grimly stubborn in his belief that it was he who had divined the enemy's intention more accurately than Kesselring. Fundamental differences of temperament in addition to those of opinion had divided von Mackensen and Kesselring. The son of a former field-marshal whose views and actions, as Westphal has remarked, were conditioned only by military and never by political considerations, complained that Kesselring 'over-estimated his prowess as a battle leader' – a comment which, it is interesting to recall, was so very similar to that of an indignant III Army Corps commander in Nürnberg in 1919. Kesselring, for his part, took the view that von Mackensen did not demand enough of his troops. The tension that had long existed between them on wholly professional matters, again as Westphal points out, never descended to personal abuse. They remained friends and it may be taken that it was with regret, *after* the defeat of von Mackensen's army was complete (though its total annihilation was averted), Kesselring took the final step of sacking von Mackensen on the 6 June and replacing him with Lemelsen.

Three days previously, when it became quite apparent that Rome could no longer be defended, Kesselring had made formal application to OKW to abandon the city, and at the same time issued orders for its evacuation which came into operation prior to approval being received: there can be no clearer example of his easy relationship with Hitler than at this time. He knew it was permissible to give up Rome without a struggle, leaving all the bridges within the city intact though demolishing those outside, before drawing off reluctantly to the north. This was his long-held policy and endorsed by Hitler. Moreover his insistent demands, couched as a plea for rescue from a desperate situation, obtained for him five new divisions from various corners of Europe, and even from France where the main Allied invasion was imminent. This was counter-productive, once more, to Germany's grand strategy of exhausting the enemy, for while it is true that the Battle for Rome had cost the Allies 42,000 men and the Germans only some 25,000, the judgement of Warlimont is entirely valid when he categorised Hitler's order 'to reconstitute the front north of Rome as far south as possible', instead of economising in manpower by rapidly pulling back to the Apennine position – the Gothic Line – as 'dancing to the enemy's tune'.

How despondent were Kesselring's genuine feelings is difficult to assess. With several of his divisions below strength, from between fifty and ten per cent in men, and badly depleted with regard to equipment, there was the mounting toll by the enemy air forces which ravaged the transport system and destroyed so many reinforcements before they reached the front. In this had to be included the inroads into his strength wrought by the partisan war. There was, too, the danger of civil war. An increasing number of scattered guerrilla incidents in April, mostly in the north, had provoked the inevitably violent SS counter-measures. These were perpetrated by Wolff on personal orders from Himmler, over Kesselring's head. He shot those who looked likely to be most responsible. On 1 May a state of partisan war, such as had riddled the Russian and Yugoslavian theatres of war for so long, had perforce to be recognised by Kesselring in Italy. At Kesselring's request, in the interests of operational and administrative efficiency, as well as, to Himmler's expressed anger, to check the SS, Keitel sent a signal precisely designating duties in the partisan struggle to come. Kesselring was made responsible for 'the highest leadership', but the underground war's conduct was placed in the hands of Wolff and his 'Guerrilla Warfare Operations Staff' who was 'subordinate directly' to Kesselring. Combat duties were shared between the SS and Police in those areas where the Army was not involved – that is within the nineteen-mile zone behind the front, the coastal areas and those districts where army units were in preponderance, located in reserve or under training. For the remainder of May the level of partisan activity had remained temperate but, concurrent with the Allied invasion of Normandy on 6 June, two days after Rome had fallen, the resistance movements received from the Allies a general broadcast enjoining them to kill Germans and disrupt communications everywhere. The fact that the scattered ambushes and demolitions which occurred merely placed a further burden on the retreat of Army Group C was of lesser importance than the principles involved. Kesselring had to keep the uprising within bounds and, as everybody who has ever been associated with such phenomena must know (as he most assuredly had), that demanded the implementation of repressive measures which, because they grew harsher, bred emotional outbursts with escalating effects of a horrific nature.

The evidence adduced at the Nürnberg Trials paints a picture of his patience being forced out of control. He felt compelled to give orders to combat a type of warfare which, by the Hague Convention, was illegal, but in so doing he compounded a struggle that had long ago relapsed into a barbarity which transcended the worst excesses of the Middle Ages. Yet, enmeshed by excesses and sorely provoked it can nevertheless be shown that he did counsel restraint.

On 17 June an order of his, recognising the threat posed by the recent deterioration, called for the fight against the partisans to be prosecuted 'with all the means at our disposal and with the utmost severity. I will protect any commander who exceeds our usual restraint on the choice of severity of the methods he adopts against partisans. In this connection the old principle stands that a mistake in the choice of methods in executing one's orders is better than failure or neglect to act.' Three days later, in yet another order for operational reasons, he spelled out his meaning: 'whenever there is evidence of considerable numbers of partisan groups, a proportion of the male population of the area will be arrested; and in the event of an act of violence being committed, these men will be shot'. At his trial he said he did not rate these orders as an incitement to violence. Without adequate rebuttal the prosecution was able to show that these lax orders, probably the products of hasty drafting, were taken as licence by some commanders in the field to commit excesses, such as the killing of 212 men, women and children under SS auspices at Civitella besides many more. Later still, on 1 July, the method and scale of taking reprisals was more closely defined in response to further calls by the Allies for intensified guerrilla warfare against the Germans, a guerrilla warfare which, after all, had been instigated by the top Allied leadership, primarily by Winston Churchill, when he had instructed Hugh Dalton in 1940 to 'set Europe on fire'. It was scarcely to be hoped that commanders in the field, hard pressed and angered by what, to them, were criminal acts by an ex-ally, should pay rigid attention to the restrictive paragraphs of Kesselring's orders. Injunctions that forbade looting in any form because, 'The good name of the German soldier requires this', and the careful qualifications demanding restraint in subsequent orders of 21 August and 24 September (by which time Kesselring realised that many of his underlings were going too far with repressive measures) came too late to avert provoking the populace to still more desperate violence. Restraint would be at a premium in connection with a foe who may well have accounted for about 15,000 Germans killed or wounded throughout June to August – far more than the guerrillas lost.

Kesselring's defence against various charges during his trial will be examined in Chapter 13. It was a defence upon which he was to dilate at length in his 'Memoirs' and, with precision, in a paper he wrote for the Americans entitled 'The War Behind the Front: Guerrilla Warfare' in which he described this combat as 'a corruption of legitimate military warfare . . . in conflict with the written and unwritten rules of international law'. In the present day, now that guerrilla warfare has become so much a part of life to so many people, along with an emotive terminology in which one side classifies guerrillas as terrorists and the other as patriotic heroes, it is much easier than it was in 1944 or 1947 to sympathise with Kesselring's genuine attempt to limit what amounted to civil war. At that time it was he and the Germans who were portrayed as the criminals and only today that people, who did not then understand, are coming to appreciate his dilemma. It is hard to comprehend the difficulty of training and controlling the polyglot forces allocated to him – German units recruited or coerced from every corner of the Third Reich and its conquered territories which included Russians, Cossacks and Turkomans – many of them riff-raff, nearly all of them speaking different languages and posing a difficult communication problem. No wonder there were tragic misunderstandings in addition to the deliberately perpetrated massacres and the burning of villages in what Kesselring decried as 'Robbers' Raids' by such SS men as *Sturmbannführer* Reder who was to lay waste to whole districts. Against the weight of horrors, however, had to be balanced Kesselring's, admittedly tactical, efforts to reduce partisan activity with truces, by propaganda and by collaboration with Vatican, church and officials, besides his broadcast appeals to the enemy to desist.

Whatever damage these German repressions may have done to humanity they certainly achieved Kesselring's military aim. Underlying everything, as he said, was military necessity. In no way were his lines of communication seriously disrupted by guerrillas and nowhere were the administrative facilities much harmed. Far more damage in this respect was done by air power. Yet despite the complementary effects of air and guerrilla attacks, the retreat of his army through 150 miles of semi-hostile territory to the Gothic Lince proceeded without collapsing into rout at any time, aided as it was by a diminution of Allied effort when troops were taken away for the invasion of Southern France. Contrary to Warlimont's opinion that a swift retreat to the Gothic Line was imperative, Kesselring once more opted to prolong the retirement by holding a succession of delaying positions, nine miles at a bound en route, each designed to make the enemy halt and deploy a set-piece assault. Unfortunately his order, worded so as to give an impression of tenacity while retaining a free hand, failed to convince Hitler. He clamped on another hard demand for implacable resistance at all points. Kesselring, as usual, protested to Jodl who could not budge Hitler and so, as usual, he put more pressure on his subordinates, telling them that the Albert Frieda Line (from Grosseto in the west to Porto Civitanova in the east) was to be held as preliminary to a final hop backwards into the Gothic Lince. Lemelsen he made 'very unhappy by my words' when he received a sharp rap for going back nineteen miles in twenty-four hours on the 14th. 'But after all', Kesselring expostulated to von Vietinghoff (who must have smiled), 'it must be possible to use strong language at times . . .'. The tension they all endured was of course tremendous, particularly for Lemelsen, a gunner like Kesselring but of relatively limited intellectual capacity, of whom it had been considered that the appointment of corps commander was about his ceiling. Lemelsen deserves sympathy, however, in the situation that he found himself, since not only was his Army in full retreat with a '30 km gap' torn in its front, but Allied bombing had hit his own, plus each corps and divisional headquarters, destroying their signals equipment. Intercommunication was made rudimentary to say the least. Neither was Army Group headquarters functioning too well. Hans Röttiger, the new Chief of Staff, had arrived on 7 June, long after Westphal had departed, to find the headquarters on the move. Inevitably it took time for the C-in-C to come to terms with his new partner and it was 20 June before the headquarters was functioning to full capacity.

For the better part of June Kesselring was helping his commanders out of successive difficulties, and giving ground without Hitler's permission while engaged upon preparing another comprehensive case in favour of his own strategy. When Hitler grew impatient with this circumlocution and again demanded a halt, Kesselring flew with his chief operations officer (Ia), Dietrich Beelitz, to put his case to the Führer in person. Hitler as usual, according to the 'Memoirs', prevaricated at which, 'Beginning to lose patience, I made a short and heated reply.' What follows is just that, a straight refutation of Hitler's arguments and an ultimatum to the effect that 'if I change my plans to meet with your ideas, sooner or later the way into Germany will be opened to the Allies'. He guaranteed – if his hands were untied – to delay the Allied advance appreciably and so prolong the war into 1945. At this Hitler gave way. To no other commander, not even to favourites such as Göring, Guderian or Rommel, did Hitler make such concessions at this stage of the war and, to all intents and purposes, keep his word thereafter. Von Rundstedt and Rommel, who at that moment were near the end of their tether under enemy pressure and Hitler's interference in Normandy, and Zeitzler the Chief of Army Staff, waging a calamitous war against the Russians, were for ever mistrusted and rarely able to uphold their requests. Perhaps Kesselring was the exception who proved a rule, but a distinct exception in Hitler's estimation he undoubtedly was. There can be very little doubt that he had his own relationship with Hitler in mind when, in later years, he commented on the decline of the power of the German General Staff in relationship to the Führer, saying

> . . . it ought not to have weakened, much less dissipated, its strength and especially its prestige in useless opposition, but rather that it should have tried to retain or even improve its controlling position by an intelligent study of Hitler's military ideas and from the confidence which it could only gain in this way . . . The second way, that of open resistance on the part of the General Staff, would have been doomed to failure in view of the structure of the *Wehrmacht* itself, *and the attitude of the German people*.

The italics are mine to draw attention to the fundamental weakness underlying the efforts of the conspiratorial group within the General Staff who, as the *Wehrmacht* fell back in Russia, in Italy and in France, concluded that only by the elimination of Hitler and the Nazi Party and SS could Germany be saved from physical as well as moral destruction. On the eve of the assassination attempt on 20 July, however, there is evidence enough to show that the people and the *Wehrmacht* still stood behind Hitler. They were unlikely to follow the lead of a group of unimportant dissident officers, most of whose leaders were malcontents who had been sacked or dishonoured by Hitler, and who, in the eyes of the vast majority of officers (Kesselring among them), were in breach of their sacred oath. Unhappily for the prospects of success, the conspirators had spread their contacts wide in order to reach for the extensive objectives they had to achieve. This, as von Senger (who knew of the plot) points out, was a serious weakness: 'I had repeatedly expressed doubts over the prospects of success. I had always realised the dangers; the secret could only be maintained if the circle of conspirators remained small, but in that case there would not be enough people in key positions with a knowledge of the plot.' Apart from that, there was the incompetence of the conspirators themselves, as demonstrated by their failure to blot out the communications from Rastenberg, when the bomb failed to kill Hitler, and their indecisiveness in exploiting an initial advantage when the Party hierarchy stood temporarily in confusion.

In company with others in the upper military hierarchy, Kesselring has sought to demonstrate that he was unaware of the conspiracy and that only a few among his officers were. Westphal, for example, admits that he knew, as did von Senger, and the latter has told Rainer Kesselring that he owed his life to an intercession on the field-marshal's part. Rainer Kesselring was left in no doubt whatsoever that his father knew something was afoot (they discussed the whole subject) and that, like so many of his kind, he was prepared to let it proceed providing adequate precautions were taken to avoid a holocaust and, above all by his way of thinking, civil war. With close knowledge of the way all three services felt and believing that Hitler still possessed the support of the vast majority of fighting men as well as that of the Nazi Party – who were, after all, the elements actually in firm control of all levels of government – he derided the chance of success. It was not mischance 'as I could not be reached' which prevented his seeing one of the arch conspirators, Dr Karl Gördeler, in 1942, but a genuine sense of repugnance at such methods of *putsch* as he had known in 1919. He knew Gördeler's business and had a keen desire to isolate his command from any such involvement, a view which he strengthened during the days in Italy. It may be that this isolation was easier to implement because, as Westphal says in a letter to me, 'We were probably too far from the centre.'

It was this remoteness, no doubt, which led von Vietinghoff, fearing the consequences of the attempted assassination when first the news came through on the night of the 20th, to suggest to Kesselring on the telephone that they should send a joint signal to Hitler expressing their loyalty, saying that the Italian Army Group stood behind the Führer. Karl-Ulrich Schroeder, who monitored the conversation at von Vietinghoff's side, recalls his amazement at Kesselring's refusal to comply and the C-in-C's pronouncement that 'this is a Black Day for the Army' adding, that it was hardly for him as a *Luftwaffe* officer to join in such conciliations. Schroeder's interpretation of Kesselring's response is that of indignation that so partisan an attitude should have been struck. It is quite likely, however, that Kesselring was playing for time. He was prepared to let the conspirators do their worst (as he made plain in conversation with his son after the war) and declined to declare his interest until he was sure that the plot had failed – which was by no means the case that evening. Only next day, when failure was confirmed, did Kesselring send a personal message to Hitler.

Non-involvement in the bomb plot was Kesselring's personal choice, an isolation related to Service loyalties and not to the commonly held view that he was irrevocably committed to Hitler and the Nazis. By now Kesselring had dissociated himself from the squabbling *Luftwaffe* cliques of 1937. His eyes were open also to the danger of the SS. Himmler's callous proposals in connection with moving the people of Rome, and the subsequent blatant outbreaks of SS brutality in April which had led him to insist upon having them under his command (and had instigated the Keitel signal on 1 May) were proof enough of their calumny, but he dealt with these things on a day-to-day basis without histrionics and without taking sides. Few people may have loved him, but he was respected by all with whom he had to deal because he had so few axes to grind – a reputation which once more brought him into the firing line of the latest outbreak of *Luftwaffe* intrigue.

Amid the paroxysm which, in the aftermath of the bomb plot, drove Hitler to dismiss or slaughter both the guilty and the innocent – Rommel, in due course, among the dead and many army officers of high calibre besides – nobody felt safe; the slightest slip threatened a horrible death: terror abounded. Not even the paladin of the *Luftwaffe*, Hermann Göring, was safe. He whose once-vaunted organisation was by now incapable of defending the Reich (upon which no bomb, according to him in his heyday, would ever drop) let alone aiding the armies at the front or the U-boats at sea, was under pressure by the Army for replacement as C-in-C by a man who would take an active part in restoring the effectiveness of the *Luftwaffe*. Matters came to a head at the end of July, in parallel with the wholesale army sackings. Indeed, it was the new Chief of Army Staff, Guderian, who had succeeded Zeitzler on 20 July, who led the campaign. But so many superior officers had been lost from one cause or another that the choice was extremely restricted. The graves of Europe and the gaols of Germany were occupied by so many competent men while many of those who survived were inelligible for consideration for one reason or another. There were but few of the original prestigious *Luftwaffe* élite left and of these von Richthofen was ill, Sperrle and Milch discredited. The latter had been dismissed as State Secretary in June because the new jet aircraft had not been developed to Hitler's expectation as a bomber – Milch well knowing that it was fighters that were most needed as the best weapon to protect Germany from the enemy bombers. There remained Kesselring and Ritter von Greim but the former, as Richard Suchenwirth points out, was indispensible in Italy where 'the entire front, long subject to inhuman demands, depended upon his contagiously inspiring temperament'. In any case Hitler had no intention of sacking Göring outright; he merely desired a senior *Luftwaffe* officer permanently at his headquarters, thus to eliminate Göring's right of interference. So von Greim got the job and Kesselring continued to conduct the defence of the outer works of the Gothic Line as the Allies neared Florence (which he was to surrender undamaged), with the prospect of another bout of hard fighting for river and mountain barriers.

Despite Kesselring's superfluous obsession about another landing in the rear (the Germans were not to know that the impending Allied invasion of southern France had subtracted Alexander's amphibious capability), he had much for which to be thankful in August, above all the slow (and confidently expected) pace of the enemy pursuit which had allowed him to save so much from the wreck and extract his men and material along minor roads where the air attacks were less prevalent. Of course there was hardly a day which passed without some crisis or another, but his Army and Corps commanders were now accustomed to his ways and generally appreciative of his efforts on their behalf. Moreover at the end of August they enjoyed the first break in intelligence work they had known for some time. For once a clear indication of the timing and placement of a blow could be deduced, this time from a captured copy of Oliver Leese's Order of the Day and Eighth Army's surprise attack towards Rimini on the Adriatic coast and the identification of the formations to which prisoners belonged. There was sufficient time to shift a complete corps to the threatened sector to meet the attack, though Kesselring, typically and parsimoniously, denied von Vietinghoff all the troops he would have liked. Despite this reinforcement a wide breach was made in the German defences, costly to the assailants but fatal to the Gothic Line in that area. As usual Kesselring was ready with last-minute reinforcements and expedients as the main body slowly withdrew, avoiding envelopment amid intricate country that was ideal for delay. Though under endless air attacks he was able to shift more formations, his last mobile reserves, from the centre to stiffen his left wing.

By 3 September all were in place and the consensus of opinion among his commanders was that the crisis was past. Buoyed up by their optimism, which matched his own, he went to spend the day with Lemelsen on the western flank where all was quiet. In his absence, however, a well-directed Canadian attack, crossing the River Conca, had shot forward a couple of miles and was threatening vital ground at Coriano. Worse still, nobody that evening could give him a clear picture of the situation. Under normal circumstances he might have behaved in his accustomed calm manner but unfortunately he found at GHQ Walter Warlimont, Jodl's deputy from OKW (another gunner like himself) who had rarely shown him much sympathy in the past. The knowledge that the Führer would hear of his failure and the realisation that his subordinates

had let things slip, provoked him, to quote Nicholson in the Canadian
Official History, 'into a towering rage. He threatened to replace corps and
divisional commanders who were able to think of nothing but
retreat . . . he expressed his vexation by creating a scene clearly intended
to exact the maximum performance from all concerned.' Shrewdly
Nicholson has evaluated the C-in-C's simulation of rage as an act, for this
was not the usual way Kesselring behaved – he was far too practised a
commander to allow temper to loosen his judgement. But Kesselring kept
it up until midnight on the telephone to von Vietinghoff and gradually the
retirement was slowed and then brought to a halt when rain began to fall
on the 6th. In the meantime Coriano held out. By sheer force of
personality Kesselring had prevailed.

As the histories point out, the Germans had reached a state by
mid-September from which only the autumn rains could save them, and
by good fortune their early arrival came not a moment too soon. The
eventual loss of Coriano on 13 September, catching von Vietinghoff before
he was quite ready to withdraw, fell short of Allied requirements since
further heavy rain prevented further pursuit by tanks. The brilliant use by
the Germans of their artillery, which was not nearly so well employed on
other fronts as in Italy, was due, no doubt, to Kesselring's personal
interest and knowledge as a gunner who emulated Napoleon by seeing fire
support applied to his own desires. It took such a heavy toll of the Eighth
Army that the Canadian History is compelled to admit 'it would not
completely recover for many months'. Elsewhere in the Apennines the
Allied attack ground to a halt against Germans who fought with
demoniacal fury spurred on by a commander who kept several options
open. Scarcely daring to hope that Allied pressure would be relaxed and
that he would long be able to hold out in the Apennines, Kesselring, while
urging his men to dig-in, had begun planning on 30 August for the next
step back, this time to the line of the River Po. The familiar processes were
set in motion – Phase I, a course of preparation for an unpalatable
decision by Hitler by the submission of statistics and arguments to
demonstrate the vulnerability of Army Group C; followed by Phase II, the
presentation of the plan (Operation 'Autumn Fog') by Röttiger to Hitler
on 23 September. As was to be expected, the plan was rejected, though
20,000 men were offered in recompense. But Hitler's response had a
different sound about it this time. For the first time to Kesselring he gave
reasons such as the Army Group commanders in the East and West had
become thoroughly accustomed to hearing as their lines were driven back
on the frontiers of 1939: '. . . for political, military and administrative

reasons [Hitler] had decided to defend the Apennine front and to hold upper Italy not only until late Autumn but indefinitely'. One reason for being so unyielding was fear of 'the shock for the German people; but of fundamental importance was the retention of the industrial output that still flowed from the northern Italian factories. They all saw the storm brewing and appreciated that engulfment could not be long delayed. But they stiffened their necks and went on fighting as if for a future that dawned in a cloudless sky. The political system permitted no other course of military action.

As it happened there was reason for characteristic optimism on Kesselring's part at this time, despite a distinct absence of it from his contemporary exhortations. The crisis receded as the weather deteriorated and the enemy counted the appalling price of the last few weeks' fighting, which had cost over 50,000 casualties, caused a reduction in the number of tanks available (almost unheard of at this stage of the war) and resulted in the disbandment of two British formations, including an armoured division. For while the Germans were down to fifty per cent of established strength in their infantry divisions, the Allies were little better off and deprived of reinforcements which were being sent to the other theatres. By chance, Hitler's demands stood a chance of being implemented providing the anarchy into which his Reich had fallen did not raise too many difficulties. But vested interests, the struggle between Party, Army and *Luftwaffe*, did not make matters smooth. For example, as the Eighth Army once more tried to push up the coast towards Cesenatico and Cesena in October, and a threat from Fifth Army in the central sector made it necessary to divert troops there, Kesselring discovered that Richard Heidrich, commander of the I Parachute Corps, was conserving 7,000 fresh reinforcements in readiness for a privately conceived plan to defend Ravenna when the enemy at last reached it. This, Kesselring told him, was not the time for a single able-bodied man to be absent from the front, but Heidrich quoted as his authority specific orders from Hitler and Göring to rebuild his corps 'for Führer and Reich'. Despite Kesselring's protests, the paratrooper prevailed for the time being as once more Göring tried to make the point that he was still to be reckoned with.

Nobody with the future of humanity at heart would wish to have seen a depraved Nazi Germany win this war, yet admiration must be spared for a man such as Kesselring who would still persevere after a succession of bitter disappointments as each industriously prepared plan fell apart. It was a strange irony, too, which robbed him of participation in the

celebration of one of the final substantial German defensive successes in
Italy, one which, on 20 October, seemed hardly attainable. For by then
the Americans were making dangerous headway in the central sector and
approaching the important route centre of Bologna, while Eighth Army
once more was making progress up the Adriatic coast. Doling out his
meagre reserves in the meanest proportions to meet each threat, he began
to recognise the usual signs of a falling momentum in the enemy progress,
indications he had so often seen before as the prologue to yet another pause
to preceed the next offensive. As of routine he shifted boundaries and
moved troops to adapt to enemy drives which, for once, were fairly clearly
revealed. The long-awaited arrival of a few of the revolutionary Arado 234
jet aircraft with a top speed of 472 mph at 20,000 ft at last made it possible
to reconnoitre the enemy rear areas to useful effect. A radical
reorganisation of the command chain and the alteration of responsibilities
was set in motion as the front to be defended began to expand.
Commanders had to be settled in and made aware of their responsibilities,
though few needed to be told of their C-in-C's implacable intentions to
obey the inflexible orders of the Führer. But a new agency by now had
intruded, that of the Fascist Italian troops which had been incorporated
within the newly created Army of Liguria under Marshal Rodolfo
Graziani, a soldier who had made his name by defeating poorly armed
colonial armies, such as the Abyssinian one in 1935, but who had been
routed by the British in Cyrenaica in 1940. To the ingredients of civil war
which were incorporated already in the partisan war there now was added
the probability of fratricidal combat between the Fascist Italians of
Mussolini's republic and the co-belligerent Italians of the Badoglio
government under Allied sponsorship.

Things at the front were beginning to stabilise when, on the 22nd, he
grudgingly gave permission for one more local retirement in the west and
spent the rest of the day (as he had the previous one) with Albert Speer, the
Reich Armaments Minister, in planning to make Italy industrially
self-sufficient at a time when it looked as if Germany itself might be
overrun from east and west. At 4 a.m. on the 23rd, in a deluge of rain, he
got into his car for a tour of the front, well knowing that the terrible
weather was good for his Army Group and for himself too since there was
no likelihood of being strafed by aircraft on the road. He spent the
morning with LXXVI Panzer Corps assessing the developments of a
Canadian attack across waterlogged ground by the River Savio and
observing that the conditions bid fair to halt the enemy, and, indeed, that
a German counter-attack was making good progress. After the usual quick

lunch he was off once more through the hills at 44 mph to visit 29th Panzer Grenadier Division near Bologna and check that hard-won American successes in capturing the mountain peaks seven miles to the south of the city were, as seemed possible, the last kick of a dying enemy offensive. Three days later Clark, by calling off the offensive, was to admit what Kesselring thought must be the truth on the 23rd. But Kesselring, by then, was no longer present to savour the victory. Travelling in the dark from Bologna towards Forli (where the British were close) his car came into violent collision with the barrel of a big gun as it emerged from a side turning. A heavy blow on the head fractured his skull, lacerated his face and rendered him unconscious for twelve hours. He was to be out of action for nearly three months, his place taken by von Vietinghoff who managed to carry on in the same style where Kesselring had left off and contain Alexander's offensive until it was completely halted at the end of the year without relinquishment of vital territory.

It is unlikely that Kesselring's mind relaxed very much during his period of physical recovery and convalescence. For the first time in years, he spent a fortnight at home but he as quickly as possible made his way back to Italy, resuming command in the middle of January. There is a comment in his 'Memoirs' to the effect that, although he had the greatest confidence in von Vietinghoff, 'it is a fretful business to be laid up inactive within easy reach of the front. The interest one takes in what is going on is a tonic but at the same time a worry.' Kesselring was of that breed who generate activity if things seemed to have fallen too quiet, the kind whose moments of meditation are integral with day-to-day bustle. Even so it is unlikely that he realised how soon it might be that he would be provided with ample time for reflection. Successful men at the top rarely have time or inclination to consider their own impending redundancy.

12

A Study in Obstinacy

Divorced from the turmoil of high command, diplomacy and politics, as he mainly was during nearly three months of enforced convalescence, Kesselring had the opportunity, commensurate with the atrophy inflicted by the damage to his skull, to reflect at length in an atmosphere of tranquillity upon the state into which his country had relapsed. To whatever sphere of the contracting Third Reich he directed his contemplation, whether it was the devastating destruction by enemy bombing or the moral desolation inflicted by the amoral agents of Himmler and the spreading influence of his malign organisation, nothing but enervating deterioration could be seen. And that which could not be seen was now more easily sensed, especially by anybody who was as closely associated with the upper hierarchy as he was. As Albert Speer, the most frank of the top Nazi leaders, has said of the Jewish subject alone, 'I could have understood about the Jews if I had wanted to'. Perhaps the enormity of the Nazi crimes was unimaginable but Kesselring, with long training and deep sensitivity, never lacked in imagination. That is only too clear from the record. Be these things as they may, he can hardly have been in doubt about the parlous state of the military situation. By day and night the air was filled with the thunder of an enemy air power which far transcended the sound that had been made by his *Luftwaffe* in its heyday. Above the bark of the anti-aircraft guns he would only occasionally detect the whine of vastly outnumbered intercepting German fighters trying unavailingly to halt an irresistible enemy air fleet. Reading between the lines of the newspapers and listening to reports from callers, he recognised the signs of collapse in the last great German offensive, aimed into the Ardennes in December, and could appreciate the meaning of its recoil at the end of the month. Kesselring might take heart in the knowledge that the prolonged lull in Italy was a measure of his own achievements, but he could not conceal from himself the realisation that the decay in Germany's state which he had recognised in 1943 had now reached the final stages of corruption. The fact that he had secretly encouraged Karl Wolff of the SS to make contact with the Americans in Switzerland during the autumn of 1944, prior to his accident, bears witness to that.

The Italian front to which he returned at the end of January 1945 was no longer of much strategic importance in the eyes of his opponents, though strong arguments divided the Allies as to its political consequences. For the time being Alexander and Clark were outnumbered by the Germans because they had been more severely starved of reinforcements than the Germans. They were uncertain of receiving sufficient resources even for a spring offensive when the weather improved. Nevertheless their position at the entrance to the Plain of Lombardy with the threat to northern Italy was enough to pin Kesselring's Army Group down. For him February was to be a month filled with delusions as he busied himself with the familiar routine of constructing defences that purchased a tenuous hold on the northern crags of the Apennines, employing the meagrest resources for a task that was controversial in purpose. Every day came the reports of a Russian horde flooding into Germany from the east through Poland and from the Balkans (which had been skilfully evacuated in the autumn) and of the Western Allies closing up to the River Rhine along its length. That these events cannot always have been clearly analysed in his mind sometimes is apparent: a certain confusion to match that of the outside world installed itself. Sudden inactivity after decades of intense industry must have relaxed his concentration. There are indications that he was already burnt out.

Siegfried Westphal instantly apprehended the change when, as Chief of Staff to the C-in-C West, he met Kesselring again on 11 March. Once more they were teamed up because, on the 8th, Kesselring had been called before Hitler (whose headquarters now sheltered in Berlin as the Russians closed up to the River Oder) to be told that he was to take over from Gerd von Rundstedt. The Americans had seized a bridge over the Rhine at Remagen and this had convinced Hitler that the change must be made. But even the spurious reasoning of the Führer with its adherence to palliative miracles could project themselves no further than the exhortation to 'hang on' as best he could. So volatile was the situation, but so emphatic Hitler's confidence in Kesselring, that his departure from Italy was to be kept secret in case it caused a collapse there.

Characteristically Kesselring put on a cheerful demeanour when meeting Westphal, saying, 'I am the new V3!' But of this introduction

Westphal (who once more demonstrates his inability to penetrate the irony of Kesselring when faced with the ridiculous) writes:

> When Kesselring arrived I reported to him the situation in the West. Immediately I noticed how he had altered. Of course, he had hardly recovered from a serious accident, but during my report he sometimes displayed rejection, sometimes disbelief and sometimes smiled thoughtfully. When I pointed out the dangerously depleted state of our forces . . . and asked him if he disbelieved me, Kesselring answered that 'the Führer had told him something different'. I requested my immediate dismissal . . . This the field-marshal rejected out of hand and assured me of his undiminished trust.

It is quite inconceivable that Kesselring did not recognise the hopelessness of it all and that he was unaware of Hitler's fallibility. Trust, of course, was at a premium in the ruling circles of Germany. Just about the last things that bore resemblance to reality were rational military strategies and tactics. In his 'Memoirs' Kesselring gives a very different version of their discussion. Maybe it was the ingrained habit of loneliness in supreme command which prevented him from disclosing his feelings; much more likely they were both too wary of the consequences of seeming to betray the Führer to be entirely frank. It is utterly impossible to imagine the reactions and fears of men who were under ceaseless suspicion and surveillance. With hindsight it is easy to ask, as Milch was asked during the Nürnberg trials, why it was that senior German leaders did not resign their posts in protest against the bad things they knew were taking place, and all too wrong to underestimate his entirely valid reply: 'For us there was only one kind of resignation – death!' One false move was enough to engineer that event, as Rommel among many more had discovered, and though there were undoubtedly those who shrank from challenging a gruesome fate, probably preceded by torture, there were the rest who responsibly looked to the day when martyrs would be but names of those who escaped into legend and the living the men of destiny who had rescued Germany from the pit. At that very moment the SS was frantically engaged in erasing evidence by killing all potential witnesses of their worst atrocities. Westphal himself declares that, had he been guilty of neglect, Kesselring, who certainly was no coward, could not have saved him. In the final analysis hardly anybody dared speak the truth openly; everything had to be arrived at by devious ways. Double talk was the language of the day and so if the post-war reminiscences of leading Germans as to their activities and pronouncements on the closing stages of the war are wrapped in contradictions, this was simply because they felt compelled to adopt those attitudes – and perhaps, later, for a host of different reasons, to fabricate stories that would excuse or justify the anomalies of their behaviour.

Although Kesselring deals at large in his 'Memoirs' with the conduct of the last campaign in the West, the subject is as academic as his various debates with Hitler as to future strategy were a charade. It is faintly possible that, for a day or two, he was fooled by the Führer's verbose presentation of the situation as he dreamed it, but the glare of insight illuminates a comment of Albert Speer when he describes Kesselring's performance early in April during an attempt by himself to persuade Hitler that an end to the war had to be made. At the time he says he was disappointed that Kesselring seemed to agree with the Führer's reasoning for continuance, enshrined as this was in the utterances of a lunatic who had long ago determined to couple Germany's destruction with his own. Later he realised 'there was no point in getting angry about battles that would never be fought'. Germany's final tragedy lay in the impossibility for all those in a dwindling authority to put an end to the war so long as Hitler was alive. It was not even a question of keeping the oath any more, though it still weighed heavily on them. The upper hierarchy was populated by sycophants, such as Keitel, and ruthless killers, such as Martin Bormann and the other SS leaders, all of whom had a vested interest in death and were bent upon ignoring or eliminating anybody who stood in their way. Guderian, in his last few weeks as Chief of Staff, had courageously but ineffectually tried, behind Hitler's back, to initiate peace overtures through the Foreign Minister, Joachim von Ribbentrop (and even through Himmler) and had been fortunate in survival when Hitler merely sent him on sick leave.

There was little room for anger and a wealth of meaning in the row which broke out with Walther Model, the Commander of Army Group B, on 11 March in front of Westphal. Kesselring, employing the expansive methods that had worked so well in Italy, made sweeping recommendations and levelled a few recriminations. Model, at the end of his tether, lost his temper and announced his refusal to be lectured by a C-in-C who could not possibly understand conditions on the West front. When Kesselring repeated what Keitel and Jodl had told him, Model exploded: 'From them I want to hear nothing. All our troubles come from them.' As Westphal writes, 'All the bitterness against the upper leadership overflowed from Model without the slightest consideration as to who might be listening.' Model would fight on and commit suicide

when surrender seemed imminent in the Ruhr in April. In his 'Memoirs'
Kesselring writes movingly of Model and it may well have been that this
uncontrolled outburst by the tempestuous commander of Army Group B
finally shattered any illusions Kesselring may have possessed. He sadly
confesses,

> 'I felt utterly at sea . . . My predecessor, von Rundstedt, rightly
> regarded himself as the heir to the tradition of the Supreme Command
> in World War One. . . . With his finger on the pulse of things, he
> issued orders from his headquarters almost never visiting the front and
> rarely using the telephone . . . Even if my ways were different I could
> still understand von Rundstedt's though I could not persuade myself to
> adopt them. . . . The laxity of discipline everywhere required personal
> contact with commanders and troops. . . . One had to have a
> glimpse . . . into men's hearts.'

But he could only oversee but little of his command because flying was out
of the question due to enemy air supremacy, and travel by road hazardous
and tortuous.

The soldiers were beginning to give up and make their way home, the
burghers of Germany to resist attempts by the Army to defend their towns
and villages. When Kesselring sought ways to enforce the rounding up of
deserters, Westphal persuaded him to let them go. When Speer asked him
to spare the bridges and public utilities from demolition, in response to
Hitler's demoniacal craving for a scorched earth policy, Kesselring would
not comply directly but ordered instead (shades of Cassino) that defence
works must not be constructed inside built-up areas, but on their
periphery – except in the Ruhr which, levelled to rubble as it was from
years of bombing, could scarcely come to much more harm and was to be
converted into a fortress. Bleakly Speer records that Kesselring adopted
the attitude of the soldier pure and simple and said that it was his prime
duty to care for the safety of his soldiers. Anomalies abounded in a crazy
situation. On 20 April Kesselring went on a last dangerous journey to
Berlin for Hitler's 56th birthday and once more the Führer declined to
face facts and call a halt. The British, Americans and French were
rampaging through the west, pushing a wedge into central Germany; the
Russians were across the Oder and the siege of Berlin was imminent. It
was the last time he was to see the Führer. As communications from
Kesselring's headquarters to both wings of his command became
increasingly difficult, a final reorganisation of OKW was planned.
Admiral Karl Dönitz, Keitel and Jodl were to set up a northern command,

while Kesselring, with General Winter from OKW, was to establish a southern command based on the Alps, thus amalgamating his old Italian command (then in process of dissolution under the impact of Alexander and Clark's last offensive) with his present one, an organisation that would include the much-vaunted but under-implemented Alpine Redoubt and the German version of partisans – the Werewolf organisation. But the former was a chimera and from the latter he dissociated himself. On 28 April, with the Russian net tight around Berlin, this plan was put into operation and Kesselring entered upon the closing assignment of his military career in an atmosphere of Grand Guignol.

It probably is true, as Westphal asserts, that both he and Kesselring were in despair and that 'Kesselring did not want to recognise what was in store for us, above all for Germany, even though he recognised it'. The fact remains that he paraded his loyalty to Hitler beyond the point of reason – nine months beyond the date when the conspirators abandoned the oath and tried to assassinate Hitler, and shortly before the melodramatic occasion when Speer flourished a pistol and claimed *that* as the only way to bring an end to the tragedy. Since March, Karl Wolff had been in close contact with Allen Dulles of the American Office of Strategic Services in Switzerland in an attempt to make a local peace, and in April had persuaded von Vietinghoff, Kesselring's successor in command of Army Group C, to agree to an armistice in Italy and that part of Austria whence the Allied forces were making almost unchecked. But when Kesselring, on the 28th, found himself placed over his old Army Group whose commander was embarked upon this course, he instantly dismissed von Vietinghoff. The Führer still lived, cut off though he was; the oath held good.

Kesselring must have felt very lonely at this time. There was nobody in whom he could safely and totally confide and there can be little doubt that, even if his judgement was not impaired by the after-effects of the fracture to his skull, his conscience was afflicted, his intellectual powers impaired. When he travelled to Innsbruck to see von Vietinghoff and Röttiger, he withheld from Westphal the purpose of his journey, preferring, so he said in repetition of an old theme, 'to spare him consternation'. In the 'Memoirs' he is evasive, omits reference to the sackings but gives, as his reason for fighting on, 'the absolute duty not to let our German brothers-in-arms fall into Russian hands'. That is difficult to correlate with his veto of surrender to the British and Americans in the south and his final timing of actual surrender which took place prior to all other fronts. His arguments in support of continued resistance are devious and unconvincing up to the moment when he comes to reveal the death of Hitler on 30 April and the policy announced by Dönitz as Hitler's legalised successor, as 'a determination to obtain peace as speedily as possible – without letting our soldiers on the eastern front fall into the hands of the Russians'. To this he added the key phrase:'My conscience was consequently satisfied.' Since surely he must have realised that any hope of the Germans in the east being allowed to escape *en masse* to the west, or the Western Allies arranging this with the Russians was unlikely, here is the strongest of hints that he was under duress from an afflicted conscience and held back only on account of the fatal oath to the Head of State and Supreme Commander. From this obligation he could unburden himself thirty-six hours after Hitler's death by the announcement of a truce on the afternoon of 2 May. But why, it is asked, was the delay so long? To which one answer appears to be that of corrupt communications and not, as has been suggested, procrastination on Kesselring's part. It took time to contact Dönitz by radio and obtain his concurrence. The messages between the Allies and the German High Command were circuitously improvised by a Czech radio operator at the SS headquarters in Bolzano. By this route, too, Kesselring offered, on 3 May, to surrender the entire command in the West, still a clear five days before the war against the Russians in their sector of the southern front could be brought to an end when they made a juncture with the Americans in Austria and Czechoslovakia. That, in the circumstances, was fast work.

Is there another reason for his insistence upon prolonging the war which falls outside the prohibition of the oath and the inhibitions demanded by duty? Is it possible, as Rainer Kesselring deduces from long conversations with his father after the war, that Kesselring, ever the deep thinker with an inherent political sense based upon background and deep historical study, was endeavouring to save something from the wreck which Germany could use at the bargaining table? It was his strongly held view, shared by many Germans, that Hindenburg and Ludendorff had accepted too quickly the famous 14 Points in 1918 and had not instantly suppressed the riots which led to the republic and the too rapid disbandment of the Army. Rainer Kesselring thinks his father held the opinion that the Allies, regardless of the unconditional surrender policy, were open to negotiation and that the longer the German Army could be held together the more tolerable might the terms of surrender be. He sees no contradiction between this attitude and the early peace contacts with Allen Dulles. Albert Kesselring knew in 1944, if not 1943, that surrender there had to be, but he did not want to accept it at any price – or simply to save his neck. It is an argument that is compatible with his performance.

To the end the conduct of the German senior officers was dictated by their training and principles in channels that they believed were straight and proper. Each was bent and tortured by a system against which there was no appeal or from which there was no redress. Clearly, in after years, Kesselring was perturbed by the evidence of his procrastination in making peace, for he goes to great lengths in the 'Memoirs' to justify his behaviour. In the process he pleads too hard and reveals once more – this time on a grand scale – the underlying causes behind the remarks of that far-sighted major in 1919 who had reported upon the 'great obstinacy' that 'hampered his activities due to a preconceived opinion' – preconceived opinions which, at this period, led him to believe he could succeed where all others had failed. There is no mention in the 'Memoirs' of von Vietinghoff's and Röttiger's abrupt replacement by two other officers on the 28th, or of Wolff's despairing attempts to swing Kesselring against his preconceived course of forbidding an armistice and his move to arrest the officers Kesselring had put in. In due course Kesselring was to recognise the folly of his obstinacy, for he withholds recriminations against Wolff, von Vietinghoff or Röttiger. At the end of the war there were more important things to attend to, though he was to be denied co-operation with General Dwight Eisenhower and the Allies in the restoration of the communications and welfare of a ruined Fatherland. That was a job the Allies had reserved for themselves, just as they had reserved prisons for all the ruling hierarchy of Hitler's broken Third Reich along with each captured member of the General Staff.

From a hotel room in Berchtesgaren on 15 May, after several abortive attempts for an interview with Eisenhower, Kesselring was moved out, bag and baggage, to Mondorf in Luxembourg, the first of many prison camps he was to inhabit during the last great campaign of his career.

13

By Trial and Error

By what stretch of imagination is it possible, more than thirty years later, to conjure up the atmosphere and attitudes of 1945 and arrive at some sort of understanding of the state of mind of those who prosecuted and those who defended in the trials of the so-called war criminals? Six years of combat that had culminated in an orgy of destruction, the overrunning of Germany, and the discovery of the death camps along with the revelation of massed genocide of Jews, besides evidence of other appalling atrocities by an element of the German people, had manufactured hatreds which, when added to the dire losses and deprivations inflicted by the war, were bound to induce a unique and volatile situation. Though it was an aim of the newly formed United Nations to create a working system of world government based on justice, what chance had justice when, as an expression of the most extreme vengeance, there were those among the Allies who demanded collective punishments by the extermination of whole sections of the German people, let alone those who had led them into war? But if this proposition, an extremists' solution that was as malignant of human values as the horrors generated by Hitler's Final Solution for the Jewish race, was fortunately cast aside, its substitute, a process based upon justice with the constructive intention of establishing world government, also included a destructive motive against the powers who had lost the war. But, as many Germans recognised, there was hardly any alternative open to the Allies since public opinion demanded retribution of a kind.

The staffs of the International Tribunals, which began their work of prosecution at Nürnberg in 1945 of what were termed Major or Minor War Criminals, were meant to create procedures for the future. It was their task to establish a new process in law based upon precedents which, in instances, were scanty to say the least. They had as their aim, in so far as the Germans were concerned and so far as the blurred intentions of the Allies permitted, to punish (within bounds) those responsible, though there are those among the prosecutors who refute the motive of retribution. They had also to draft principles of international justice and show what had happened and why; to act as an instrument of deterrence to future transgressors; to bring home to the German people, without resort to collective measures, their responsibility for the war; and to condemn those organisations, like the leadership corps of the Nazi Party, the SS, the Gestapo, the General Staff and the High Command of the *Wehrmacht*, who had promoted the worst offences. Speed was considered essential: the Allies wished to deal only with ringleaders and they wanted to start and complete the trials as quickly as possible. In consequence there was but little delay between the end of the war, the apprehension of wanted men and a start in gathering evidence concomitant with intensive interrogation of those same men – the war criminals.

At the camp at Mondorf, Kesselring found himself in company with many old comrades, chief among them Göring – a broken wretch, addicted to drugs, who was described by the American Camp Commandant, Colonel Andrus, as 'a simpering slob . . . but we took him off dope and made a man of him'. According to Westphal, Kesselring was 'without compare' and stood like a rock among the bewildered and downcast German prisoners, encouraging, helping and guiding them into resistance of the 'enemy', as Kesselring still called the Allies. He alone stood by Hitler's old right-hand man whom the Führer had renounced at the end, and persuaded his previous commander to come to terms with his fate and assume the leading role he must play in the trials to come. He told Göring that 'only one thing counted, to stand by that for which he was responsible and, if necessary, die with dignity'. It is impossible to corroborate this story, though there is little reason to doubt its veracity, for Göring was to perform in accord with these principles and to strive hard to carry his fellow major war criminals with him. As he put it, himself, to one of them as he strove to wield them into a corporate organisation, pledged to give nothing away: 'You must accept the fact that your life is lost. The only question left is whether you are willing to stand by me and die a martyr's death . . . some day the German people will rise again and acknowledge us as heroes and our bones will be moved to marble caskets in a national shrine.'

Whether or not Kesselring was entirely responsible for thus inspiring Göring is open to question. The fact remains that, as a witness at Nürnberg for Göring (the man who had once called him the *Luftwaffe*'s enemy Number One) he was unshakeably calm and composed and, indeed, gave nothing away. These things the Allies recognised. Once they appreciated that Göring was unifying his fellow defendants, they took measures to prevent his influencing them further and segregated the prisoners. No sooner had Kesselring given his evidence than he was transferred from among the witnesses to the prisoners' wing where he, too, was segregated in solitary confinement for five months without explanation. As a witness he impressed all who heard him, and it may well be that it was the strength and validity of his testimony which helped deter any charges being brought concerning the conduct of air bombing in Poland in 1939, at Rotterdam or upon Coventry in 1940, for example. But he also ensured his own fate. For even if the Allies, by their own bombing of cities, had placed themselves in an impossible moral position and could hardly claim one law for themselves and apply another against somebody else – even against a defeated enemy – they had to hand self-made laws of their own which were readily adaptable against Kesselring. By his arrogant dominance he drew attention to himself. As a minor war criminal he was eligible for trial in the country where his alleged crimes had been committed and was subject to the London Agreement of the Allied Powers that had been signed on 8 August 1945. For Article 8 of the Agreement decreed that a defendant was not free of responsibility for a crime even if he could prove he had acted under the orders of a superior. And Article 9 adopted the Anglo-Saxon system of criminal procedure in all trials – a disputable arrangement but one which nevertheless could operate as much to the advantage of the defence as the prosecution. Kesselring, for one, would turn its meaning to propaganda usage against the Allies even when it aided his own case.

To understand the significance of Kesselring's trial it is essential to relate his treatment and experience prior to its opening and recall, also, the advice he had given to Göring and the manner of its adaptation for himself. Conditions in the camps for the war criminals were themselves provocative to a personality of Kesselring's proud and unyielding nature. His deprivation of a table in his room, once he had completed his evidence at Nürnberg in March 1946, stiffened his resolve and concentrated a mind still suffering from the accident. He was moved from camp to camp in the American sector and in each the conditions were hard. Rules for the prisoners at Nürnberg were strictly enforced by Colonel Andrus, Westphal claiming that the American soldiers were incited against them. It was inevitable, of course, that there should be prejudice on the Allied part, since qualified officers to deal with denazification (as it was called) were in short supply and therefore a great many were bound to be German nationals or Jews who had been forced to leave Germany prior to the war. It is scarcely surprising if they exuded hatred or were upset by the horror of German atrocities. A charge of bias could be levelled at all nationalities though there were peaks and troughs of behaviour depending upon the commandant of the camp in question. For example, at the Dachau camp where Kesselring shared a minute cell with von Brauchitsch, Milch and two others, there was barely room to move and exercise was restricted. The surprising thing is that things were not worse.

Several fellow officers of Kesselring's from his Italian command were also selected for trial on the grounds of atrocities alleged to have been committed in 1944 and 1945, and were sent for interrogation to London. Here von Mackensen as well as Mälzer joined him, but they received treatment of such relative clemency that, quite likely, they tended, with unsuspecting frankness, to write statements about their previous activities that were damaging. Colonel Alexander Scotland, who commanded the so-called 'London Cage', was a past master in extracting information from his prisoners, but scrupulous in his treatment of the generals who fell into his care. Yet it seems to have come as a surprise to him when von Mackensen and Mälzer made frank confessions in describing the events connected with the Via Rasella explosion and the execution of hostages in March 1944, just as it came as a surprise to them when he explained their culpability. To him it would have been more natural if these officers had tried to conceal the facts or place the responsibility elsewhere – as was the practice of so many of his prisoners. Scotland's attitude to Kesselring and von Mackensen must, however, be treated with reservation since, both in his book, *The London Cage*, and as a witness he exhibited a distinct and, in parts, misplaced sympathy for the two soldiers, besides faulty knowledge of Kesselring's role in Italy, the field-marshal's nationalistic motivations and high-minded intentions. Scotland, indeed, was seriously in error. When he held the view that neither man was guilty because they were not responsible for the orders which had led to the acts under investigation, he seems to be uncomprehending of the provisions of Article 8 of the London Agreement, and he is completely wrong in stating that Kesselring in 1944 was 'merely an officer on Mussolini's staff . . . far from supreme in the matter of executive powers'. Moreover, to express his amazement at Kesselring's insistence upon accepting full responsibility since 'I now knew that if ever a man's exaggerated sense of his own importance was leading him to his doom, that man was Kesselring', simply goes to show how Scotland had underrated the German and how little he understood the man he had under examination. Indeed he had failed to understand the Keitel signal that gave Kesselring complete command over partisan operations, reading it in precisely the opposite sense that was meant.*

Nevertheless, Scotland's liking for Kesselring was fully reciprocated, though probably the field-marshal laughed to himself when he presented Scotland with his signed photograph, for beyond doubt he had charmed his gaoler as he had charmed other men, and he often had given in better days a signed photograph to his German subordinates. But Scotland is true when he transmits a sense of unease at the treatment of the three Germans, and was fairly representative of a rising swell of public disquiet among the Allies as to the nature and manner of these trials. Critical letters began to appear in the press as it became evident that dubious practices were being introduced and that, *prima facie*, certain generals such as Halder, Milch, von Manstein and Kesselring were being used as scapegoats. Why was it, Scotland asks, that Britain after the war concerned herself with the indictment of Germans in Italy? 'To this day I remain convinced that our intervention was unnecessary, unjust and wholly untenable.' After all, he could have added, Kappler of the SD, who actually committed the crime in the Ardeatine Caves, had been handed over to the Italians for trial and, in 1948, would receive life imprisonment. Could it be that the British already feared the Italians might be too lenient? Or was it really, as declared in court, that the British sincerely believed soldiers of their standing should be tried by soldiers and not by civilians? In which case why not go the whole hog and compose the court of officers of a requisite seniority and experience of high command, not just a major-general and five lieutenant-colonels guided by a civilian Judge Advocate.

By the time Kesselring was brought to trial in February 1947 a British military court in Rome had sentenced von Mackensen and Mälzer to death. Kesselring had given evidence on their behalf, trying by all means in his power to divert the blame upon himself. It was to no avail and so, before facing his own trial in Venice, Kesselring was convinced that sentence of death upon himself was also guaranteed, a belief which, within an hour of the trial's commencement, had been heavily substantiated. For the four German lawyers, headed by Dr Laternser, who were to conduct his defence had only arrived the previous night (their delayed appearance

*The signal read in this connection: 'The Supreme head of the SS and Police will be responsible for conducting operations against the partisans in Italy and will follow the guiding principles laid down by GOC in C South West and will be subordinated personally to him. The operations area and the coastal area to a depth of 30 km outside the operational zone are excluded from his responsibility.'

by no means a German error) and thus were denied an opportunity to consult their client or prepare their case in detail. Despite this the prosecuting officer, Colonel Richard Halse, pressed hard for the trial to go ahead at once. It was even suggested that the defence might be placed in the hands of a judge who had already been subpoenaed as a witness for the prosecution! Small wonder was it that one member of the court protested that 'This trial must not be allowed to become a farce from the very start', and all the more damaging that there ensued a prolonged argument before the court finally granted a week's adjournment.

There is insufficient room in this book to treat upon the Kesselring trial at length. Here it is possible only to concentrate upon its special features, to sense the atmosphere and describe its outcome as the evidence and procedures affected the central character, the accused. The disquiet of officers of the court, besides members of press and public who heard the proceedings, has long been apparent. Notes by one member of the court, Lieutenant-Colonel P. M. Marjoribanks-Egerton, illustrate the confusion there must have been over the accurate translation of many documents to and from English into German and vice-versa. Anybody who has any experience of sitting in judgement when problems of translation from the German are involved (as has the author) will understand only too well the damaging misunderstandings that can arise with so ambiguous a language. A standing objection by Kesselring that he was at a disadvantage because Germans were unused to the Anglo-Saxon methods of cross-examination is difficult to sustain, however. Kesselring had several times already been subject to this revealing form of questioning and his counsel, from much experience at Nürnberg and subsequently, was well versed in the process by this time.

Kesselring is on much firmer ground when he complains about what he calls 'sergeant affidavits'. These sworn statements, it transpired during the hearing, had been made by military police sergeants of the British Special Investigation Branch (SIB) based on statements they had taken from Italian citizens after the liberation of Italy. The sergeants themselves had been ordinary British policemen conscripted into the army during the war. At the time they were out of their environment. By now they had returned to civilian life and were not available for cross examination. Moreover the statements themselves, as Kesselring points out in his 'Memoirs', were suspect, having been taken from people who were under pressure from the agents of the vying ideological partisan groups whose struggle had been directed rather more towards post-war political supremacy than eviction of the Germans. It had been shown in the Italian courts that such statements were often wildly exaggerated and invalid. Upon these biased statements, which were freely accepted by the court, the prosecution rested almost entirely for support of the second charge of having killed over 1,000 patriots. But, as Colonel Halse rather lamely admitted in court regarding a similar document, it had been prepared 'from statements to enable the Field-Marshal to be interrogated in the same way as the affidavits have been prepared from statements'.

It was on the twelfth day of the trial that Kesselring at last was able to speak for himself and then call witnesses such as Westphal, Beelitz and Lemelsen in his support on matters of fact. All spoke on oath and each was subjected to a protracted and exhaustive cross-examination. At times they faltered but for the most part, despite the difficulties imposed by interpretation (which sometimes was corrected by Mr. C. C. Stirling, the Judge Advocate General (JAG)), they maintained a coherent front. Kesselring argued, as was the standard German practice, that in the case of the Ardeatine Caves killing, the responsibility lay with Hitler who, as Supreme Commander, had issued the order. It was always the German view that an order legally given could not be refused and it is worth noting that, in the trial of Kappler, the Italians accepted the legality of that order. Not unreasonably Kesselring was to hold that since, at the time of the offences, he was subject to German law, it was only upon German law – not a newly imposed Anglo-Saxon version – that he could be judged. With clear logic, speaking, as he said at the time, as a 'not professional lawyer' when discussing the mechanics of taking reprisals,

I could only take notice and be influenced by purely military reasons. In cases of emergency, German Law authorised the confirming authority and also the convening authority to set aside existing instructions. He had to act as his duty dictated at that time. . . . if he acted as his common-sense and his sense of duty as an officer commanded and if he thought it was right, then it was right . . . In extraordinary emergency cases I, as supreme commander, had the right to order that reprisals should be taken and could disregard the whole legal machinery.

Kesselring's defence was based squarely in relation to the charge in connection with the Ardeatine Caves on the belief that he had executed, on Hitler's order, a just reprisal that was in accordance with international law and as a matter of urgent military decision. In relation to the second charge he asserted that 'I never issued orders which were contrary either to the laws or usage of war and those alleged happenings cannot be represented as originating because of my orders'. Indeed, he quoted an official

American pamphlet, *The Rules of Land Warfare*, which laid down that 'Hostages . . . may be punished or put to death if illegal actions are nevertheless committed' and also allowed summary execution of guerrillas and partisans. He could also show that, no sooner was he aware of atrocities taking place than he had taken steps to prevent malpractice. Perhaps he had been a little late: at least he had not *deliberately* perpetrated the outrages. At another moment he quoted rules to be found in every German soldier's pay book saying spies and partisans should not be executed but brought before a court-martial.

The trial dragged on with each of Kesselring's witnesses submitted to a gruelling examination. Reputable Italians came forward to vouch for his part in trying to mitigate the effects of war upon their country. Doggedly the prosecution stuck to arguments that the JAG, at times, found indigestible:

JAG: But surely, Mr Prosecutor, you are not saying, are you, that in the case of a reprisal it is not permissible to take the lives of perfectly innocent people?

Col. Hasle: I do not quite follow that; I am sorry.

JAG: . . . Is it not permissible in international law, as a reprisal, to take the lives of perfectly innocent people, that is to say, people who have had nothing to do with any other crime at all?

Col. Halse: I say, no, it is not legal . . .

Dr Laternser: And I say it is legal . . .

. . .

JAG: (to Halse a few moments later) Are you drawing a distinction that reprisal cannot take the form of an execution?

Col. Halse: Yes; there are certain circumstances, I agree, when possibly – I say 'possibly' – an innocent life might be taken as a reprisal.

JAG: But you have just said the very opposite!

Always in the background could be felt the political forces leaning upon the members of the court, the witnesses and the accused. To this day the conduct of the Italian campaign hangs over the European political scene, since the partisan war, as Kesselring so aptly put it in a letter written immediately after the trial, 'could not be allowed to go down in history as a criminal operation'. Neither the British nor American official histories of the last phase have been published – and for political reasons, no doubt, it is so. It had been a struggle for political supremacy of right or left in that volatile country, one without much chivalry which Kesselring obviously understood far better than his opponent, Field-Marshal Sir Harold Alexander. For while Alexander might say 'I think that the warfare in Italy was carried out fairly and, from a soldierly point of view, as well as it could be done' (an opinion Laternser was to quote in his client's favour) the JAG, in his summing up, was to denigrate Kesselring's chivalry because he had said, 'Also General Alexander put himself beyond all military honour by issuing this proclamation' (the one of June 1944 calling on the Italian people to arise and 'kill Germans').

In his summing up Dr Laternser was to rise to heights of eloquence in his appeal to the members of the court to appreciate that 'Field-Marshal Kesselring faces this court with a clear conscience' and in arguing the case for the defence demonstrated his grasp of the tribunal's procedures besides the essentials of the case itself. It cannot be said that Laternser missed a trick or failed his client. Quite clearly he won the respect of everyone who heard him in action. At the heart of his argument was the implied question: 'Would you rather believe unchallenged affidavits by young British police sergeants or the evidence of senior and honourable German officers after withstanding the test of intensive cross examination?' As Laternser said, 'I am firmly convinced that each of the witnesses would have fallen victim to these long cross-examinations . . . as the Field-Marshal was in the witness box for twelve days, other officers for a week or several days . . . would not contradictions on the major points have had to occur *if* the untruth had been spoken?'

Kesselring has waxed highly indignant over the prejudice of Stirling, the JAG – accusing him of earlier 'fighting desperately' for the conviction of von Mackensen and Mälzer during the Rome trial and quoting a Swiss newspaper in its reference to the JAG as 'the second and the better prosecutor', and of dropping his pen in boredom when witnesses for the defence were speaking. To read the JAG summing up does not uphold this conclusion, though it is understandable that continental nationals, who were accustomed to a different way of administering justice, might have been puzzled by the procedures which, to the military members of the court (who were little more than a jury of intelligent army officers with special rights of intervention), was standard practice. The court record was taken by stenographers and the JAG had only to record those matters of law or points he needed immediately. It was his task to explain the case in the conventional Anglo-Saxon way and point out the courses open to the court and the lines along which they might act and decide. It is true that he spent a long time in explaining the law as it affected the case for the prosecution, but this is hardly surprising when one recalls that *every* prosecution, as designed by the London Agreement, was in some way a departure from conventional juridical proceedings and the Nürnberg Trial had created new and tenuous precedents. It is insufficient to lay all the blame for any miscarriage of justice which may or may not have taken place on JAG or Court President, and important to remember that this jury, composed of educated men, should have been perfectly capable of seeing through and rejecting, if necessary, any prejudice from the JAG. Moreover, the JAG gave them clear instructions to study the defence's case, laying stress on their duty to consider whether or not Kesselring's intentions, in the second charge, were *deliberate*. 'There is a very clear issue for you to decide,' he said. 'It is for the prosecution to prove it and if you are not satisfied, well, Gentlemen, you will acquit the accused on the second charge.'

It is easy to understand Kesselring's diatribe in his 'Memoirs'. When he wrote them in gaol, he was genuinely incensed by an apparent injustice which provoked the most virulent reaction in him. He was not only pleading in the 'Memoirs' for a cause, in which he believed with the utmost sincerity, but trying, also, to pass a message to posterity. Under the demand of these requirements the traits of character and method which had been glaringly evident in his struggles against Communism, Milch and Rommel – similar obscenities (in his view) – were fully exposed. In his vituperation he was prepared to distort the facts in order to attain an object. Here was the blemish on his character, the propensity to resort to an almost unreasoning acrimony and unscrupulousness when engaged in rectification when the principles of good, as he saw them, seemed to be threatened by evil. He would pursue a vendetta, if need be, to reduce or destroy the opposition. Once in this state of mind he seems to have lost sight of his inborn generosity. When, for example, the JAG, in his closing remarks, paid a compliment to Kesselring, Kesselring chose to misquote and misconstrue the sentence in his 'Memoirs', to make it appear as another of Stirling's alleged cynicisms. Stirling's conclusion was, indeed, as generous as could be expected. Having referred to Kesselring as waging as 'stubborn and determined a battle for the life – it might even be – but certainly the honour . . . as ever he fought in those long days he was retiring through Italy' he added by way of peroration: 'These are the twilight hours of a great fighting soldier. It is for you, Sir, and your members to say . . . Whether that twilight is to deepen into the gloom and darkness of a conviction or whether you are going to say: "No, that twilight must give way to an acquittal to the dawn of better things for

Albert Kesselring, one-time Field-Marshal" . . .'

As things turned out the result was to be all things to all men. For when the court returned to deliver its verdict it was indeed to find Kesselring guilty on both charges, a verdict which completely astounded the defence lawyers – though not their client, who was prepared already to fire a parting shot of contempt at those he felt had misjudged him, and heard the fatal words without a sign of emotion. Though implored by Laternser to make a statement prior to the sentence* – condemnation to death by shooting – was passed, he would have none of it. So it was for Laternser to say the closing words on the Field-Marshal's behalf.

'It was his idea when deciding to defend himself to defend the ideas for which he stood and not his own person.'

Scarcely a person in that court room was unmoved. Nobody who witnessed that final scene can have doubted that Kesselring had won his last victory. British soldiers expressed their open admiration. He was perfectly well aware, however, that public opinion was moving to his side (even though the London *Times* referred to the scrupulous fairness of the court) and that, as the weeks passed while he awaited the decision of the confirming officer (none other than General Sir John Harding who, as staff officer and commander, had been among his toughest opponents in Africa and Italy), there were insistent voices in Britain and elsewhere speaking out against the trial and its outcome. Neither the members of the Court, nor the Confirming Officer may, of course, divulge their opinions or reasons in relation to a case. Rightly we are prevented from understanding why or how it was that the original verdict was reached or by what criteria General Harding determined his final conclusion to commute the death sentence on Kesselring (and the other two generals) to life imprisonment. Insight into how Harding may have tackled the problem can be obtained, however, by reference to the instructions Confirming Officers were given to guide their consideration of such cases. They laid down that the state of public feeling must be taken into account and, in this case, there were pronounced expressions of public perturbance in the weeks prior to Harding announcing his decision on 4 July. In so far as Kesselring was concerned the punishment was bearable. After a short spell spent gumming paper bags he was sent to Werl, there to begin the labours which were to result in a voluminous compilation of experience and opinions for the American Historical Division.

Move into the twilight though he had, this almost monastic period

*Probably well knowing that Kesselring's intention to make one after sentence would not be allowed on procedural grounds – as was the case.

became richly illuminated by study and reflections which are of immense value to historians as well as regenerative to Kesselring himself. Employing his excellent memory to its fullest extent he was able within his cell to reconstruct events which might otherwise have been buried among the dry war diaries compiled by his staffs. Denied, though he was, access to original documents, he was given the opportunity to explain and instruct with striking clarity and remarkable objectivity the events he had witnessed. At the same time he secretly wrote, and had smuggled out of prison, the pages of his 'Memoirs' – in all its imperfection the least reliable source of information he penned but, treated with scepticism, a useful guide as to the way his mind was working.

*   *   *

The man who emerged from prison in July 1952 was but a shadow of the one who had entered captivity seven years before. Rainer Kesselring, from close observation of his father, goes so far as to say that he was broken. Despite the remedial benefits provided by his task as historian and the brave, almost gay, front he erected in his 'Memoirs', he really had endured and suffered from the exacting privations of prison life with its inevitable antagonisms with fellow prisoners in a closely confined community. For many years the habits he acquired in Werl would persist in, for example, the prison routine of pacing up and down his room or on a veranda, five steps one way and five steps back, to the drill he had become accustomed in his cell. They let him out of gaol for a completely successful operation upon cancer of the throat and released him for ever three months later as an act of clemency. His return to freedom was, in its day, a sensation that thrust him into the forefront of public notice as a symbol of changing European attitudes at the very moment when moves to restore Germany's armed forces were well advanced. The Americans exerted influence to provide him with a small flat at Wiessee where he was joined by Pauline and Rainer. At once he was the target for a deluge of telegrams of congratulation as well as the barrage of requests that is invariably attendant upon celebrities. A retreat into repose was positively denied him in the crucial moment when, for the first time in two decades, he was seeking a basis for family life and finalising, too, a matter that was very important to him, the completion of the details in connection with Rainer's adoption from Kurt Kesselring, his second cousin.

With Pauline, in the closing years of her life (she was to die in 1957), he was to achieve a gentler and rewarding understanding. With Rainer he succeeded in building a close personal relationship between men of widely disparate ages. The eighteen-year-old youth, as he then was, was adopted as compensation to Kesselring for his disappointment at not fathering a child of his own. Rainer testifies that they soon struck up an excellent relationship and recalls Kesselring's sympathetic understanding and the way he did not mind disagreements and would tirelessly discuss the simplest of problems in trying to arrive at a solution. He speaks, as well, of his father's immense generosity, of the way he had done all in his limited power to help his fellow prisoners and how he had turned over the money he had saved during the war for the assistance of old comrades. His inherent kindness also found expression in the efforts he made to restore broken friendships, to rebuild bridges with the Rommel family and effect a full reconciliation with Milch. It would be pleasant to record that the years in prison helped him towards the only true period of tranquillity of his whole life in compliance with the emotions he expressed in his 'Memoirs' when commenting upon his feelings at the time of being sentenced to death. Admitting that a rich life lay behind him, 'in which there could be no further peaks of experience', he added, 'To-day, five years later, I must confess that this life, so outwardly defamed, has been enriched by new springs of comfort . . . I now try to judge, objectively, to regard my disappointments as symptomatic of the malady of the age and to subdue revenge and hatred to understanding.' But the old compulsion to become energetically involved in the action and to take an initiative had not been quelled and would remain rampant to the end.

During the stay at Werl, contact had been made with him by an old comrades' association called the *Stahlhelms* which had worked to have him released and of which he had been made honorary president. Odious to many people though the name was because of a similarly named right-wing para-military organisation of the 1920s and 30s which had turned from its original conservative orientation to become among the supporters of the Nazis, to Kesselring this objection appears to have been unimportant. In an ill-informed state of mind when harried by all kinds of supplicants and confidence tricksters who gave him no peace, after his recovery from the operation, he probably failed to recognise its monarchist tendencies or sense the political forces involved or even come to understand, until it was too late, that membership of this group of veterans would exclude him from association with the others. Foremost in his mind, when he accepted the appointment of President in full, was a sense of gratitude for what the members had done for him while he was in gaol.

Misjudgements of the current state of national and international opinion, allied to unwise statements, marred a genuine attempt on Kesselring's part to come to terms with the current situation from which he had become divorced while in prison. In his first speech as President of the *Stahlhelms* in 1953 he invited them to call him 'Comrade Kesselring'. On another occasion he said, 'I believe that the term "war criminal" is no longer a shameful one.'

Naturally an organisation such as this had a hearing in the public debates relative to the constitution of the new *Bundeswehr* and of the European Defence Community. Inevitably he found it impossible to stand aside or remain silent. He stated his clear preference for the integrated European force suggested by EDC and in the process fell into argument with, for example, his fellow Bavarian Franz-Josef Strauss. Some of those hostile to the Germans as a race would interpret his efforts as those of an archetypal apologist for the German armed forces and their General Staff, as an old voice pleading for the creation of a new *Wehrmacht*. At the same time, having realised the narrow and restrictive nature of the *Stahlhelms*, he tried after rearmament was started to turn the organisation into a truly conservative body with an appeal to younger people, allied to a disclaimer of the out-fashioned and unpopular image of the past that was redolent in its tactless naming.

All his aims were impossible to achieve, of course, and not only for the political conflicts that caught him in a cross-fire between the advocates of the West under Konrad Adenaur (of whom he approved), and those who were Nazi and who believed fervently in the re-unification of Germany. Good health now deserted him in his declining years with a heart complaint that demanded that he spend recurringly more frequent spells in a sanatorium. Each re-emergence would at once be the cue for renewed efforts on his part for the *Stahlhelms*, interspersed with a series of appearances in court to give evidence on behalf of one or other of 'war criminals' in West Germany who had pleaded with him as the last C-in-C for assistance. The whole feverish process to which he dedicated those final years was rather sad, a trifle bizarre to watch, even if the motives which guided his actions were of the highest integrity stimulated by his innate sense of duty to those who, like himself, had been condemned. He was at war until the end came in the sanatorium at Bad Nauheim on 20 July 1960.

The pall-bearers were members of the *Stahlhelms* who fired a volley over the grave as part of a funeral which, though quasi-military, was without military honours in the formal sense. General Kammhüber spoke on behalf of the *Luftwaffe* and *Bundeswehr* and took the opportunity to say that the field-marshal would be remembered as he was but forgotten in connection with his recent activities. Siegfried Westphal spoke for the veterans of Africa and Italy in praise of 'a man of admirable strength of character whose care was for the soldiers of all ranks'. A storm was brooding throughout and a few mourners took shelter as the rain came down. But most stayed to the end, as the wind howled and a great spirit seemed to pass them by.

14

A Man on His Own

Placing Albert Kesselring in his correct place on the roll of great military commanders is difficult due to the wide variety of tasks he fulfilled. At various stages of his heterogeneuos career he had been involved in so many different kinds of project that it is almost impossible to draw an exact parallel with any of his illustrious forebears or his contemporaries. Like Gerhard von Scharnhorst, he took part in several campaigns as a staff officer, suffered the trauma of defeat and subsequently played a leading role in reconstructing a broken army. Also in the manner of von Scharnhorst, who had died as Chief of Staff in the Napoleonic Wars prior to victory being achieved, Kesselring was among the most accomplished schemers and administrators produced by the German Army, matching the creator of the German General Staff in his understanding of the social and administrative influences that forged the links between the nation and the fighting men. They raised modern forces that could more than hold their own against the best in the world. But, of the two, it was Kesselring alone who had the distinction of commanding his own creation.

There was a similarity, too, between Kesselring and the elder Helmuth von Moltke, in that von Moltke's fundamental reorganisation of the Army engendered such over-confidence that its later masters committed it to campaigns during the First World War that overstretched its capability. It was much the same again after 1939. No sooner had the *Wehrmacht* demonstrated its proficiency in Poland than it was given tasks beyond its strength. The blame for this cannot be laid at Kesselring's door (any more than it can at von Moltke's), but it was he who created the administrative organisation upon which was laid the foundations of an army that was superior to all its opponents, and he who performed the same service for the *Luftwaffe*, a force that was, in many respects, strikingly original. For, in designing and implementing the basic structure of the *Luftwaffe*,

247

Kesselring, as one of the master builders of a brand new concept of warfare in a new dimension with a philosophy all of its own, went far beyond the scope of von Moltke's work. Indeed, the *Luftwaffe* reflected Kesselring's image to a truer extent than those of his principal collaborators, for although Wever and Milch were pre-eminent in its initial creation, it was Kesselring, through the decisions forced on him as Chief of Staff by a rapidly changing political situation of 1936 and 1937, who fixed upon the actual nature of the instrument that went to war in 1939 and enabled the *Wehrmacht* to win so many outstanding victories. And, like von Moltke, it was Kesselring who played a leading part in winning those victories in the battle arena.

It is necessary to look back to von Scharnhorst and von Moltke for suitable personalities with whom to compare Kesselring because there are few generals of the First or Second World War who matched their accomplishments in the widest sense. Not one among the principal military leaders of any nation involved in the First World War can boast of having commanded land, sea and air forces and none could claim to having created the forces which they came to direct in battle. In effect, each, in his way, was a specialist while Kesselring had the training and the opportunity, as well as the ability, to embrace and master almost every nature and phase of activity with distinction. As to his contemporaries, the genuinely creatively minded German generals such as Wever, Guderian and Student, who matched Kesselring in the brilliance of their command and staff work, were denied his opportunities for the simple reasons that circumstances or their temperaments precluded it; in the case of Wever his personal error as a pilot was fatal and, in so far as the other two were concerned, they were found wanting in maintaining their aims without coming into headlong and immolatory collision with superior authority. Kesselring was superior to all three in adaptability and survival, supreme in the arts of persuasion, compromise and, as required, dissimulation. Besides that he was endowed, as an administrator and a high commander in situations of exacting political and diplomatic complexity, with extraordinary strength of purpose.

In effect Kesselring stands apart and fulfils the stiffest tests demanded of any man who aspires to the list of Great Captains. As a confirmed addict of offensive warfare and a master of envelopment by air and land, he was able to operate in an environment which Alfred von Schlieffen would have envied when, in the years preceding 1908, he designed his assault on the West. Finally, as a master of prolonged defensive warfare, Kesselring has few rivals in history unless one looks as far back as Belisarius. Of what other general can it be said that, over a period of two and a half years, he fought a virtually incessant delaying action against desperate odds, managed to impose his will upon strong-minded and sceptical subordinates, and yet emerged unscathed by serious rout, leading his men in fighting to the last gasp?

Therefore to propose Kesselring for an exalted position among the highest of the past military hierarchy is valid, a postulation which gains in credibility if it is accepted that his methods of command, based upon forceful administrative procedures, were original in application if not in concept. It is unlikely that Franz-Josef Strauss's assertion to the *Bundestag* in 1957 that 'An army cannot be administered. It must be led', was aimed specifically at Kesselring, but it could be said that the system which the new *Bundeswehr* had inherited from the old *Wehrmacht* gave grounds for concern on that account, since there were precious few great administrators available who combined (within themselves) powers of command and leadership such as Kesselring embodied. Here, indeed, is to be detected the dangerous paradox in Kesselring of a dedicated professional who thrived upon responsibility, whose way, in the words of Karl von Clausewitz, 'always takes me across a great battlefield; without my entering upon it no permanent happiness will come to me'. His tendency towards over-centralisation in the execution of authority was the negation of the flexible de-centralised business and command practices he promoted. Nevertheless, by the application of brute personality, he was able to extract quick and positive results from subordinates who otherwise might have dragged their feet in emergency situations.

The fact that almost every one of Kesselring's moments of crisis and major decision were associated with sudden emergencies must, however, be taken into account in assessing his performance. If Westphal is just in adversely commenting upon Kesselring's tendency to deny himself adequate time for reflection, the criticism is one of degree, a matter of a fast brain stealing a few minutes, extra contemplation. The situation into which Hitler plunged Germany, through the revolutionary turn of his policies, inevitably was productive of a swiftly moving drama of rapidly assembled traumatic events which almost invariably precluded long and deep analysis. Yet in attracting criticism upon himself, Kesselring very often has only himself to blame. He who endeavours, at length, to counter disapprobation by a profusion of excuses is assured of contradictions, and Kesselring's diverse apologia, written in the years of atrophy, is no exception to that rule. In judging Kesselring through his own depositions it is essential to understand the secretive idiosyncracies that were the products of bureaucratic and diplomatic experience, and to be aware of his concealments as well as his disclosures.

Naturally there were good reasons for deceptiveness on Kesselring's part. He was hardly the sort of character to act upon emotional or sensory causes. Because he worked his way into the centre of a web of intrigue in a governmental system which thrived upon circumlocution that created secret organisations and dealt, almost exclusively, with obscure subjects, it was inevitable that he should acquire matching habits as of second nature. Of the oblique phrase, the digressive allusion in debate, he was as much the master as he was captain of the indirect approach in battle. With a sardonic remark he could inflict hurt on his colleagues in the same manner as he wrought havoc on his enemies. Verbal barbs were his armour, allied to a coolly deliberated ambition in an environment that, so frequently, he felt was hostile to him. There were, for example, those among the 'Old Eagles' who denigrated Kesselring because, in their sectional opinion, he was ignorant of the subtleties of aviation and could not possibly attain for them their objectives. On the other hand, in a later period, after Kesselring had satisfied the Old Eagles as to his loyalty to the *Luftwaffe* and was recognised as an Eagle himself, there were the soldiers in North Africa and Italy who persisted, both during and after the war, in vilifying Kesselring's soldierly talents on the grounds that he was only an airman – quite overlooking that he was first a soldier as well as being one of quite outstanding and proven competence. To be placed in authority over so many dissident subordinates and to be compelled to struggle against their bigotry and prejudice while performing the onerous tasks of a Commander-in-Chief in the most perilous situation that was as much due to inadequate resources as enemy pressure, were reasons enough for a prickly attitude. His plight certainly evokes sympathy, his truly remarkable resistance to such harmful denigration, in retaining lonely mastership of his own opinions and decisions, the profoundest admiration.

Settled upon a lofty peak in the upper strata of command, the weight of responsibility could never once be relieved by turning to a help-mate who could assuage the tension. The lack of a wife or mistress to whom he was sympathetically attuned and from whom he could extract the relaxation and tenderness which, history demonstrates, is of such vital importance to people who are brought to the utmost stretch of nervous and physical strain, must of itself have been harmful. Yet rarely would he admit it. Probably it was the tyranny of loneliness which, to a large extent, impelled him to develop highly the sense of duty that he demanded of others: there had to be some sort of compensation and with him it appeared as a frenetic application to the task in hand, a total absorption in work. Undoubtedly his misfortune in being identified in close association with the demagogue Adolf Hitler was a wedge that drove him still further apart from his contemporaries. Loyalty to authority, one of the mainsprings of his actuation, was the magnetic force that would set him on course, no matter what the destination might be. It is all too easy to overlook, among the clouds of calumny that enshrouded him after the war, that it was he, by his devious circumlocutions, who managed to apply a touch of the brake upon a few of Hitler's ghastly schemes. Under these circumstances it would have been surprising had he been easy to work with. It is the more astonishing that he persevered, to the end, in unchallenged control of his realms of responsibility, and came as near as did anybody to solving the dilemma of survival in resistance to Hitler without fatally sacrificing integrity. And since it has been the fate of those who stood close to the Führer to be accused (and most justly accused in many instances) of condonation of his excesses, it is all the more important to be aware of the several occasions when a stand against evil was taken and a corrective applied. Kesselring was just about the only C-in-C who, after 1941, managed to change Hitler's ways – and survived. And if by survival and by his pronounced loyalty to the Third Reich he damaged his personal reputation, it is also true to say that he stands straight in the record as a moderating influence whose lapses were mostly the products of provocations and historical associations. That his revulsion against civil war and the observed consequences of partisan combat was sincere is incontrovertible; that they led him to the dock hardly surprising since no man so involved can escape from that kind of imbroglio with clean hands.

What chance of survival in integrity has a lonely person who is subject to a multiplicity of overbearing stresses? To what extent can anybody who is denied the tenderness of a close and affectionate home life, achieve balance of judgement? What sort of price has to be paid for unshared power vested in a man of ingrained secretive habits who is inhibited within a closed system to share fully his innermost thoughts with anyone? Enigmatic as Kesselring emerges from the pages of so many contemporary histories and slandered as he frequently has been, he paid a very high price for his principles. The unique combination of brilliant administrator, astute diplomat and accomplished commander, alloyed with a physical and moral courage of exemplary merit, may have placed him at the tip among the military leaders of the Second World War, but it also exacted a severe penalty. Fortunate he was to inherit the civilised instincts of his forebears to counteract the dehumanising influences among those with whom he found himself in Hitler's hierarchy. Had it not been so it is more than likely that he would have been sucked much deeper into the mire of depravity which engulfed so many of his contemporaries. Then he would have swung on the end of a rope as a convicted major war criminal instead of escaping death in imprisonment as one of the minor kind. That his reprieve was due, to no small extent, to the respect he won from the prosecutors themselves is probable and due, no doubt, to the good impression he made as a man of honour. Indeed it was in the implementation of justice by the Venice Tribunal that the record was placed in perspective. Thereafter, with the passage of time, the opportunity to arrive at calmer judgements helped define the real attributes besides the defects of this controversial figure. Yet he had to be laid in the grave before it became possible, unemotionally, to assemble a balanced picture of this hard man whose stiff sense of duty, loyalty and prejudice fabricated an intractable integrity that was moulded with absolute independence in all things to the end.

Bibliography

ANON. *The Rise and Fall of the German Air Force.* HMSO, 1948.
  The Trial of the Major War Criminals. International Tribunal, 1949.
BEKKER, C. *The Luftwaffe War Diaries.* Macdonald, 1966.
BLUMENSON, M. *Salerno to Cassino.* U.S. Army Dept., 1969.
CHURCHILL, W. S. *The Second World War.* 6 Vols. Cassell, 1948–54.
CIANO, G. *Diary, 1939–1943.* Heinemann, 1947.
COLLIER, B. *The Defence of the United Kingdom.* HMSO, 1957.
CUNEO, J. R. *Winged Mars.* M.S.P., 1942.
DEICHMANN, P. *German Air Force Operations in Support of the Army.* Arno, 1962.
DÖNITZ, K. *Memoirs.* Weidenfeld & Nicolson, 1959.
ELLIS, L. F. *The War in France and Flanders 1939–1940.* HMSO, 1953.
FALLS, C. *Military Operations, France and Belgium 1917.* Macmillan, 1940.
GALLAND, A. *The First and the Last.* Methuen, 1955.
  The Battle of Britain. Forces Aerienne Francaises, 1951.
GARLAND, A. AND SMYTH, H. *Sicily and the Surrender of Italy.* U.S. Army Dept., 1965.
GÖBBELS, J. F. *Diaries.* Hamilton, 1948.
GUDERIAN, H. *Panzer Leader.* Joseph, 1953.
HALDER, F. *Kriegstagebuch.* Kohlhammer, 1962.
HOWE, G. F. *North West Africa, Seizing the Initiative in the West.* U.S. Army Dept., 1957.
IRVING, D. *The Life of Erhard Milch.* Weidenfeld & Nicolson, 1973.
KAHN, L. *The Nuremberg Trials.* Ballantine, 1972.
KENNEDY, R. *The German Campaign in Poland 1939.* U.S. Army Dept., 1956.
KESSELRING, A. *The Memoirs of Field-Marshal Kesselring.* Kimber, 1963.

LEWIN, R. *Rommel as Military Commander*. Batsford, 1968.

MACDONALD, C. *The Mighty Endeavour*. Oxford, 1969.

MACKSEY, K. *Crucible of Power*. Hutchinson, 1970.
  Guderian, Panzer General. Macdonald, 1975.

MASON, H. M. *The Rise and Fall of the Luftwaffe 1918–1940*. Cassell, 1973.

MELLENTHIN, F. W. VON. *Panzer Battles*. Cassell, 1955.
  German Generals as I saw them. Norman, 1977.

MOLONY, C. ET AL. *The Mediterranean and Middle East*. vols. II-V. HMSO.

MOSLEY, L. *The Reich Marshal*. Weidenfeld & Nicolson, 1974.

NICHOLSON, G. *The Canadians in Italy*. Cloutier, 1956.

NIELSEN, A. *The German Air Force General Staff*. Arno, 1959.

PITT, B. (ED.), *Purnell's History of the Second World War*. Purnell, 1966.

PLOCHER, H. *The German Air Force versus Russia, 1941*. Arno, 1965.

ROMMEL, E. (ED. LIDDELL HART). *Papers*. Collins, 1953.

RUGE, F. *Sea Warfare, A German Concept*. Cassell, 1957.

SALEWSKI, M. *Die deutsche Seekriegsleitung 1935–1945*. vol II. Bernard und Graefe, 1975.

SCOTLAND, A. *The London Cage*. Evans, 1957.

SEATON, A. *The Russo–German War 1941–45*. Barker, 1971.

SENGER UND ETTERLIN, F. VON. *Neither Fear nor Hope*. Macdonald, 1963.

SPEER, A. *Inside the Third Reich*. Weidenfeld & Nicolson, 1970.

SUCHENWIRTH, R. *Command and Leadership of the German Air Force*. Arno, 1969.
  The Development of the German Air Force 1919–1939. Arno, 1968.

VÖLKERS, K. H. *Dokumente und Dokumentarfotos zur Gesschichte der deutschen Luftwaffe*. DVA, 1968.
  Der Deutsch Luftwaffe 1933–1939. DVA, 1967.

WAITE, R. L. *Vanguard of Nazism*. Harvard UP, 1952.

WARLIMONT, W. *Inside Hitler's Headquarters*. Weidenfeld & Nicolson, 1964.

WESTPHAL, S. *The German Army in the West*. Cassell, 1951.
  Erinnerungen. Hase und Koehler, 1975.

WHEELER-BENNETT, J. *The Nemesis of Power*. Macmillan, 1953.

WILMOT, C. *The Struggle for Europe*. Collins, 1952.

WINTERBOTHAM, F. W. *The Ultra Secret*. Weidenfeld & Nicolson, 1974.

WOOD, D. AND DEMSTER, D. *The Narrow Margin*. Hutchinson, 1961.

Index

Adenaur, K., 245
Aircraft
  British
    Hawker Hurricane, 75, 84
    Supermarine Spitfire, 73, 75, 84, 115, 126
  German
    Arado 234: 222
    Dornier D17: 48
    Feisler Storch, 114
    Focke-Wulf FW 189: 95, 97
    Focke-Wulf FW 190: 202
    Heinkel 51: 48, 49
    Heinkel III: 48
    Junkers 52: 48, 63, 71, 124, 156
    Junkers 86: 48
    Junkers 87: 48, 50, 63, 75, 94
    Junkers 88: 51
    Messerschmitt Bf 109: 48, 62, 75, 77, 83, 100
    Messerschmitt Bf 110: 48, 75, 77
    Messerschmitt 323: 156
    Ural bomber, 47, 51, 52, 134
  Polish
    PSL P11, 62
  Russian
    Polikarpov I, 15 94
    Polikarpov I, 16 94
Akarit Line, 153, 154
Alam Halfa, 124, 133
Alban Hills, 198, 210
Albert Freida Line, 215
Alexander, H.
  Anzio attacks, 195
  in Cairo, 128
  Churchill and, 140

Gothic Line, advance to, 219
Gustav Line attacks, 206, 207, 209
Italy, final campaign in, 225
Kesselring and, 240
in Tunisia, 153
Algiers, 133–36, 141
Alpine Redoubt, 229
Ambrosio, V., 147, 148, 157, 159, 164, 167
Anderson, K., 137
Andrus, Colonel, 233, 234
Anzio, 195–99, 201–4, 207–11
Apennine Mountains, 163, 182, 193, 199, 211, 220, 225
Ardeatine Caves, 204, 236, 238
Ardennes Offensive 1944, 224
Arnim, J. von, 105, 140–45, 147–55, 157
Arras, Battles of, 24, 25, 27, 198
Artillery
  in general, 21
  88mm, 50, 63, 89
Auchinleck, C., 122
Aurunci Mountains, 208
Austria, 229, 230
Autumn Fog, Operation, 220
Avalanche, Operation, 174
Axis, Operation, 169, 174, 176

Baade, 171
Badoglio, Marshal, 167–69, 173, 176, 222, 223
Barbarossa, Operation, 89 *passim*
Barré, General, 137
Barsewisch, K-H von, 67, 95
Bastico, Marshal, 110, 121, 139, 143
Bayerlein, F., 97, 146, 155
Beda Fomm, 105

Beelitz, D., 190, 204, 238
Benghazi, 106, 111, 114
Berndt, I., 121, 141
Bernhardt Line, 183, 184, 187, 192, 195
Bizerta, 113, 134, 136, 137, 175
Blaskowitz, H., 65–67
Blomberg, W. von, 41
Bock, F. von, 63, 68, 90, 95, 97, 100, 102
Bologna, 200, 222
Bomb Plot of 20 July 1944, 216–18
Bône, 135
Bonifacio, 179
Bonin, Colonel von, 184
Bormann, M., 227
Bougie, 136
Brandenburg, E., 35
Brauchitsch, W. von, 34, 90, 100, 102, 195, 235
Brenner Pass, 104, 169
Britain, Battle of, 74–88
British Army
  Eighth Army, 118, 122, 128, 151, 154, 166, 173, 174, 180, 193, 219, 221, 222
  Xth Corps, 196, 198
Brooke, A., 140
Bundeswehr, 245, 249

Caesar Line, 210
Canadian Army, 206, 209, 219, 220, 222
Canaris, W., 129, 141, 169, 196
Carboni, G., 176–78, 182
Casablanca, 133
Casibile, 1, 174
Cassino, 192, 196, 199–201, 204, 208, 228
Castellano, G., 173, 174
Catania, 166
Caucasus, 121, 127, 128, 156
Cavallero, U., 109–10, 113–16, 121, 122, 124, 139, 147
Cesena, 221
Cesenatico, 221
Churchill, W., 69, 133, 140, 213
Ciano, U., 69, 102, 135, 155
Cintella, 213
Clark, M., 180, 193–95, 198, 199, 210, 223, 225, 229
Clausewitz, K. von, 249
Codes, 73, 106, 207
Comando Supremo, 107, 114, 122, 127, 144, 145, 147–51, 165, 167
Commissars, Russian, 90
Communications, 72, 73, 75, 78, 206, 207

Concentration Camps, 44
Condor Legion, 50, 83
Coningham, A., 171
Coriano, 219, 220
Corsica, 129, 167, 179
Coventry, 72, 87, 234
Crete, 98, 105, 106, 115
Crüwell, General, 118
Czechoslovakia, 32, 54, 57, 58, 59, 230

Dachau, 235
Dalton, H., 213
Danzig, 62
Darlan, Admiral, 135
Deichmann, P., 115, 124, 127–29, 133, 134, 147
Derna, 110, 114
Destourian Movement, 141
Dietrich, S., 186
Djedeida, 141
Dnieper River, 97
Donitz, K., 156, 228, 230
Dora Line, 208
Douhet, G., 46, 57, 116
Dowding, H., 81
Dulles, A., 229, 230
Duna River, 26, 27
Dunkirk, 73, 74, 89, 154, 172
Dutch Air Force, 68, 71

Eisenhower, D., 128, 140, 147, 176, 195, 230
El Alamein, 123, 128–32
Elba, 179
El Hamma, 154
Elnya, 97, 99, 100
Enfidaville, 152
Enigma, 73, 76, 209
Enna, 166
Epp, R. von, 29
Esteva, Admiral, 135
European Defence Community, 245

Faid, 148
Fascist Council, 167
Felmy, H., 35, 65, 67, 68
Fiebig, M., 96, 97
Fili, 37
Fink, J., 77, 79
Florence, 200, 218
Foggia, 183
Fondouk, 149

Forli, 223
France, 32, 59, 73, 74, 198
Freikorps, 28, 29, 34
French Army, 143, 183, 207, 209
French North Africa, 128 *passim*
Frölich, S., 106, 111, 112

Gabes, 137, 139, 141, 153
Gafsa, 147–49
Galland, A., 86, 161
Gambarra, General, 110
Gari River, 194
Garigliano River, 183–85, 187, 193, 195, 196
Gause, A., 127, 137, 139
Gazala Line, 114, 117, 122
German Air Force, Imperial (see also *Luftwaffe*), 25, 35, 116
German Army
   Army Groups
      Afrika, 145 *passim*
      B, 68, 164, 179, 227, 228
      C, 186, 212, 220
      Centre, 90
      North, 60, 63
      South, 60
   Armies
      Fifth Panzer, 140, 144, 145, 150
      Fourteenth, 196, 198, 207, 210
      Panzer Afrika, 114, 127, 132
      Second, 99
      Sixth, 23, 26, 144
      Tenth, 172, 179, 184, 195, 200, 208
   Groups
      Afrika, 145
      2nd Panzer, 90, 96, 99
      3rd Panzer, 97
   Corps
      Afrika, 102, 107, 111, 122, 130, 149
      II Bavarian, 26
      III Bavarian, 26, 28–30
      XIV *Panzer*, 164, 171, 173, 184, 210
      LXXVI *Panzer*, 173, 193, 222
      I Parachute, 196, 198, 221
      XC, 137
   Divisions
      2nd Bavarian *Landwehr*, 26
      10th *Panzer*, 149, 150
      21st *Panzer*, 147, 149, 150
      26th *Panzer*, 209
      29th *Panzer*, 208, 222
      15th *Panzer Grenadier*, 165, 166

      90th *Panzer Grenadier*, 208
      1st Parachute, 166
      2nd Parachute, 168
      4th Parachute, 202
   Wehrkreis
      VII, 39
   Regiments
      1st Bavarian Foot Artillery, 23
      2nd Bavarian Foot Artillery, 19, 21
      3rd Bavarian Artillery, 24
      4th Artillery, 41
      Lehr, 202
German Navy, 115, 127
Gestapo, 159, 204, 233
Gibraltar, 129
Göbbels, J., 106, 117, 121, 133, 141, 181
Gördeler, G., 217
Göring, H.
   air force, calls for, 41
   Battle for Britain and, 74, 78, 82–86
   in captivity, 233, 234
   C-in-C Luftwaffe, 42 *passim*
   in decline, 158, 159, 172, 218
   financial support and, 45
   invasion of the west and, 1940, 71–74
   Kesselring and, 52–55, 158, 163, 221
   Malta invasion and, 107, 114, 115, 117, 121
   North Africa, planning defence of, 138–40
   Poland and, 58
   Russian invasion and, 92, 94
   war, preparations for, 50 *passim*
Gothic Line, 211, 214, 215, 218–23
Grandi, Count, 167
Grazianni, R., 222
Greece, 104, 105
Greim, R. von, 218
Grosseto, 215
Guderian, H.
   Army Chief of Staff, 218
   Hitler, sacked by in 1941, 102
   Panzerwaffe and, 39, 42, 58
   Rommel, preferred by as successor, 123
   in Russia, 90, 94–97, 99
   in *Truppenamt*, 34
Gustav Line, 193–96, 198–201, 203, 206–8
Guzzoni, General, 166, 169

Haack, R. von, 34
Hague, The, 71
Hague Convention, 212

Halder, F., 90, 99, 100, 134, 236
Halse, R., 237–39
Hamburg, 172
Harding, J., 242
Harlinghausen, M., 136
Hasse, J., 34, 37
Hasse, O., 41
Heidrich, R., 221
Heinkel, E., 45
Hercules, Operation, 115, 117, 119, 121–23, 134
Herr, T., 193
Heye, W., 41
Himmler, H., 159, 188, 189, 204, 211, 217, 227
Hindenburg, P. von, 26, 230
Hitler, A.
  Anzio, defence of, 202, 203
  Battle for Britain and, 74, 82
  bomb plot, 216–18
  comes to power, 41
  death of, 230
  Dunkirk and, 73
  Germany, defence of and, 225–30
  Gothic Line, defence of, 214, 215
  Gustav Line and Cassino, defence of, 200, 210
  Italian armistice and, 174, 177
  Italian defection and, 160
  Kesselring and, 59, 65, 158, 160, 161, 168, 181, 183, 186, 215, 251
  Luftwaffe, authorises, 42 passim
  Malta invasion and, 107, 114, 115, 117, 121
  North Africa, French, and, 129, 134, 135, 138
  Russia and, 85, 90, 96, 98, 99, 155
  weapons philosophy, 44, 45, 58
Hitler Line, 208
Holland, 68–73
Horn, General, 17
Hoth, H., 97
Hube, H., 164, 169
Husky, Operation, 165
Hutnicki, 63

Irving, D., 52
Italia, 179
Italian Air Force, 49, 107
Italian Army, 104ff, 144ff, 163ff, 176ff, 222
Italian Navy, 104, 127, 128, 134, 139, 152

Italy
  armistice negotiations, 160 passim
  campaign in, 174 passim

Japanese Air Force, 91
Jeschonnek, H.
  Battle for Britain, 74, 78, 83, 85
  campaign in the west, 66–68, 73
  Hitler and, 59
  Kesselring sent to Italy by, 102
  Luftwaffe Chief of Staff, 55
  Russian campaign, 88, 89, 95, 100
  suicide of, 172, 173
  von Waldau sent to Rommel by, 112
Jews, 66, 189, 204, 224, 232, 234
Jodl, A., 134, 155, 163, 166, 172–74, 176, 179, 185, 186, 210, 227
Junkers, H., 46
Junkers works, 37

Kammhüber, General, 245
Kappler, H., 189, 204, 236, 238
Kasserine, 148, 150, 153, 155
Kayssler, Pauline, 22, 33, 40, 41, 66, 243
Keitel, W., 39, 134, 145, 174, 195, 204, 211, 218, 227, 235
Keppler, General, 24
Kesselring, A.
  trial, 15–16, 204, 213, 234–43, 252
  family, 16, 17, 22, 40, 66
  education, 17, 18
  Jews and, 18, 66, 204
  Prussians and, 18
  Army, early service, 19–22
  artillery methods and, 21
  balloons and, 21
  in First World War, 23–28
  Crown-Prince Rupprecht and, 23, 26, 189, 198
  at Arras, 24, 25
  on air power, 24, 25, 50, 57, 106
  Communists and, 26–29, 241
  in General Staff, 26, 31
  Friekorps and, 28, 29
  in Reichswehr, 32–41
  Nazi Party and, 33
  in Truppenamt, 34–41
  Luftwaffe, 35, 39, 42ff, 46–52, 172, 218
  Wehrmacht and, 37
  concentration camps, 44
  Hitler and, 44, 160, 182–86, 202, 203, 215–17, 251

Chief of Air Staff, 48–51
Milch and, 48–55, 103, 244
Spanish Civil War, 49
preparations for war, 50 *passim*
commands an Air Fleet, 54 *passim*
four-engined Ural bomber and, 51, 134
Czechoslovakia and, 57–59
Poland and, 56, 59–68
Warsaw bombing, 62–65
shot down, 62, 158, 197
Luftflotte II, 67 *passim*
1940 company in the west, 67 *passim*
Field-Marshal, 78
Battle for Britain and, 74–84
night bombing and, 82, 86–89
Russia and, 26, 88 *passim*, 98
C-in-C South, 101, 102
Malta, invasion of, 106 *passim*
Tobruk, attack on, 117
Rommel, 103, 112, 113, 119, 130, 133, 146
Egypt, invasion of, 119–23
Alam Halfa, 124
command, powers of, 127
French North Africa, invasion of, 128, 129, 133–36
El Alamein, 129–32
Tunisia, defence of, 135 *passim*
Nehring, 136, 138, 141, 142
Comando Supremo and, 144, 145, 147–51
Kasserine, 148–51
defence tactics, 152, 153, 162
Mareth, 153–55
Italy, 157, 160, 163–65, 167–69, 173, 174, 176, 179, 186–88, 190–92
Calabria, defence of, 168, 174, 176
Salerno, 173–83
islands, evacuation of, 179
scorched earth policy, 182
C-in-C South West, 185, 186
SS intrigues and, 188, 189, 211, 217, 218
working methods, 190
Allied assessment of, 194
Gustav Line, defence of, 190–204, 206–10
Anzio, defence of, 195–99, 210, 211
Cassino and, 200, 201
partisan warfare, 203–5, 212–14, 238–40
Rome, fall of, 211
Gothic Line, defence of, 211, 214, 215, 219–23
Bomb Plot of 20 July 1944 and, 216–18

injured, 223
peace feelers, 225, 229–31
C-in-C West, 225
West Germany, defence of, 226–31
Southern Command, 228, 229
captivity, 231, 233–45
American Historical Division, 242, 243
retirement, 243–46
Stahlhelms and, 244, 245
as a great commander, comparisons, 247–50
Kesselring, C. A., 17
Kesselring, Killian, 16
Kesselring, Kurt, 243
Kesselring, R., 13, 53, 72, 118, 216, 217, 230, 243, 244
Kesselring, Rosina, 17
Kiev, 95, 99, 100
Kreppel, General, 21
Kressenstein, K. von, 34
Kursk, 163, 166

Lampedusa, 162
Lang, Colonel, 154
Laternser, Dr H., 15, 16, 236, 239, 240, 242
Laval, P., 135
Lederer, O., 136, 137
Leese, O., 219
Leghorn, 207
Lemelsen, J., 184, 192–94, 215, 219, 238
Le Kef, 149, 150
Liri River, 193, 196, 200, 208, 209
Lipetsk, 37
Loerzer, B., 109, 114, 135
London, 83–85, 87, 88
London Agreement, 234, 235, 240
Lucas, J., 198, 199
Ludendorff, E., 26, 31, 230
Lufthansa, 38, 42
Luftwaffe, 35
    Luftflotte I: 56, 57, 59–65, 100
        II: 67 *passim*
        III: 78, 82, 90
        IV: 100
        V: 78, 81
    Flieger Korps I: 92
        II: 92, 96, 97, 109, 114
        IV: 92
        V: 92
        VIII: 92, 97, 99, 100
        X: 105

XI: 176
Luftkreis III: 54, 56
Kampfgeschwader 2: 77

Mackensen, E. von, 196, 198, 199, 201, 208–11, 235, 236, 240
Mackensen, H. von, 167
Malta, 105, 106 *passim*, 152
Mälzer, General, 198, 235, 236, 240
Mareth, 139, 144, 151–55
Marjoribanks-Egerton, P. M., 237
Marne, Battle of, 23
Marshall, G., 140
Mechili, 110
Medenine, 151, 152
Medjez el Bab, 137, 141
Mellenthin, F. von, 118
Mersa Brega, 132, 136, 137, 139, 142
Mersa Matruh, 122
Messe, G., 144, 146, 155
Messina, 166, 168
Messines, Battle of, 25
Metz, 20–23
Mignano Gap, 193, 195
Milch, E.
    dismissed by Hitler, 218
    Göring and, 53–55
    Luftflotte V, commands, 67
    Lufthansa and, 38, 42
    Luftwaffe, 159
    Kesselring and, 48–55, 244
    Nürnberg trial, 226
    Spanish Civil War and, 49–51
    State Secretary for Aviation, 42 *passim*
    Ural bomber and, 51
Minsk, 95
Model, W., 227, 228
Mollke, H. von, 247, 248
Moltke, H. von, 21
Mondorf, 231, 233
Monte Camino, 194
Monte La Difensa, 194
Monte Lungo, 194
Monte Maggiore, 194
Montgomery, B., 11, 128, 130–33, 139, 140, 142, 153, 166, 180, 193
Moscow, 92, 95, 98–102
Mügge, K. A., 157
Munich, 21, 28, 29, 32, 39, 57
Mussolini, B.
    deposed, 167
    Egypt, invasion of, 121

French North Africa, invasion of, 129
Geneva Convention and, 146
Kesselring and *Comando Supremo*, 144
last days in power, 160, 161, 164, 165
Malta, invasion of, 115, 117, 121
North African Defence, 138, 155
rescued from captivity, 179
Second World War, 104, 105
Spanish Civil War and, 49

Nancy, Battle of, 23
Naples, 139, 173, 175, 183
Nehring, W., 97, 122, 136–38, 141, 142
New Zealand Division, 201
Normandy invasion, 162, 206, 211, 215
Nürnberg, 28, 29, 30
Nürnberg Trials, 15, 44, 52, 63, 134, 212, 226, 232–34

Oran, 133
Orient, Operation, 102
Ortona, 193

Pantellaria, 162, 164
Panzerwaffe, 39, 46, 58
Parachute troops, 63, 69–71, 74, 98, 137
Partisan warfare, 28–30, 141, 159, 188, 203–5, 212–14, 229
Patton, G., 154, 165, 166
Peenemunde, 172
Petain, Marshal, 135
Pichon, 150
Po, River, 220
Pohl, von, 110
Poland, 32, 54, 58–68, 79, 89, 234, 247
Polish Air Force, 60, 62, 63
Polish Army, 60–63, 206
Porto Civitanova, 215

Radar, 76, 79
Radio beams, 47, 87
Raeder, E., 74, 115, 143, 156
Ramcke, H., 132
Rapallo, Treaty of, 35
Rapido River, 194–96
Ravenna, 221
Reder, *Sturmbannführer*, 214
Reichswehr, 31 *passim*
Remagen, 225
Rheinfelden, Battle of, 17
Rhine, River, 225
Ribbentrop, J. von, 227

Richard, Plan, 197
Richthofen, M. von, 25
Richthofen, W. von, 105, 161, 163, 171,
  172, 179, 218
Rimini, 219
Rintelen, E. von, 110, 159, 169, 173, 174
Ritchie, N., 118
Roatta, General, 173, 175, 176
Roma, 179
Rome, 107, 163, 169, 173, 175, 177, 178,
  182, 183, 185, 193, 195, 196–98, 200,
  210–12, 217, 218
Rommel, E.
  Afrika Korps and, 102, 107, 111
  Army Group Africa commander, 146
  death, 218
  El Alamein, 129–33
  Egypt, 121
  Field-Marshal, 119
  Gazala, 114, 117, 122
  Göbbels and, 106, 133, 181
  Italian armistice and, 178
  Italy, excluded from command, 182–86
  Kasserine, 148–51
  Medenine, 151
  Mersa Brega, retreat to, 110
  new Army Group and, 161, 162, 164,
    168, 178
  Panzerarmee Afrika and, 114
  Tobruk, 116, 117, 119
  Tunisia, 132, 133, 138, 139, 141–43, 151
Roosevelt, F., 140
Rote Kapelle, 158
Rotterdam, 71–73, 234
Rottiger, H., 215, 220, 229, 230
Royal Air Force, 71, 74–88
Royal Navy, 74
Ruge, F., 156
Rundstedt, G. von, 215, 225, 228
Rupprecht, Crown Prince, 23, 26, 161, 189
Russia, 33, 35, 59, 85, 88 *passim*, 211, 216
Russian Air Force, 37, 90, 94
Russian Army, 26, 225, 228

Salerno, 173, 175–82, 199
Sangro River, 183, 187, 193, 199
Sant 'Ambrogio, 197
San Pietro, 192
Sardinia, 156, 164, 167, 173, 179
Sbiba, 150
Schacht, H., 46
Scharnhorst, G. von, 247, 248

Schlieffen, A. von, 248
Schliecher, K. von, 34, 44
Schmundt, R., 194, 195
Schroeder, K-U., 217
Schweinfurt, 172
Scotland, A., 235, 236
Schutz Staffeln (SS), 159, 188, 211, 216,
  226, 233
Seeckt, H. von, 12, 32, 34–38, 41, 161
Senger und Etterlin, F. von 166, 169, 179,
  184, 186, 196, 206, 209, 210, 216–18
Senger Line, 208, 209
Service Manual No. 16, 50, 57, 60, 63, 98
Seyler, Major, 29, 30
Sfax, 147
Sicily, 105, 110, 113, 117, 134, 139, 153,
  156, 162 *passim*, 183
Sidi Barrani, 119
Sidi bou Zid, 148
Sirte, 142
Skortzeny, O., 179
Smolensk, 95, 97, 98, 105
Souk el Arba, 137
Spanish Civil War, 49, 51, 57
Speer, A., 162, 195, 222, 224, 228
Speidel, W., 60
Sperrle, H., 35, 65, 78, 82, 83, 90, 218
Stahlhelms, 244, 245
Stalin, J., 91
Stalingrad, 121, 127, 138, 144, 154, 156,
  158
Stirling, C., 238–42
Strauss, F-J., 245, 249
Student, K.
  Holland, invasion of, 69–71
  Italy, 176, 177
  Malta, invasion of, 121
  Truppenamt, in, 34, 35
Stumme, G., 125, 129, 130
Stulpnagel, J. von, 34, 39
Stumpff, R., 55
Suchenwirth, Professor R., 49, 51, 218
Suez, 115

Taranto, 181
Tebessa, 149, 150
Thala, 150
Theseus, Operation, 117 *passim*
Tobruk, 105, 117, 119, 121, 136
Trenchard, H., 42
Tripoli, 106, 110, 139

Index

Tunis, 134, 137, 138, 152, 156, 159
Tunisia, 134 *passim*

U-boats, 156, 162
Udet, E., 36, 47, 48, 103, 134
Ultra, 73, 79, 87, 122, 137
US Army
  Armies
    Fifth, 193, 195, 221
    Seventh, 165, 166
  Divisions
    1st Armoured, 149, 150
    36th Infantry, 196, 197, 201
    34th Infantry, 201

Valmontone, 210
Vatican, 214
Venice Tribunal, 13, 15, 16
Versailles, Treaty of, 31, 42
Via Rasella, 204
Victor Emmanual III, 159, 167, 168
Vietinghoff, H. von
  Anzio, 195–98
  armistice negotiations, 229
  Bomb Plot, 217
  Calabria, defends, 176
  Cassino, defence of, 196–201, 207–10
  Cassino, retreat to, 184, 185
  C-in-C Army Group C, 223, 229
  Gothic Line, defence of, 219, 220, 223
  Kesselring, 210
  Salerno, defends, 176, 178 83
  Tenth Army, commands, 173
Vimy Ridge, 23, 24, 193
Volturno River, 184, 185
Voronezh, 98

Waldau, H. von, 112
Warlimont, W., 146, 211, 214, 219
Warsaw, 60, 62, 63, 72, 90, 95

Weichold, E., 114, 127, 143, 156
Weichs, General von, 99
Wentzell, F., 208
Werewolves, 229
Werl, 242–44
Westphal, S.
  Bomb Plot and, 216, 217
  captivity, 233
  C-in-C West, at HQ, 225–29
  commands a division, 142
  Hitler, mission to, 202
  Italian armistice and, 176–78
  Italy, leaves, 210
  Kesselring and, 112, 118, 127, 130, 142, 145, 162, 190, 211, 226, 238, 245, 246, 249
  Rommel's staff officer, 111
  Via Rasella incident and, 204
Wever, W.
  air power, 50, 51, 57
  General Staff and, 46–48
  Luftwaffe Chief of Staff designate, 42–48
  Panzerwaffe and, 39
Wheeler-Bennet, J., 34
Wilhelm II, Kaiser, 21, 26
Wilberg, H., 35
Wilson, M., 199
Wimmer, W., 35
Winter, General, 229
Winterbotham, W., 43, 44, 56, 73, 126, 152
Wolff, K., 188, 211, 225, 229, 230
Wolverhampton, 87

Yartsevo, 97
Ypres, Battles of, 23
Yugoslavia, 105, 187, 198, 205, 211

Zeigler, H., 141
Zeitzler, K., 215, 218